THE LIFE
OF THE
EMPEROR
FRANCIS JOSEPH

by

Francis Gribble

NATAL PUBLISHING LLC

ARS LONGA, VITA BREVIS

Copyright[©] 2024 Natal Publishing

All rights reserved

The Emperor Francis Joseph.

Contents

Baron Otto von Seefried zu Buttenheim

probable future of the House of Habsburg—Questions both
personal and political which will be raised when Francis Joseph
dies—The extent to which he has been "in the movement"—
The faithful companion of his old age

PREFACE

There exist plenty of surveys of the modern history and
political conditions of Austria. Mr. Henry Wickham Steed's
"The Habsburg Monarchy" is the most recent, and probably
the best, though Mr. R. P. Mahaffy's "Francis Joseph I.: His
Life and Times"—a smaller and less pretentious book—is
also very good. One knows equally well where to turn for
gossipy compilations—some of them authoritative, and
others devoid of authority—dealing with the inner life of the
Austrian Court. Sir Horace Rumbold has treated the subject
with the dutiful reticence of a diplomatist in "The Austrian
Court of the Nineteenth Century"; Countess Marie Larisch
and Princess Louisa of Tuscany, occupying positions of
greater freedom and less responsibility, have in "My Past"
and "My Own Story" lifted the veil with indignant gestures,
and pointed fingers of scorn at the intimate pictures which
they have revealed. M. H. de Weindel, again, has written of
"François-Joseph Intime"; while the enterprise of an
American journalist has contributed "The Keystone of
Empire," "The Martyrdom of an Empress," and "The Private
Life of Two Emperors—William II. of Germany and Francis
Joseph of Austria."

This bibliographical list—to which additions could
easily be made—might seem to indicate that the ground has
already been well covered; but that is not the case. There
exists no life of Francis Joseph, and no History of Austria, in
which the personal and political aspects of the subject are
considered in their relation to each other. The assumption of
writers who have previously treated the theme has been that
tittle-tattle is tittle-tattle, and that history is history, and that
the two can never meet. The two things, however, are liable
to meet anywhere; and in the country and period here under

review they are continually meeting. Austria is not one of the "inevitable" countries, like England and Spain, bound to have a separate existence under some form of government or other because of their geographical situation and the national characteristics of their inhabitants. There is no Austrian nation: only a medley of races which detest each other, bound (but by no means welded) together for the supposed convenience of the rest of Europe, and unified only by the fact that its component parts all appertain to the dominions of the House of Habsburg.

It follows that the personality of the Habsburgs matters in a sense in which the personalities of rulers who are mere figure-heads does not matter; and that personality—the collective personality as well as the separate personalities of individual members of the House—can only be gauged by those who study their private lives in conjunction with their public performances. The history of the property (seeing that it comprises peoples as well as lands) includes and implies the history of the owners of the property. Our spectacle, in so far as one can sum it up in a sentence, is that of an Empire continually threatened with dissolution under the control of an historic family continually displaying all the symptoms of decadence. The political and the personal factors in the problem are perpetually interacting; and one of the questions which the political prophet has to consider is: Will not the decadence of the family hasten the dissolution of the Empire?

Whence it follows, as a secondary sequence, that, in the history of modern Austria, tittle-tattle matters; for it is only by the careful study of the tittle-tattle that we can hope to discover whether the Habsburgs of to-day are true or false to the proud and impressive traditions of their House. In their case, as in that of any other House, a stray story of a romantic or scandalous character might properly be ignored as appertaining to the domain of idle gossip; but when stories of that kind meet us at every turn—and meet us with increasing frequency as time proceeds—we are no longer entitled to dismiss them with superior indifference. They are significant; the key to the situation is to be found in them. Tittle-tattle, in short, when one encounters it, not in sample but in bulk, ceases to be tittle-tattle, but attains to the dignity of history, and furnishes the raw material for the generalisations of the political philosopher.

The annals of the House of Habsburg furnish a case in point—the best of all possible cases. There is no House in Europe whose annals are richer in incident and eccentricity; and the eccentricities, whether romantic or scandalous, are such as to challenge the scientific investigator—whether he be a student of eugenics or of politics—to group them and see what inferences he can draw. The present writer has decided to take up the challenge; and, in order to take it up, he will be obliged to deal with a good many matters besides the political manœuvres of the Emperor and his Ministers. "John Orth" pelting the Emperor with the insignia of the Order of the Golden Fleece; "Herr Wulfling" cracking nuts in a tree with Fräulein Adamovics; Princess Louisa of Tuscany, first bicycling with the dentist in the Dresden Park, and then appealing to her son's tutor to come and "compromise" her in Switzerland—all these are matters which may suggest reflections quite as far-reaching as anything that we read about Francis Joseph's skill in extricating his country from embarrassments with rival Powers and keeping the peace (in so far as it has been kept) between Ruthenians and Galicians.

It would be presumption, of course, to represent this biography as the full and final portrait of Francis Joseph as he really is. The complete material for such a definite portrait of a sovereign is never made available during the sovereign's life-time; and the portraits drawn by people who have occupied privileged positions at Court are generally the most colourless of all: misleading—and, as a rule, designed to mislead—by excess of eulogy. Discretion, in such cases, takes the place of criticism; the "selection" is not that of the artist, but of the courtier. The illustrious personage thus officially or semi-officially portrayed "comes out" not as an individual, but as a type: as conventional and as unconvincing as the stock "heavy father" or "gentlemanly villain" of melodrama. Sir Horace Rumbold's polite portrait of Francis Joseph is one of many marked by those limitations. The popular Austrian portraits are still more distinctly marked by them.

One need not wonder, and one must not complain. The

path to candour was blocked by the obligations, in the one case of hospitality, and, in the other, of loyalty; but there is no reason why the historian who is not under such obligations should not criticise more freely. His object is neither depreciation nor flattery, but truth—as much of the truth as is attainable at the given moment; and he must therefore resist the common tendency of the biographers of contemporary rulers to credit their subjects, not only with their own particular virtues, but with all other people's virtues as well. The only result, in moral portraiture, of attributing virtues with too heavy a hand is to produce a picture in which the wood cannot be seen for the trees.

That error must be avoided, as much in the interest of the subject of the portrait as in that of the public to which it is to be submitted. The real virtues will be more conspicuous if no imaginary virtues are allowed to block our view of them, and if other miscellaneous qualities which contrast with them are given their due tribute of attention. Cromwell, it will be remembered, insisted that the artist should paint him "warts and all,"; and if the Life of an Emperor is not to be written in that spirit, one might just as well refrain from writing it, for there would be nothing to be learnt from it when it was written.

Francis Gribble

Chapter I

The collapse of the Holy Roman Empire—The impossibility of reviving it—The German Federation—The Holy Alliance—The policy of sitting on the safety valve—The consequent explosions—The problems consequently prepared for Francis Joseph—The Head of the House of Habsburg—Inseparable connection between the events of his public and private life.

In order to clear the way, and set the stage for the drama of the Emperor Francis Joseph's life, we must go back to the dissolution of that Holy Roman Empire of which the Emperor of Austria was, at the end, the titular head. Happily, we have not very far to go.

The Holy Roman Empire—in fact, as a cynic has said, neither Holy nor Roman, and scarcely worthy to be called an Empire—collapsed in the Napoleonic wars. The Battle of the Nations at Leipzig, the "world's earthquake" at Waterloo, the Congress of Vienna: none of these things availed to set the Holy Roman Empire on its feet again.

Perhaps a really great man might even then have been able to restore it and make something of it, using it as a decorative setting for glorious achievements; perhaps not. The experiment was not tried, because there was no great man available to try it. The sovereigns of those days, with the sole exception of Alexander of Russia, were pitifully lacking in personal prestige. Whatever Napoleon had failed to do, he had at least succeeded in destroying the prestige of the hereditary representatives of ancient dynasties. The House of Habsburg, in spite of Napoleon's marriage to a daughter of the House, had suffered as much indignity as any other royal family, and more than most. That marriage, indeed, was itself esteemed an indignity; even the old friends of the House were doubtful whether it still deserved respect.

Moreover, while Austria was rather weak, Prussia was very jealous—not altogether without reason. In the earlier stages of the final combination against Napoleon, Prussia had borne the burden and heat of the day, while Austria sat, with a double face, shilly-shallying on the fence. Now, it might be said, Austria represented the Past and Prussia the Future of the German world; and the Future was in no mood to tolerate proud airs or lofty pretensions from the Past. In the absence, therefore, of a commanding personality among the sovereigns, the revival of the Holy Roman Empire was impossible; and the centre of gravity of the German world was shifting.

Still, something had to be done; some organisation had to be contrived to give cohesion to the medley and provide the Continental Concert with a reasonable prospect of a quiet life. So there sprang into being two organisations which concern us:—

- 1. The German Federation.
- 2. The Holy Alliance.

Their detailed history need not delay us; but we must pause to see how they created the difficulties with which Francis Joseph, coming to throne as a boy of eighteen, had to cope, and posed the problems which he would have either to solve for himself or to see roughly, and even violently, solved for him by others.

Just as the Holy Roman Empire was scarcely worthy to be called an Empire, so the German Federation was scarcely worthy to be called a Federation. It was loose and cumbrous, inefficient and inert. There was no Federal Tribunal, no Federal army, no Federal diplomatic machinery; in all these matters the component States—ruled by thirty-eight separate sovereigns—retained their independence. The Federal Assembly, which met at Frankfurt, was, in effect, only a Congress of the Ambassadors of those States, with the Austrian Ambassador in the chair. No important step could be taken without the unanimous consent of the Ambassadors; and there was no important piece of business on which they were all of one mind. The position of Austria at the head of the Assembly was one of dignity without authority, conferring little more actual power than falls to the president of a debating society.

So loose an arrangement obviously could not endure. One of two things was bound to happen; the bonds of union must, in the course of time, either be tightened or be broken. The seeds of destruction were present in the organisation from the first in the shape of Austro-Prussian jealousy: that jealousy between the Past and the Future to which we have referred. The interests and aspirations of these two dominant States conflicted. Neither of them was strong enough to bring the other to heel; neither of them was weak enough, or humble enough, to acquiesce in the other's hegemony. It remained only for one of them to turn the other out of the Federation, and fashion a real Federation—a real Empire, perhaps—out of the remaining constituents. That inevitable process—delayed for more than fifty years, but eventually altering the whole outlook of Austrian policy—was to provide the central problem of Francis Joseph's reign; but many other problems, hardly of less significance, were first to arise out of the programme of the Holy Alliance.

The Holy Alliance, of course, was, in fact, no more Holy than the Holy Roman Empire, and was, perhaps, hardly worthy to be called an Alliance. It was an agreement, or mutual understanding, rather than an Alliance, inspired by hatred and terror of the new ideas disseminated by the French Revolution; and those are hardly unjust who describe it as a conspiracy, suggested by Metternich, and acquiesced in by the principal Continental sovereigns, for keeping all subject peoples in the places which the Congress of Vienna had assigned to them. And that in a double sense. In the first place, autocratic forms of government were to be maintained in all countries which the Holy Three regarded as within their sphere of influence. In the second place, subject nationalities were to be kept in subjection to the Powers which the Settlement of 1815 had placed in authority over them.

It follows that the policy of the Holy Alliance was a policy of sitting on safety valves; and its history is the history of a series of Conferences and Congresses held to decide who should sit on which safety valve in the name of all. It was agreed, for instance, that Austria should sit on the safety valve in Naples, and that France should sit on it in Spain; and there was much talk—though also much difference of opinion—about sitting on the safety valves in Portugal and Greece. The Holy Alliance fell to pieces, after a much shorter life than that of the Holy Roman Empire, because Russia maintained against Austria, and England maintained against France, that certain safety valves should not be sat upon.

Moreover, safety valves were many, and the upward pressure was of a continually increasing force. If Metternich and Castlereagh, and the Emperors of Austria and Russia, and the King of Prussia, had, like the Bourbons, "learnt nothing" from the French Revolution and its sequel, the common people, from university professors to artisans, had learnt much. They might desire a breathing-time before committing themselves to desperate courses. The breathing-time might be protracted because the despotisms were reasonably benevolent towards people who did not meddle with politics; because the administration was honest, and the taxes were not oppressive. Still, sooner or later intelligent men were bound to tire of submission, and clamour for Parliaments and the recognition of "nationalities." Byron—the friend of the Carbonari before he was the friend of Greece—was hounding them on to do so.

In England Byron was notorious for his indecorum; but, on the Continent, he was famous for his audacity. The improprieties of "Don Juan" did not shock Continental Liberals; but its courageous political criticisms stirred them. The lines over which they gloated—though they must have had a difficulty in translating them—were such lines as these:—

Lock up the billy bald-coot, Alexander!
Ship off the Holy Three to Senegal!
Teach them that sauce for goose is sauce for gander,
And ask them how *they* like to be in thrall!

Such passages—and there are plenty of them—express the temper to which the Continental Liberals were gradually coming. When they came to it, and found such men as Metternich, and Bomba of Naples, and Charles X. of France, sitting on the safety valves, explosions could by no means be prevented. The political history of the period is the history of those explosions and their consequences; and we all know that there were two principal series of such explosions—the explosions of 1830, and the explosions of 1848. The noise of the first detonations was, as it were, a salute fired in the year of Francis Joseph's birth; the louder roar of the second greeted his accession.

First Italy and then Hungary exploded; and Francis

Joseph, as a boy of eighteen, had to face the confusion and try to calm it. The story of his bearing in the presence of the turmoil must not be anticipated; but we may look sufficiently ahead to note that a new Austria, differently constituted, and looking out of a new window in a new direction, had gradually to be re-created out of what might very well have been a wreck. The old Austria over which Francis Joseph began to reign in 1848 was a Teuton Power holding the most prosperous provinces of Italy in its iron grip. That grip has been reluctantly relaxed until only the pressure of one little finger remains; and the new Austria over which Francis Joseph rules to-day has only a small Teuton nucleus, associated with a Magyar nucleus nearly as large, trying in conjunction with it to assert predominant partnership in a large and increasing community of Slavs, and casting envious, but not very hopeful, glances across the Danube towards the Balkan States and the Ægean harbours.

So great has been the evolution accomplished within the reign of a single ruler: a ruler who, at the beginning of his reign, did not dare to set his foot in his own capital, and, long before the end of it, had come to be regarded as the one indispensable man in the Empire—the one man whose life must be preserved and prolonged at all hazards, for fear lest his death should entail the collapse of the edifice which he had reared—the one man who sometimes appeared to command the affection of all his subjects. It would be a striking story, even if one related the Emperor's political achievements without reference to his personal life; but the two things, though commonly separated by political historians, are not really separable.

Certainly they are not so separated by his own subjects. They not only admire the statesman who has acquired a prestige to which he was not born, and has used it to recover by diplomacy what he has lost in war; they also cherish an affectionate sympathy for the man at whom calamity has dealt blow after blow, whom no blow, however cruel, has struck down, and who, in spite of innumerable sorrows, has continued to confront the world with a dignified, if melancholy, composure. He has had, they perceive, no less trouble with his family than with his Empire; and they have sometimes thought of him—or at least been tempted to think of him—as the one splendidly sane member of an eccentric and decadent House.

It follows that one must write of Francis Joseph, not only as an Emperor, but also as a Habsburg—the head of the most interesting of all the royal houses: a House whose members, unpredictable in their insurgent extravagances, have, again and again, moved the Courts and Chancelleries of Europe to consternation. Our picture must be, not only of a great and successful ruler, but also of a brave old man, tried in the fire but not consumed by it, bowed down by sorrows but not broken by them, maintaining the mediæval majesty of royal caste in the presence of his peers, at a time when other Habsburgs—one Habsburg after another—were flinging the prejudices of royal caste to the winds and making, as it must have seemed to him, sad messes of their lives, after the manner of those reprobate relatives who, even in middle-class families, are spoken of, if at all, with bated breath.

That being our theme—or a portion of it—we may next speak of the Habsburgs collectively; and we will begin by considering what the eugenists have to say about them.

CHAPTER II

The House of Habsburg from the standpoint of Eugenics—The "Habsburg jaw"—Degeneracy the consequence of consanguineous marriages—Sound physiological instinct of King Cophetua—And of those Habsburgs who have followed his example—Morganatic marriages—The family organism fighting for its life—Has Francis Joseph understood?—Indications that he has understood in part.

The House of Habsburg furnishes the "horrible examples" in two recent works on the new science of Eugenics: *L'hérédité des Stigmates de Dégénérescence*, by Dr. Galippe, and *L'Origine du Type familial de la Maison de Habsburg*, by Dr. Oswald Rubbrecht. The arguments in both cases are based, not only on a study of history, but also on a collation of portraits; and though the writers differ on some points of detail, their general conclusions are identical. For both of them the Habsburgs are "degenerates"; both of them attribute the degeneracy to the same cause. It is, they agree, the cumulative effect of what is technically called "in-breeding"—of a long succession of inter-marriages among comparatively near relatives.

One hears of the physiological law thus violated, whenever the question of a marriage between cousins is mooted. The tendency of such a marriage, we are always told, is to perpetuate and accentuate typical characteristics and weaknesses, both physical and moral. A single marriage between cousins may produce no perceptible evil result; and one can cite cases in which it appears to have produced remarkably brilliant results.[1] But a series of such marriages, continued through generation after generation, invariably and inevitably tells. The family, or the community, in which such unions are the rule, loses vigour and develops peculiarities— a special, readily recognisable, physiognomy, and an unstable mental equilibrium. The transmitted eccentricities—more

---

[1] Darwin married his first cousin, and all his sons were men of remarkable ability.

particularly the mental eccentricities—may skip a generation or leave an individual exempt; but they are always lurking in the background—always to be expected to reappear.

It has been so, and is so, according to Drs. Rubbrecht and Galippe, with the Habsburgs. We have all heard of the "Habsburg jaw"; and Dr. Rubbrecht traces it to its mediæval source, and, standing before a long row of family portraits, carefully and scientifically depicts the Habsburg face:—

"In addition to the underhung lower jaw and the large lower lip, the Habsburg physiognomy presents the following characteristic features: excessive length, and, sometimes, excessive size of the nose; 'exorbitism,' more or less pronounced, with a forehead often of considerable height. One would say that the head, squeezed in by lateral pressure, had undergone a concomitant vertical allongation, and had been stretched, and pulled up and down at the same time. According to Dr. Galippe, the lateral flattening of the skull is the fundamental characteristic, and all the other abnormalities follow from it."

That is what Dr. Rubbrecht makes of the portraits. He generalises only as a student of physiognomy, and does not discuss mental and moral issues, or presume to predict the future. Dr. Galippe is more outspoken:—

"The Habsburgs" (he writes), "having, by their intermarriages, developed a degenerate taint, and having transmitted it, either separately or in conjunction with other taints, both physical and psychical, to the families matrimonially allied with them, have brought into existence a specific type of human animal, by the same means which the breeders of dogs and horses employ for the creation of a new sub-species."

As for the general consequences of such in-breeding, he continues:—

"Even those aristocratic families which present no original mark of degeneracy disappear quickly. It follows, *a fortiori*, that those families which, possessing such characteristics, perpetuate them by contracting marriages within the degrees of consanguinity, are doomed to a still more speedy extinction."

As for the case of the Habsburgs in particular, he

concludes:—

"The Habsburgs of Spain have long since been swept off the stage of history, disappearing in sterility or insanity. The Habsburgs of Austria, numerous though the representatives of the House are at the present time, will end by disappearing in their turn as an historic family, if they persist in their errors,—that is to say, in their marriages with blood relations."

It is a new way of looking at an old problem,—a new thought suggested by the latest of the sciences; and it opens the door to reflections of great and urgent moment to many other royal houses besides that of Habsburg. In a general way, it has long been held to be almost as improper for Kings and Queens to marry their subjects as for angels to marry the daughters of men. A purer and bluer blood ran in their veins than in the veins of their subjects; and to adulterate that blue blood with red blood was to degrade it. They must, therefore, seek their brides and bridegrooms within the magic circle. Kings must marry Queens, and Princes must marry Princesses; and the distinctive exclusiveness of reigning houses must be maintained by a succession of unions between cousins.

That view of the matter has continued to prevail in royal circles—and also in high political and diplomatic circles— long after the students of heredity have established conclusions unfavourable to such courses. The arguments can hardly have failed to reach the ears of those whom they concerned; and the feeling—tacit, if not avowed—has presumably been that Kings, and Queens, and Princes and Princesses are so great and good and glorious that the laws of Nature do not apply to them. But that is not the case. Science shows that Kings cannot override the laws of Nature even in the countries in which they are permitted to override the laws of the land; that the price which Nature exacts for exclusiveness is degeneracy; that hardly any royal family anywhere has failed to pay that price; that the percentage of insanity has, through the ages, been higher among hereditary rulers whose blue blood has thus been protected from admixture than in any other class of the community; and that the sound physiological instinct is that on which King

Cophetua acted in the legend, when the bare-footed beggar-maid appeared before him:—

> As shines the moon in clouded skies,
> She in her poor attire was seen;
> One praised her ankles, one her eyes,
> One her dark hair and lovesome mien.
> So sweet a face, such angel grace,
> In all that land had never been:
> Cophetua swore a royal oath:
> "This beggar maid shall be my queen."

It is this example of King Cophetua—and the moral which the eugenists read into it—that we shall need to bear in mind when we endeavour to appreciate those incidents in the latter-day history of the House of Habsburg which are commonly supposed, whether rightly or wrongly, to have been most distressing to the head of the family. That history has largely, and indeed mainly, if not quite entirely, been a history of revolt on the part of the sons—and even the daughters—of the House against the splendid restrictions and inherited obligations which hedged them about as members of an uniquely illustrious race.

The revolt has expressed itself in many ways: some of them, in the world's view, creditable and even honourable; others in a greater or less degree scandalous. We have seen—and we shall see yet again in these pages—one Habsburg throwing off the panoply of state, to live his own mysterious life in the remote Balearic Isles, and another Habsburg disappearing for ever—unless those are right who assure us that he bides his time, in hiding, for some dark political reason, and will "come again"—as the navigating officer of a merchant vessel. There have also been intrigues which have ended in tragedy, and morganatic marriages with actresses and other persons deemed "impossible" in imperial circles; and there has been at least one elopement of a Habsburg Princess, who, having failed to live harmoniously with a Crown Prince, found that even a professional pianist could not permanently satisfy her craving for romance.

One knows the ordinary comment on these proceedings: "All the Habsburgs are mad,—all of them except Francis Joseph; and here is another Habsburg proving himself (or herself) as mad as the others, if not madder." The remark is not profound; but it is often, in a rough way, true. John Orth, "Herr Wulfling," Princess Louisa of Tuscany:—all these (and not these only) have done strange things,—things which one would hesitate to put forward as the sole and unsupported proofs of the possession of well-balanced minds. This is not the page for the detailed account of such proceedings; but it is pertinent and proper, even here, to remark the startling frequency of their occurrence. It is not a case of the discovery of a single skeleton in a single cupboard—a phenomenon which any research into any family history is apt to bring to light. The impression, when one reviews the recent annals of the House of Habsburg, is of continuous rattling of skeletons in all the cupboards, and of one sane and strong man—the accepted and now the hereditary Head of the House—going gravely through his troubled life, not unmoved, indeed, by the ghostly noises, but, at least, without allowing his composure to be too visibly disturbed by them: a man of whom one may say, giving a somewhat new sense to old and hackneyed lines:—

Si fractus illabatur orbis,

Impavidum ferient ruinae.

But that is not the only view of the matter which it is permissible to take. One may also, with the conclusions of science to back one, regard the eccentricities of the more eccentric Habsburgs, if not as the best proofs of sanity that they are capable of giving, then as instinctive and desperate, if not always very intelligent, endeavours to escape from the imminent fate which the eugenists have foretold for them. The family, we may take it, no less than the individual, is an "organism," albeit only partly conscious of itself; and our spectacle, we may add, is that of an organism blindly fighting for its life. The fight may not be very wisely conducted, not having been begun until the work of destruction was too far advanced; but it is nevertheless a fight worth fighting, and one of which we should follow the vicissitudes, not with horror or with merriment, but with intelligent sympathy. For degeneracy *is* too high a price to pay for haughty exclusiveness; and it is better to flee from the City of Destruction late in the day, followed and attended by the cry of scandal, than to remain in it and be overwhelmed.

That, at any rate, is the appreciation of the Habsburg scandals—or of a good many of them—which will commend itself to eugenists and sociologists, who will esteem the revolts sound in principle, even though they allow them to be occasionally extravagant in detail. The individual makers of the scandals need not be assumed to have acted from any higher or deeper motive than the satisfaction of what has more than once proved to be only a passing inclination. The whole circumstances of their upbringing, and the precepts of duty and propriety impressed upon them from childhood, make that unlikely. But the physiological instinct behind the admitted motive has been a sound one. Looked at from the viewpoint of the individual, it had been the instinct of King Cophetua; looked at from the point of view of the race, it has been the instinct of self-preservation.

It has been the tragedy—or one of the tragedies—of Francis Joseph that the years of his reign have coincided with the years of this stage in the Habsburg struggle for continued existence. Chosen for his august and exalted post as the sanest and healthiest Habsburg available—albeit the son of an epileptic father and the nephew of an epileptic uncle—he has looked down from above on the exciting incidents and varying vicissitudes of that struggle. One does not know whether to regard his tragedy as the greater on the assumption that he understood the inner meaning of the spectacle or on the assumption that he did not understand it. In the former case there would be more of pathos, in the latter case more of irony, in the drama; but it is impossible to say for certain whether he has understood or not.

The probability, in the lack of direct evidence, is that he has understood in part. One might draw that inference from his occasional indulgence, as well as from his occasional severity, towards the rebels against the laws, both written and unwritten, of his House; and one has no right to infer the contrary from the fact that he himself has not rebelled. He is a Habsburg as well as an Emperor, and may very well have felt the impulses which appear to have become common to the race, though he has had both exceptional reasons and exceptional facilities for repressing them. One knows, at any rate, that he, like so many other members of his family, has sought, and won, the friendship of women outside the charmed circle of the royal families, and that the lady in whose company he seems, in the last years of his long life, to find the most agreeable respite from the cares of State, is not an Archduchess, and was once an actress. That fact must surely have helped him to understand.

But these are matters for subsequent consideration. The ground is now clear; and we may proceed, without further delay, to genealogy and biography.

CHAPTER III

Francis Joseph's ancestors—Francis, Duke of Lorraine—Francis II.—Leopold II.—Collaterals—The Spanish marriages of the Habsburgs—Their alliances with Portugal, the various Bourbons, and the Wittelsbachs of Bavaria—Moral and mental defects thus perpetuated and emphasised—Francis Joseph as the sane champion of a mad family.

The Habsburgs can be traced back to the seventh century before we lose them in the crowd of common men. The branch of the family to which the Emperor Francis Joseph belongs is that known as the House of Habsburg-Lorraine, founded by the marriage of the Empress Maria Theresa to Francis, Duke of Lorraine, in 1736; and the House of Lorraine has an independent genealogy, only less ancient and illustrious than that of Habsburg itself, being descended, through the House of Anjou, from Hugues Capet, the ancestor of the royal house of France. Anjou was given, in 1246, by Saint Louis, to his younger brother Charles, whose granddaughter married her cousin, Charles de Valois; and the House of Anjou kept the Duchy of Lorraine until Francis abdicated on the occasion of his marriage, in favour of Stanilas Lecszinski, whose daughter married Louis XV.

This Francis seems to have been a mixed character, not entirely commendable. He is credited with virtue in his private life; but it is also related of him that he farmed taxes, lent money at usurious rates of interest, and acted as a kind of army contractor to Frederick the Great, at a time when that monarch was at war with Austria. He was the father of Marie-Antoinette, and also of the Emperors Joseph II. and Leopold II. Joseph left no issue, but Leopold, who married Marie-Louise, daughter of Charles III. of Spain, had a large family, only two members of which need be mentioned here:

1. Francis II., who became Emperor in 1792, and was on the throne when Napoleon broke up the Holy Roman Empire.

2. The Archduke John, whose romantic marriage with the daughter of a postmaster set a precedent for those morganatic unions which have recently become so frequent in the House of Habsburg.

Leopold II. is described by the historians as a benevolent

despot—a reformer according to his lights—who displayed great intolerance in religious matters, and died young through the unbridled indulgence of his amorous proclivities. Francis II. is an Emperor of whom it would be necessary to speak evil at length, if he, and not his grandson, were the subject of this narrative: a double-faced and incompetent ruler, who needed all the help he got from Metternich; a petty domestic tyrant, who behaved abominably towards his daughter Marie-Louise, his son-in-law Napoleon, and his grandson the Duc de Reichstadt. How he deliberately threw Neipperg at his daughter's head for the express purpose of undermining the affection which her husband had, to his disgust, inspired in her, is a story which belongs to other pages than these. Here we will merely note that he married four wives, and by the second of them—Marie-Thérèse-Caroline-Josephine de Bourbon—had two sons, who now concern us:—

1. The Emperor Ferdinand, who succeeded to the throne in 1835, but bowed his head before the storm and abdicated in 1848, though he did not die until 1875.

2. The Archduke Francis Charles, who, as Ferdinand had no children, should have succeeded him, but whom his wife, the Archduchess Sophie, daughter of Maximilian I. of Bavaria, persuaded to resign his rights in favour of his eldest son, the present Emperor, Francis Joseph.

That is all the genealogy which we need for the moment. It shows us the Habsburgs as a feeble folk—getting feebler as times got more tempestuous; and it also shows us Francis Joseph launched upon his stormy political career at the age of eighteen—launched upon it as the rising hope of a decadent family—a youth of energy and promise, with no sign of decadence about him, supple but strong, exempt, as far as could be judged, from the family taints of physique and character, and designed to restore the threatened dignity of the Austrian Empire, by confronting the new era in a new spirit. His accession will be our historical starting point; but, before we come to it, we must turn aside for a brief glance at some of those collateral ancestors whose traits, if there be anything in heredity, we may expect to see reappearing—not invariably, but here and there, and now and then—in their descendants, the Habsburgs of the nineteenth and twentieth centuries.

The list of the allied houses includes, of course, practically the whole of Catholic Europe, and a portion of Protestant Europe as well. To attempt to review them all would be to lose oneself in an interminable maze; but the collateral sources of particular contamination can be noted, and we shall see house after house contributing—some of them only on one, but some of them on several occasions— its strain of madness to the great family with which it was its privilege to intermarry. We may begin with the House of Burgundy, and end with that of Bavaria, taking on our way the Houses of Spain, Portugal, Medicis, and Bourbon Parma.

Charles the Bold of Burgundy fell into a melancholy madness after his defeat by the Swiss at Morat, and died a madman. His daughter Marie, Duchess of Brabant and Countess of Flanders, married Archduke Maximilian of Austria, son of the Emperor Frederick IV. Their son, Philippe le Bel, married that daughter of Ferdinand of Arragon who is known to history as Joanna the Mad. Those are the unfavourable circumstances in which we see Habsburg blood introduced into the royal family of Spain; and the subsequent history of the family presents two features pertinent to our survey:—

1. A long series of degenerates among the Kings and Infants of Spain.

2. A long series of marriages between Spanish and Austrian Habsburgs.

No full account of the manifestations of the madness of Spanish rulers, Princes, and Princesses can be given here; they are too numerous, and also too gross for general reading. The briefest of summaries must suffice. Joanna the Mad travelled all over Spain with her husband's coffin, wailing and lamenting, at the top of her shrill voice, whenever the funeral procession halted. Joanna's son, the great Emperor Charles V., lived on the border-line which separates genius from insanity, and was, at any rate, an epileptic, like that Archduke Charles whose campaigns against Napoleon were punctuated by untimely fits. His son, Philip II.—known to English history as the husband of our Bloody Mary—is described by the historians as "half-mad"; and Philip's brother Charles was notoriously a homicidal maniac. Philip III. was comparatively sane; but even he tried to poison his sister. Charles II. was nicknamed "the bewitched," and was so afraid of the dark that three monks had to sit every night at his bedside, in order that he might sleep in peace. Philip V. was, for years, a bedridden imbecile; and Ferdinand VI. was a victim of religious melancholia, Etc. The catalogue is far from complete; but it may suffice as a preface to the statement that one finds eight or nine Spanish marriages in the Habsburg matrimonial annals.

One encounters a very similar list of lunatics in the annals of the royal House of Portugal; and with that house also the Habsburgs have again and again intermarried. The pathology of the Medicis and the multitudinous Italian Bourbons, whose blood also runs in the Habsburg veins, is hardly better; and it can scarcely have been in the expectation of introducing a healthier strain that they sought alliances with the Wittelsbachs of Bavaria. Sanity, in that house, is represented by the King who sacrificed his kingdom to the beautiful eyes of Lola Montez; madness by the Kings Louis and Otto, whose extravagances and eccentricities have been related in innumerable volumes of memoirs and newspaper articles, and who are Francis Joseph's cousins.

Assuredly no Eugenist will assert that that heredity is good. On the contrary, the impression derived from a close examination of it is that of several strains of insanity and decadence converging, much in the way in which a multitude of Swiss mountain torrents converge to form the Rhone. But even that analogy is unduly favourable; for the sources from which fresh blood has been introduced into the family have not been indefinitely numerous. The same source has been tapped over and over again by the renewal of consanguineous marriages in one generation after another, with the result that the Habsburg type—with all its peculiar physical, mental, and moral characteristics—has been perpetuated and emphasised.

The physical characteristics were long ago recognised by the family itself with pride, and by outsiders with a curious wonder akin to envy and admiration. Napoleon so remarked it at the time of his betrothal to Marie-Louise, as M. Frédéric

Masson relates:—

"When" (M. Masson writes) "Lejeune, who had just arrived from Vienna, showed him a sketch of the Archduchess which he had made at the theatre, 'Ah!' he exclaimed in delight, 'I see she has the Austrian lip.'"

In Brantôme, again, we find a much earlier reference to the feature. He tells us how Eleanor of Austria, the wife of Francis I. of France, examined the sculptured tombs of her ancestors at Dijon; and he proceeds:—

"Some of the bodies were in so good a state of preservation that she could distinguish many of their features, and, among other things, the shapes of their mouths. Whereupon she suddenly exclaimed, 'Ah! I always thought we got our mouths from our Austrian ancestors; but I now see that we get them from Marie of Burgundy and the other Burgundians. If ever I see my brother the Emperor I will tell him so. Indeed, I think I will write to him on the subject.' The lady who informed me of this told me that the Queen spoke as one who took pride in the characteristic; wherein she was quite right."

That this physical peculiarity was, in the case of the Habsburgs, the outward sign of mental and moral divergences from the healthy norm was evidently as little suspected by Napoleon as by Brantôme. It is the discovery of the students of a comparatively new science; and it is a discovery of which the biographer must be careful to make neither too little nor too much. Eugenics is not yet an exact science; and the laws of heredity remain obscure. They are laws, it would seem, which, though generally true, cannot be relied upon to operate in any particular way in any particular case. The life of a family almost invariably confirms them, whereas the life of an individual may often appear to confute them; and we may often see genius flowering on the same plant as insanity.

The history of the Habsburgs in general—and the life of Francis Joseph in particular—supports that view of the matter. The Archduke Charles, who was so nearly a match for Napoleon, and actually beat him at Aspern, was not a very distant relative of the Archduke Otto who used to dance in a Vienna café, attired only in a képi, a pair of gloves, and a sword-belt. The Archduchess Christina, who proved such an admirable mother to the little King of Spain—though she has transmitted a double portion of the Habsburg jaw to him—was no less a Habsburg than the Princess who so signally and so publicly failed to find happiness in the love of Signor Toselli. And so on, and so forth; for the contrasts of the kind to which one could point are endless. One is left with the impression that the family, taken as a family, is mad, but that certain isolated members of it have been as sane as the rest of us, and abler than the majority; and one needs the impression before one can justly appreciate the drama of Francis Joseph's life.

He has stood before Europe, for more than sixty years, as the picked champion of the Habsburgs: picked not only for his ability, but also for his strength of character and conciliatory tact—for all those qualities, in short, which one looks for from a sane man in an exalted station. He started, as we have seen, under the burden of a singularly bad heredity; and he has carried that burden through life with patient endurance—and with an air of dignity—as if personally unconscious of the taint, while the lives of those nearest and dearest to him were furnishing undeniable proofs of it at every turn. He has shown himself, to conclude, the true head of the house, by nature as well as by pragmatic sanction.

So much made clear, we may proceed to chronicle the bald facts of his birth and childhood.

CHAPTER IV

Francis Joseph's childhood—The severe education which prepared him for his *rôle*—Difficulties of that *rôle*—The Liberal revolt against the Metternich system—The idea of nationality—Hübner's surprise that anyone should object to Austrian rule—Every Austrian a policeman at heart—The Italian rising of 1848—Francis Joseph in action—Radetzky's remonstrances—Francis Joseph's return to his studies.

Francis Joseph was born at Schönnbrunn on August 18, 1830. His father was the Archduke Francis Charles, and his mother the Archduchess Sophie, daughter of Maxmilian I. of Bavaria. He grew up and was educated in the period of peace between the two great revolutionary storms which shook Europe free from the Metternich system: a period which begins with Metternich supreme, and ends with Metternich in flight from an angry mob. He owed his throne, the steps of which he mounted, as a lad of eighteen, in the midst of the second epoch of turmoil, to his mother's influence. She was an able and imperious woman; she made up her mind that her son would make a better Emperor than either her brother-in-law or her husband; she pulled the wires and got her way.

The boy's education was thorough and practical: just the sort of education which he would have been given if his destiny had been in view from his birth. He was taught the whole duty of a soldier in each of the several branches of the service: to point a cannon as well as he could mount a horse; to dig a trench as well as he could handle a sabre or a rifle. He was also taken through complete courses of history, literature, mathematics, chemistry, astronomy, and natural history, instructed weekly in the maxims of statecraft by Metternich himself, and compelled to acquire innumerable modern languages: Hungarian, Czech, and Polish, as well as French, Italian, and, to a limited extent, English. It was an intellectual preparation which might easily have addled his brain, and does appear to have made him prematurely serious. Even before the troubles of his family compelled him to shoulder its responsibilities, he was remarked as being grave, earnest, and reserved: the good boy of his family, it was thought—and as clever as he was good.

Of course, there are anecdotes indicating that he loved his people—and, above all, loved his army—from his earliest years. The most famous of them shows him to us, moved to pity by the sight of a sentry sweltering in the August sun, stealing up behind him, and dropping a small coin into his cartridge-box, to the delight and admiration of his aged grandfather: a subject picture by Kriehuber keeps the memory of that incident alive. "Poor man! But now he is not a poor man any longer," he is said to have said, jumping about with joy at the thought that he had made someone happy. Very likely it is true; very likely it is also true that he, who was soon to be one of the best horsemen in his dominions, began life with a horror of horses. Those about him knew what sort of a man they wanted him to be, and did their best to make him such a man. There was a regular Habsburg system of education, though not all the Habsburgs have done credit to it. The great Maria Theresa had laid it down that "they must not be coddled or spoiled"; and the Emperor Joseph had expressed similar sentiments in emphatic language:—

"It may be enough for one of my subjects to say that, whereas his son will be of service to the State if he is well educated, the neglect to educate him does not matter, as he will have no public functions to perform. The case of an Archduke—a possible heir to the throne—is very different. The most important of all public functions—the government of the State—is absolutely incumbent on him. The question, therefore, whether he is or is not well educated, is one which it should be impossible to raise. He *must* be well educated; for there is no branch of the administration in which he might not do infinite harm if he had not the necessary knowledge to cope with his task and were unprovided with fixed principles of conduct."

It is a prescription as admirable as any to be found in the copy-book; though the rigid application of it has not prevented a good many Habsburgs from turning out, from the Habsburg point of view, badly. It is a call to every Habsburg in turn to "be a Habsburg," in the sense in which George III.'s mother appealed to him to "be a King"; and it rests upon a conception of the House of Habsburg as a house specially and divinely called into being in order to practise the art of government in central Europe. One may almost say that it assumes a caste of anointed rulers differing from their subjects as angels differ from the children of men; but it stops short of the corollary that rulers are born, not made. It lays down, rather, that the caste, in order to retain and exalt its qualities as a caste, must always be specialising from infancy to age. In that way, and in that way alone, its members might dispense with genius.

On the whole, they have had to dispense with it: their figures do not tower above the figures of their ministers, like those of Alexander I. of Russia and Frederick the Great of Prussia. Metternich is not the only Austrian minister who has been infinitely greater than any of the Emperors whom he served. Not all of them, again, have continued to specialise a day after the compulsion of tutors was withdrawn. A great many of them, on the contrary—a constantly increasing number of them in these latter times—have openly revolted against every restriction which made the caste characteristic. But the caste has continued, buttressed by the system, an object of regard, and almost of veneration, thanks to certain model Habsburgs, who have consented to the restrictions, and profited by them. Francis Joseph steps on to the stage of history as such a one: a specialised Habsburg, approaching nearer to genius than the others, but also gifted with a tactful adaptability which has enabled him to realise that the dead past must be allowed to bury its dead from time to time. Let us indicate the political troubles which called him into activity.

The revolutions of 1830 had been, in the main, abortive: a symptom of general discontent, but not its complete and successful expression. The work done at the Resettlement of 1815 had been shaken by it, but had not, except here and there—in Belgium, for instance—been upset; and that resettlement had been planned in the interest of reigning houses, not of peoples. The reigning houses continued to sit on the safety valve; and the steam which was trying to find vent through the safety valve consisted of:—

- 1. Liberal ideas in general.

• 2. The idea of nationality in particular.

To both those groups of ideas the Austrian Government was bitterly opposed; with both of them it was to have trouble. Its political prisons were famous throughout Europe as the homes of distinguished men, and its subject populations seethed with discontent. The idea of nationality was particularly obnoxious to it because it did not itself repose upon a national basis. "Austria," said Mazzini, with a gesture of disdain, "is not a country, but a bureaucracy"; and Austria was, in fact—what Metternich said that Italy was—a geographical ex-pression. It simply comprised the possessions of the House of Habsburg, which had, for generations, added field to field by means of prosperous marriages,[2] or accepted territory as the recompense of services rendered in war. The Emperor of Austria was also King of Hungary, King of Lombardy, King of Bohemia, etc., etc.: the head, as it were, of an ancient firm formed to carry on the general purposes of government in central Europe, and regarding men and women merely as material to be governed.

The system had its advantages—it kept the peace provisionally in what might otherwise have been one of the cockpits of Europe. That was what the French diplomatist meant when he said that, if the Austrian Empire had not existed it would have been necessary to invent it. But it was not popular, and it tended to make every Austrian statesman a policeman at heart. Even Metternich was a policeman at heart: a policeman of genius—a policeman of wide culture and charming manners—but still a policeman. He and his subordinates simply could not understand that people of other races might object to being policed by Germans. The Germans, they considered, were the best policemen in the world; and that should be an end of the matter. Count Hübner—a most intelligent Austrian—threw up his hands in amazement at the obstinate prevalence of the contrary opinion:—

"To-day" (we find him writing in his diary) "the magic word which moves the masses—not the proletariate, but the

---

[2] The idea was set forth in the famous hexameter line: *Bella gerant alii: tu, felix Austria, nube.*

intelligent public—is *nationality*. Germans, Italians, Poles, Magyars, Slavs! It is a formula capable of throwing the universe off its hinges—the lever which Archimedes sought in vain. The ringleaders have discovered it. With this lever they have, in the course of a few days, upset the old social system, and dazzled the eyes of the purblind with the deceptive promise of the perpetual happiness of the human race."

The peoples of central Europe, in Hübner's opinion, should have been as proud of their subjection to the House of Habsburg as the domestic servants whom Thackeray met on the top of the coach were of their position as the flunkeys of the Duke of Richmond. Italian national aspirations, in particular, seemed to him merely comical. He derided the Italians as mongrels—a medley of Gauls, Celts, Goths, Germans, Greeks, Normans, and Arabs; he recalled the internecine strife which had raged among their Republics in the Middle Ages. He comforted himself with the reflection that they spoke different dialects in different parts of the Peninsula, and he concluded: "I cannot believe in a United Italy."

Yet Italy was being united—and the Austrian Empire was apparently crumbling into its component parts—at the moment when he wrote, in July, 1848. Already, from the beginning of that year, anxiety had been widespread; and, in February, events in France had given a signal of unmistakable significance. "If Guizot falls," Mélanie Metternich exclaimed, "then we are all lost." Guizot did fall; and Louis-Philippe fell with him. The news reached Vienna; and it seemed as if Austria was in the melting-pot, though the trouble began, not in Vienna, but at Milan, where an Archduke reigned as Viceroy, and that sturdy octogenarian Radetzky commanded the army of occupation.

Charles Albert, King of Sardinia—the great-grandfather of the present King of Italy—had promised to be "the sword of Italy," on one condition. He would not collaborate with mere conspirators, but if there were an insurrection he would march to the aid of the insurgents. His terms were accepted, and there was a riot which became a revolution, though, in its inception, it presented some of the distinguishing characteristics of comic opera.

The revolutionists began by decreeing that as the Austrian Government depended largely for its revenues on the tobacco monopoly, no one in Italy should smoke. Austrian soldiers retorted by swaggering through the streets of Milan, smoking several cigars at once. Female patriots knocked the cigars out of their mouths, and pelted them from the house-tops with flower-pots and other missiles; while male patriots, armed with various weapons, molested them in other ways. There was street fighting, and there were killed and wounded. The patriots were many; the garrison was small; Charles Albert was known to be coming. Radetzky had no choice but to withdraw his troops within the famous Quadrilateral of Fortresses, leaving the provisional government set up by the revolutionists in possession. It seemed to the sapient Hübner a case of black ingratitude towards the admirable Austrian police.

But Austria was not, this time, to be beaten. Within the Quadrilateral Radetzky was safe; and, in due course, he marched out and defeated Charles Albert at Custozza. Few reinforcements had reached him, but they sufficed; and among the officers who came to serve under him was included Francis Joseph—not yet eighteen years of age. It was his first appearance in the field; and Radetzky was not particularly glad to see him. The scene which passed between the stripling and the veteran is best described in the Life of Radetzky included in General Ambert's *Cinq Epées*:—

"Radetzky addressed the new arrival in peremptory military language. 'Imperial Highness,' he said, 'your presence here is exceedingly embarrassing for me. Consider my responsibility in case anything should happen to you! If you should be taken prisoner, for instance, the accident would annihilate at a stroke any advantage which the Austrian army might have gained.' 'Marshal,' replied Francis Joseph, 'it is quite possible that it was unwise to send me here; but, as I am here, honour forbids me to depart without facing the enemy's fire'; and his eyes filled with tears as he spoke.

"No objection could be taken to an explanation so simple and gallant; and it was agreed that the Archduke should take part in the next battle, which was fought a few days later (the battle of May 6, at Santa Lucia). Here are the precise words of the report, addressed by Radetzky, immediately after that sanguinary struggle, to the Minister of War: 'I was myself an eye-witness of the intrepidity displayed by the Archduke, when one of the enemy's shells burst quite close to him.'"

"Austria does not lack Archdukes," he said gallantly, when implored not to expose himself to danger; but his battle was only of the nature of a holiday treat. He was still *in statu pupillari*—occupied with the severe studies by which he was preparing himself for his great *rôle*; and when he had done enough for honour, he returned to them. It was then, or soon afterwards, that he was confidentially informed of the great trust about to be reposed in him; but the intimation neither puffed him up with pride nor disturbed his diligence. He brought out his books again—immense tomes dealing with Roman, civil, criminal, and canonical law—and resumed his reading, almost as if everything depended upon his passing an examination in high honours. Not if he could help it should the arrival of his hour find him unready for it.

And his hour was near, for the times were critical. Trouble at home had followed hard on the heels of the trouble in Lombardy, and, being more complicated, had been more difficult to deal with.

CHAPTER V

The risings of 1848—Princess Mélanie Metternich's excited account of it—Disorderly flight of Metternich from Vienna—The House of Habsburg saved by "three mutinous soldiers"—Abdication of the Emperor Ferdinand in favour of his nephew, Francis Joseph—Hübner's description of the ceremony.

If we want to look at the disturbances which broke up the old order in Austria through contemporary eyes, our most helpful document will be the Diary of Metternich's wife, Princess Mélanie—so called, *tout court*, as an indication that she ranked, like the Archduchesses, as one of the Olympian goddesses of Viennese Society. One seems, as one reads it, to be listening to the shrieks of a fluttered bird; for Princess Mélanie understood as little as a bird would have understood, the true significance of the uprising. Sheer wantonness was, for her, the sole motive of the revolutionists; black ingratitude towards good rulers was their distinguishing characteristic; and the outcome of the agitation could only be "the end of all." All that because the students and the artisans had announced that they desired a "Constitution."

Already we have seen Princess Mélanie predicting that, if Guizot fell, all was lost; and, after the events of February, 1848, in Paris, she saw horrors accumulating on horror's head:—

"Poor Germany is already in a blaze. Never were times graver or more solemn. Every hour brings forth a fresh event, and fresh troubles are perpetually being added to those already in existence."

All the thrones in Germany were, in truth, being shaken, though they were all eventually to recover; and now the privileges of the Austrian throne itself were being challenged:—

"Kossuth has moved a resolution which the Chamber of Deputies has approved. These people actually demand nothing less than a Constitution for Austria!... The agitation is general, and the terror is great. People are so alarmed—

especially the great financiers—that they propose concessions to the popular demand, and see no chance of safety except in making them. One would say that Hell had broken loose. God alone can dam the torrent which threatens to swallow up everything."

At first, the trouble was confined to Hungary; but the contagion spread:—

"Here, too, the public is very much disposed to ask for a Constitution, and our various provincial assemblies are beginning to pass the most regrettable resolutions. May God enlighten us and give us the strength to be firm! That is all that I pray for."

And then:—

"The news from Germany gets worse and worse. There no longer *is* any Germany in the true sense of the word, for all the German sovereigns have been compelled to make concessions.... One really needs superhuman moral force to withstand this popular agitation."

So the trouble came nearer and nearer; and it became clear that Metternich himself was the object of popular hostility. Threatening letters were received. A piece of paper was found affixed to Metternich's door, bearing the words: "Down with Metternich. We want concessions!" Princess Mélanie herself received a significant warning, at one of her own receptions, from Félicie Esterhazy:—

"She let fall the following laconic remark: 'Is it true that you are going away to-morrow?' 'Why?' I asked her. 'Because we were told that we had better buy candles in order to be able to illuminate to-morrow, as a great event was about to happen.'"

A great event did happen on the morrow—though not the event which Félicie Esterhazy had in view; and Princess Mélanie witnessed it. She saw a demonstration on the Ballplatz, and heard an agitator, lifted on to the shoulders of his companions, shouting:—

"Long live the imperial house! We want concessions in conformity with the spirit of the times (cheers). Give us freedom of the press (cheers); let justice be administered publicly (cheers); let there be freedom of thought (cheers)! Let those who have outlived their usefulness resign and go (tremendous acclamations)!"

And Princess Mélanie complains that "no one interfered with this indecent demonstration," and that "no one attempted to silence the brawlers."

She called the demonstrations "indecent" because they were obviously aimed at her husband, who, far more than the Emperor, symbolised that *ancien régime* which the students and artisans were resolved to end. The Emperor, indeed, was merely a weak-minded, good-natured old gentleman to whom no one wished any harm. He was as ready to grant concessions as to give alms; and his subjects knew it, cheered him when he drove through the streets, and decorated their barricades with his portraits. Their objection was not to him, but to his police, who took Princess Mélanie's old-fashioned view of concessions: notably, therefore, to Metternich, the policeman of genius.

It was idle for Metternich to protest, as he sometimes did, in after years, that, though he might sometimes have governed Europe, he certainly had never governed Austria. The people knew—or thought that they knew—better. The chief article in their simple creed was that Metternich must go; and the sole question for Ferdinand and his Court and Ministers was whether Metternich should or should not be thrown overboard as a Jonah who brought ill luck to the Austrian ship of state. The upshot appears from these entries in Princess Mélanie's Journal:—

"At half-past six, Clement was sent for to the Palace."

"Yes, Clement has resigned."

The circumstances of the interview in which he did so were afterwards related by him to Hübner:—

"The Archduke Louis came to me and said: 'These gentlemen tell me that, if you could make up your mind to resign, order could be re-established.' I asked, 'What is it that your Highness desires me to do?' He replied, 'It is for you to decide what to do.' Thereupon I instantly resigned the office of Chancellor, and went into the adjoining apartment to inform the Delegates of the States that I had done so. One of these gentlemen spoke of generosity, and said that my resignation put a worthy coping-stone upon a long career. 'No, no,' I said. 'It is merely a concession to the revolution.'"

But he not only had to quit office; he also had to leave Vienna, where his life, in spite of his resignation, was not safe. He could not even leave at his leisure, but had to depart in a hurry without packing, dining with his friends, the Taaffes, and then driving off, in great haste, to Feldsberg, whence he made his way through Germany and Holland to England, where he landed just in time for his son Richard to be sworn in as a special constable, and bludgeon the Chartists, shoulder to shoulder with the future Napoleon III. The fluttered Diary records it all in a succession of shrill screams: What has Metternich—once the policeman of Europe—done to deserve such treatment! How black is the ingratitude of man! But Princess Mélanie might as well have exclaimed against the black ingratitude of water, which, under the exciting influence of heat, expands into steam, and blows up the man who sits on the safety-valve, without the least regard to his personal charm and intellectual culture.

So ironical is fate; and there was a still more cruel irony in the fact that the House of Habsburg, which owed so much to Metternich, seemed rather relieved to be rid of him, regarding his policy as an asset but his personality as an incubus. Alone among the members of the Imperial House, Francis Joseph's mother remembered to write a polite letter, inquiring how he was getting on, and confiding to him the hopes which were concentrated in her son, his political pupil:—

"My poor Franzi has been my sole consolation in our hours of trouble. In the midst of my anguish and despair, I have continued to bless God for giving me such a boy. His courage, his firmness, his judgment have been unshaken—altogether beyond what one would expect from a lad of his age—and have encouraged the hope that God will grant him a great career, since He has given him the strength to face all the risks of life."

But though the Archduchess Sophie wrote in that charming vein, she was herself one of those who had agreed that Metternich had better be sacrificed, as he was so inconveniently unpopular; and Metternich replied, not without a sense of bitterness, that he thought very highly of Francis Joseph, and had a great affection for him, and was quite confident that he would succeed in life as well as his mother could wish, if only he remembered and applied the maxims of statecraft which he himself had taught him. But he also, at the same time, chuckled through his tears, observing that the jettisoning of the Jonah did not seem to have saved the ship.

For order did not yet reign in Vienna; on the contrary, the revolution was going from bad to worse, and the Court had to leave the capital. First it went to loyal Innsbruck, in loyal Tyrol—whence Francis Joseph paid his visit, already mentioned, to the Army of Italy. Then it returned, under the illusion that things were going better; and then it went off again to Olmütz. Hungary and Bohemia, as well as Italy, were in open rebellion; and Vienna continued to throw up barricades from time to time. Unwelcome Ministers were forced on the Emperor, made concessions, and then gave place to others who promised still more concessions. The conditions of 1789, said the people who knew history, were giving place to the conditions of 1793. At any moment they might expect to see the guillotine "going always," and the Emperor's head rolling from the block into a basket.

Nor did the House of Habsburg, in that dark hour, save itself. On the contrary. "The monarchy," as Felix Schwarzenberg put it, "was saved by three mutinous soldiers": Radetzky, the octogenarian who would not grow old; Alfred von Windischgraetz, the unbending aristocrat, who was vastly more imperialist than the Emperor; Jellaçiç, the swaggering and self-sufficient Ban of Croatia. They agreed, to put it bluntly, that the Emperor Ferdinand was an old fool who had been bounced by his Ministers into giving orders which it behoved them to disobey. So Radetzky, being ordered to evacuate Lombardy, remained there; and Windischgraetz, being ordered to hold a portion of his forces at the disposition of the War Minister, replied that he could not spare them; and Jellaçiç, being dismissed from his command, refused to give it up. In that way, they collared the situation and saved it.

The Hungarians, marching on Vienna, were met by Jellaçiç and driven back. Windischgraetz, after first putting down the rising in Bohemia, marched down to Vienna and laid siege to it. Radetzky reinforced him, and then the end was near. Windischgraetz, in truth, had other reasons besides his loyalty to make him furious. His own wife had been one of the victims of the insurrection—shot while she stood at an open window to watch the rioting; so that it was not in the least likely that he would hesitate to shoot, or allow the insurgents to surrender otherwise than at discretion. First, therefore, he bombarded Vienna; and then he forced the gates and stormed the barricades. There was a certain show of resistance, but then, after a few military executions, order did really reign, and the House of Habsburg was really saved, except in so far as the Hungarians were still a menace to it. And the Emperor Ferdinand's first act, when his safety was assured, was to abdicate in favour of his nephew, Francis Joseph.

It was an abdication which had, long since, been contemplated, and even arranged. Metternich, the Empress, and the Archduchess Sophie had put their heads together and settled it. None of them had any illusions about the Emperor, and it does not appear that the Emperor had any illusions about himself. None the less, the secret had been well kept. Hübner, Schwarzenberg, and Windischgraetz were the only people who knew what was going to happen, or for what purpose the members of the royal family, and the functionaries connected with the Court, were suddenly summoned to assemble in the imperial residence at Olmütz at eight o'clock in the morning:—

"At half-past seven" (writes Hübner, whose function it was to take the minutes of the meeting) "the apartments adjoining the throne room were gorgeous with civil and military uniforms. There were present all the Archdukes and Archduchesses, with their ladies and gentlemen in waiting, the Canons of the Chapter of Olmütz, and a few ladies belonging to the aristocracy. Intense curiosity was imprinted on every countenance. The most remarkable guesses passed from mouth to mouth at this brilliant gathering, but—strange to say—no one guessed the truth. The Archduke Maximilian asked me what it was all about. The Archduke Ferdinand of Este addressed the same question to the War Minister, and received, as did the brother of the future Emperor, an evasive answer."

Soon the proceedings began:—

"Punctually at eight o'clock, the folding doors of the throne-room were thrown open to give admission to the Archdukes Maximilian, Charles Louis, and Ferdinand of Este, to the Archduchesses Maria Dorothea, widow of the Archduke Joseph, and Elizabeth, wife of the Archduke Ferdinand, to the Ministers, to Marshal Windischgraetz, to the Ban of Croatia, and to Count Grunne, Master of the Horse of the Archduke Francis Joseph.... When the door was closed on us, their Majesties, followed by the Landgrave Frederick of Furstenberg, Prince Lobkowitz, the Emperor's aide-de-camp, and the Landgravine of Furstenberg, grand mistress to the Empress, together with the Archduke Francis Charles, the Archduchess Sophia, and their son, the Archduke Francis Joseph, entered. Their Majesties took their places on two armchairs in front of the throne, and the Archdukes and Archduchesses took theirs on chairs arranged in the form of a rectangle on either side of the throne. The Ministers, Marshal Windischgraetz, and Ban Jellaçiç stood facing the Emperor. There was a deep and solemn silence."

The silence was broken by the Emperor himself, reading the statement prepared for him: the simple statement that important considerations had decided him to transmit his crown to his nephew. Then it was the turn of Felix Schwarzenberg. Ordinarily an impassive man, he now read, in a voice shaking with emotion, the three documents which gave legal validity to the transaction: the declaration that Francis Joseph had attained his majority; the declaration that Francis Joseph's father renounced his own rights in his son's favour; the Emperor's formal act of abdication. One after the other, the three documents were signed by those whom they concerned; and Francis Joseph knelt—for the last time—to Ferdinand, to receive his blessing.

Sei brav, es ist gerne geschehen, were Ferdinand's words. Literally it means: "Be good; I did it willingly." Practically it meant: "Never mind me. I don't feel hurt in the least. On the contrary, I'm well out of it." He ceased, and the retiring Empress embraced the boy Emperor. According to Hübner, the Archduchesses sobbed aloud, and there was not a dry eye in the room; and while the eyes of the company were still moist, the door was once more opened, and the courtiers, assembled in the ante-chamber, were informed of what had passed. That done, Francis Joseph rode out to review the troops, and receive their acclamations; while the Emperor Ferdinand and the Empress Marianna quietly took the afternoon train to Prague.

Thus the change was effected, quite simply, and almost without ceremony. It almost looks as though everything was done in a hurry, so that no one might have time to question the wisdom of doing it. "Farewell to my youth!" said Francis Joseph when, addressed for the first time as "Your Majesty," he realised the change in his condition, and the responsibilities to which he was committed, so soon after his eighteenth birthday. But he had never known what it was to be young, as boys of humbler station know it; and his opportunities of unbending, as some monarchs unbend, were to be few. He was the sole hope of the Habsburgs; he had to shoulder the whole burden of the Habsburgs; and he was to find it heavy. Princess Mélanie, when the news of his accession reached her, trembled for him:

"How is an Emperor of eighteen years of age to steer his course amid such conflicting currents? I shudder when I think of him—the last hope which now remains to us. May God bless him, and give him energy, while giving his counsellors the wisdom which they will need!"

The grounds of her anxiety—particular as well as general—appear on the same page of her Diary:

"They tell me that a Republic has been proclaimed in Hungary, with Kossuth as Dictator."

Which meant that Ferdinand had indeed reason to regard himself as "well out of it," and that Francis Joseph had not ascended an undisputed throne, but one for the defence of which he would have to fight desperately hard.

CHAPTER VI

Attitude of the Hungarians towards Francis Joseph—They denounce him as a traitor, and banish him from Hungary—Contempt of Austrians for Hungarians—The conquest of Hungary with Russian help—Repression and atrocities—Women flogged by order of Marshal Haynau—Marshal Haynau himself flogged by Barclay and Perkins' draymen in London, and spat upon by women in Brussels—Popular song written on that occasion.

The state of things which Francis Joseph found on his accession was this: In Vienna, all was over except the shooting and the shouting. Tyrol—the Vendée of Austria—was, as it always had been, loyal. In Bohemia, Windischgraetz had crushed the insurrection as he might have cracked a nut. But Italy and Hungary were still formidable, and had to be reconquered.

In Italy there was a renewal of the fighting; and the work done at Custozza had to be done over again at Novara—Charles Albert then taking a leaf out of the book of the Emperor Ferdinand and abdicating in favour of his son, the famous Victor Emmanuel. In Hungary, the work of conquest had hardly even been begun; and though Jellaçiç had held the Hungarians up at the gates of Vienna, they were in a position to hold him up many times before he could get to the gates of Buda-Pesth. So that the position was extremely critical.

It had been hastily assumed that Francis Joseph would be popular in Hungary. He had once been sent there, as a boy, to represent the Emperor at some public function, had made a fluent speech in the Hungarian language, and had been vociferously cheered. No doubt the precocious *bonhomie* of his manner had made a favourable impression; but that was not enough at a time when the old Hungarian privileges and the new Hungarian constitution were at issue. The affability of the sovereign was no substitute for the rights of his subjects; and the Hungarians would only consent to love, and be loyal to, the Austrian Emperor "on terms."

And those terms could not be granted. Francis Joseph, brought up in the school of Metternich, would hardly have been disposed to grant them if his hands had been free; and the men who stood by him—and over him—such men as Windischgraetz and Felix Schwarzenberg—would not have let him grant them if he had wanted to. As they had already saved Vienna for him, so they now proposed to save Austria and Hungary for him—but in their own way, and not in his. Knowing what they wanted, they told him what he wanted; and they had control of the machinery. In order to understand their proceedings, we must define their attitude, noting that they were, in the first place, aristocrats, and, in the second place, Teutons.

As aristocrats, they held that, as Windischgraetz put it, "mankind begins with the baron," and that no men except the nobly born had any rights which it was proper to take seriously—that they themselves belonged, in short, to a divinely designated ruling caste. As Teutons they regarded themselves as belonging to a divinely designated ruling race—the natural superiors of Italians, Hungarians, and Croats. Their conception of a sound imperial policy was, therefore, to employ the Hungarians to cut the throats of the Italians, and the Croats to cut the throats of the Hungarians; while they, directing operations, unified and Germanised the Empire.

The Hungarians, however, were a stubborn race who had no desire to be Germanised. They were, they urged, an independent people whose relations to the Habsburgs were defined by the Statutes of 1723; and they should not recognise Francis Joseph as their ruler until he had been crowned by their Archbishop at Pesth, and had sworn to obey the laws of the Kingdom of St. Stephen. That was the reply which they flung in Francis Joseph's teeth when he issued a proclamation indicating his intention to "unite all the countries and tribes of the monarchy into *one integral State.*" Hungary, they maintained, was not part of a State, but a State in itself, and should remain one. The Habsburgs, in trying to incorporate them in Austria, were "traitors to the liberties of Hungary," and should be banished from Hungarian soil for evermore. On those pleas issue was joined, and the Hungarian war of 1849 began.

THE EMPEROR FRANCIS JOSEPH AT THE TIME OF HIS ACCESSION
IN 1848.

It is one of the forgotten wars of European history: a particularly savage war, and one of which the issue hung for a long time in the balance. The heroic Georgei, whose name was then a household word, proved himself very nearly a match for the swaggering Ban of Croatia; and it looked, for a time, as though, even if Francis Joseph did reconquer his Kingdom, the days of Austria as a first-class Power were numbered. Palmerston, for one, thought so, and said so, declaring, in the House of Commons, that "if, the war being fought out to the uttermost, Hungary should, by superior forces, be utterly crushed, Austria, in that battle, will have crushed her own right arm."

But Palmerston was wrong; and Austria, neither for the first nor for the last time in her history, defeated the predictions of the prophets. She has been called the Sick Woman, as Turkey used to be called the Sick Man, of Europe; but the Sick Woman has had a wonderfully elastic constitution, and has been wonderfully favoured by the chapter of accidents. Again and again in her history we have a vision of *disjecta membra* re-attaching themselves, as it were, to the disabled trunk, so that it could once more get up and walk. It was so in 1849, when, the Poles having risen to help the Hungarians, the Russians, knowing what they themselves might have to fear from victorious Poles, crossed the frontier to Francis Joseph's rescue. That accident—happy or unhappy as one likes to regard it—turned the scale in the nick of time; and the rest was butchery, akin to that of the White Terror in France, but worse—a blood bath which scandalised Europe: the campaign of Haynau—called the Hyaena because of his grim chuckles at the sufferings which he caused—against the defenceless.

Certain excesses had been committed, in the early days of the revolutionary excitement—the War Minister, Latour, among others, had fallen a victim to mob violence. Those excesses were now avenged, not merely on the mob, but on the middle classes and on the Magnates. Croatian soldiers were turned loose on Hungarian towns, with a free hand to loot and ravish. Hungarian officers—officers who were also noblemen—were impressed as private soldiers, and placed in Austrian regiments, with the deliberate purpose of breaking their spirits. That was the treatment meted out even to some members of the great Hungarian houses of Esterhazy and Batthyany; and a Baron Podanitzky, who had been impressed in the artillery, was actually flogged in the streets of a Hungarian town on some absurd charge of having lost part of a bag of corn entrusted to his care.

Even women were flogged. Here is the deposition of one of them, published at the time in every newspaper in Europe—the truth of the story being confirmed, after inquiry on the spot, by the special correspondent of *The Times*:—

"Some imperialist troops entered Ruskby. It is probable that my enviable family happiness had created enemies at Ruskby, and that they were resolved to destroy it, for I am not aware that any of us had committed any fault. I was suddenly, without a previous trial or examination, taken from my husband and children. I was dragged into a square formed by the troops, and in the place in which I reside, and in the presence of its population, which had been accustomed to honour me, not because I was the Lady of the Manor, but because the whole tenor of my life deserved it, *I was flogged with rods*. You see I can write the words without dying of shame; but my husband took his own life. Deprived of all other weapons, he shot himself with a small cannon."

The story was contradicted, on the ground that no such place as Ruskby could be found on the map; but the only error was the printer's. The scene of the outrage was Ruskberg. The punishment was inflicted by the orders of a Captain Graber; and its victim was Mme. de Madersbach, the widow of a partner in the ironworks of Hoffmann and Madersbach. It was, of course, only one of the informal, and, as it were, accidental outrages. The formal outrages took the form of military executions. Generals and Colonels of the Hungarian Army, and Members of the Hungarian Chamber of Deputies were put to death—some of them hanged and others shot—until hardly one of them was left; and most of those who were left were sentenced to long terms of imprisonment in irons; while diplomatic machinery was set in motion—happily in vain—to obtain the extradition of the few fugitives who had succeeded in taking refuge with the Turks. The demand for their surrender, addressed to the Sultan, on behalf of the Austrians, by the Tsar, gave the Moslem an opportunity which he did not miss of administering a rebuke to the Christian:

"Your adjutant" (the Sultan wrote), "has demanded the extradition of the Hungarian refugees. The demand being made to excite hate against yourself as well as against me, I desire Your Majesty will not insist on carrying that point."

The most cruel of all the cruelties—the one, at all events, which made the greatest stir in the world—was the execution of Louis Batthyany, some time Prime Minister of Hungary. He was the grandson of the Batthyany who had saved the great Maria Theresa, when Frederick the Great chased her on to Hungarian soil, raising the cry—it was raised in Latin—*Moriamur pro rege nostro*; but the memory of that great service did not save him; and Countess Marie Larisch's statement, in "My Past," that "he eluded the executioner by poisoning himself in prison," is incorrect. He attempted to cut his throat with a blunt penknife, and failed; and was only shot, instead of hanged, because the dragging of a wounded man to the gibbet might have made too great a scandal. His widow made his son swear an oath that never, in any circumstances, would he speak to Francis Joseph, or in any way acknowledge his existence; and the handsome young Elemar Batthyany kept his oath, and long years afterwards used to cut the Emperor in the hunting field, while making love to the Empress behind his back.

If one could hold Francis Joseph personally responsible for these atrocities, one would, indeed, have to regard him as a sinister youth who has since grown into a sinister old man. One must hope, on the contrary—and one may fairly hope, as he was less than nineteen at the time—that he was only the dummy of a sanguinary camarilla, and the obedient son of a hard-hearted, ambitious, and self-righteous mother. But he assumed the posture of a sinister youth, whether he assumed it consciously or not, by refusing mercy even when mothers, who had succeeded in obtaining audience, knelt weeping at his feet, and pleaded for the lives of their sons, and replying cynically to a remonstrance against Louis Batthyany's execution that "the Imperial word had been pledged that every Austrian subject without distinction should be equal in the eye of the law." So that the Vienna correspondent of the *Kölner Zeitung* wrote:—

"Hanging and shooting—shooting and hanging. Such is at present the manner in which the men in power say good morning and good night to the nations of Austria. The strong hand in Austria is a bloody hand, and the slaughter once begun is so tempting that our rulers cannot think of leaving off. The whole of the civilised world protests against the present doings in Hungary. Schwarzenberg and his fellows cause public opinion to extend its imprecation to a greater person—to the Emperor whom the people ought not to be taught to associate with cruelties and deeds of blood, violence, and vengeance. Under the absolute government of former times, the people of Austria were fond of their Emperor; for whatever they suffered they threw the blame on the aristocracy and the bureaucracy. They said: 'If the Emperor could but know of it, he would help us.' At present nobody thinks of saying such a thing. They say, 'The Emperor knows it and he does it.'"

Cynicism reached its height—one cannot say whether it was Francis Joseph's own cynicism or not—in the attempt to maintain the gaiety of the Court in the midst of this Reign of Terror. As Baroness von Beck puts it:—

"Ball followed ball, *soirées* were announced, and assemblies were held, but Rachel wept still for her children, and refused to be comforted. The *Lloyd* published day after day the most magniloquent reports of the Court festivals, long lists of the beauties who assisted at them, descriptions of the gorgeous costumes with which they were adorned; but they were read without any emotion. It would not do; the city was in mourning; such fantastic attempts at mirth were out of season. They jarred upon the public feeling. If they ever won a moment of public approbation, it was like a smile upon a widow's countenance, speedily followed by a blush of reproach at her momentary forgetfulness of the one great sorrow."

When the Archduchess Sophia drove out, in fact, the common people often surrounded her carriage, in order to shout the names of the murdered Hungarians in her ear; and Countess Karolyi, whose son had been one of the victims of the repression, cursed Francis Joseph in scathing words which seem to sum up all the possibilities of human hate:—

"May Heaven and Hell blast his happiness! May his family be exterminated! May he be smitten in the persons of those he loves! May his life be wrecked, and may his children

be brought to ruin!"

A memorable curse truly, and one which one might, if one chose, take for the text of this biography, showing how time has brought the fulfilment of it, drawing the punishment out slowly, relentlessly, unceasingly. The tragedy of the Square of Queretaro, where Francis Joseph's brother faced a firing party of Republican executioners; the tragedy of the Vatican, where his sister-in-law lost her reason; the tragedy of Meyerling, where his only son perished in his shame; the tragedy of Geneva, where his wife was struck down by the dagger of the assassin—all these things, and many others also, might be represented as so many stages in the untiring and undeviating march of Nemesis—fulfilments of the curse, and illustrations of the familiar lines:—

Raro antecedentem scelestum Deseruit pede poena claudo.

Perhaps; but, if Francis Joseph's punishment was to come slowly, that of his instrument, Marshal Haynau, was to come quickly.

The day soon arrived when the Emperor realised that he must break his instrument. The butchery could not go on for ever, and the butcher—this Hyaena of Brescia—could not always be kept in evidence. When he had served his purpose, he must go. So his command was withdrawn from him; and he retired into private life, and went upon his travels. His travels took him to London, whither his reputation had preceded him. He called upon the banker Rothschild, who gave him an introduction to the brewers Barclay and Perkins, whose brewery he had expressed a desire to "go over."

Whether the banker deliberately set a trap for a hyaena or merely wished to oblige a client remains uncertain, even after a careful perusal of the letters of explanation which he sent to *The Times*. What is quite certain is that the draymen employed by Messrs. Barclay and Perkins knew that Haynau was coming, knew that he was responsible for the public flogging of women, and resolved to deal with him accordingly. Hardly had the brewery gates closed on him, when a truss of straw fell on his head from above, and then the trouble began.

A coherent account of the adventure might be difficult to

give; but there are certain details of it concerning which all the witnesses are agreed. Marshal Haynau was beaten with rods, as his victims had been beaten, and some of the rods were broken across his back. He fled for refuge into a dustbin, and was pulled out of it by the beard. Somehow or other, he escaped from the brewery and ran like a hare down the street; but he was caught, knocked over, and dragged along the ground by his fierce moustaches. A woman threw a pair of scissors out of the window of an upper chamber, appealing to the men to cut those moustaches off. Ultimately he ran into a public house, and there managed to evade his pursuers until the police delivered him.

The story was a nine days' wonder. *The Times* arose in its majesty and rebuked the draymen for their presumption in imagining that the misdeeds of people of importance were any concern of theirs; and *The Times* might as well have rebuked a volcano for forgetting its dignity and giving way to eruptions. The general sentiment found expression in a public meeting—also reported by *The Times*—whereat a vote of thanks to the draymen was carried unanimously, and Messrs. Barclay and Perkins themselves were warned that, if any one of their employees was punished for his part in the transaction, no British workman, from Land's End to John o' Groat's House, would ever again drink a glass of Barclay and Perkins's beer.

Then the writers of popular songs took the matter up, and this sort of thing was circulated on broad-sheets:—

> There was an Austrian General strong,
> Who flogged the ladies with a thong;
> He had a beard twelve inches long,
> His name was Marshal Haynau.
> He from his country had to run:
> He loved the knife, the cat, the gun,
> And cruel deeds of late was done
> By this old Marshal Haynau.
> From Barclay's brew-house he did scout;
> The women bawled, the men did shout;
> His hat fell off, and his shirt hung out,
> Oh, poor old Marshal Haynau!

At length he found a place to hide,
All at the George by Bankside,
But not till they'd well tann'd his hide,—
Barclay and Perkins's draymen.
Then for Barclay's men we'll give a cheer.
May they live long to brew our beer!
And from their masters nothing fear,—
Barclay and Perkins's draymen.

Nor was it in England only that Marshal Haynau was visited by public opprobrium. His offences were still remembered, two years afterwards, when he ventured to visit Brussels. There also, at the Vauxhall Gardens, the police had to protect him from the mob; and public opinion did not allow the punishment of the women who spat in his face in public, hissing at him the word "Hyaena." So intensely had the Austrian excesses stirred the indignation of Europe; and the only way in which Francis Joseph was able to express his resentment at the rough handling of the butcher who had done his dirty work was by refusing to send a representative to London to attend the funeral of the Duke of Wellington.

CHAPTER VII

Why Francis Joseph was called "The child of the gallows"—His affront to Napoleon III. and its consequences—The Bach system and the objections to it—Francis Joseph's *bonhomie*—The attempt on his life—Impressions formed of him by the King of the Belgians, and Lady Westmorland—The story of his romantic marriage.

It is a curious fact that Francis Joseph, who was to find the hangman so much work to do, was given, at his birth, the nickname of "the child of the gallows."

The story is that his mother, in the later days of her confinement, threw the scalding contents of a coffee-cup in her husband's face, and declared that she could be safely delivered of a child on one condition only—that a free pardon were granted to some criminal lying under sentence of death; and there was nothing for it but to satisfy her whim. The only Austrian subject fulfilling the conditions was clearly guilty of the blackest crimes; but he was let out of prison, to his amazement, at the hysterical request of the Archduchess Sophia, whose bowels of compassion then closed, never to be reopened.

Assuredly neither she nor anyone else prompted her son to compassion when Italy and Hungary lay helpless at his feet. The clemency accorded to a vulgar criminal was not to be extended to political offenders until the heads of all the tallest poppies had been cut off for the greater glory of the Habsburgs and their bureaucrats; and the policy of repression enjoyed an illusory success. If the strong hand was a bloody hand, the bloody hand was a strong hand; and Austria did not "muddle through" her difficulties, but carved her way through them. She had nothing as yet to fear from Prussia; she strode with jack-boots through Hungary and northern Italy; and the House of Habsburg—bankrupt, but with the most effective army in Europe—could once more afford to be arrogant. So that we find Francis Joseph, as soon as his position was secure, manifesting his family pride by a proposal that Napoleon III. should be insulted.

Napoleon—the triumph of his *coup d'état* having been confirmed by a plebiscite—had written to his royal and imperial cousins to announce his accession; and the question arose whether he should be welcomed as a member of the family, or snubbed as a *parvenu* intruding in exclusive circles. Should he be saluted, according to the time-honoured formula, as "Sir and Brother," or should he be rebuffed by a cold and contemptuous mode of address? Francis Joseph and his advisers favoured the latter course. The Emperor, that is to say, who had waded to his throne through the blood and slaughter of his subjects, despised the Emperor whose subjects had merely elected him, and proposed to keep him in his place by addressing him curtly as "Sir."

It was to have been a concerted insult, simultaneously administered by the Heads of the Houses of Habsburg, Hohenzollern, and Romanoff; and the Foreign Ministers of the three countries exchanged despatches on the subject. In the end, however, only the Romanoff showed the courage of his arrogance; and the Habsburg, after going far enough to offend, allowed himself to be intimidated into an appearance of courtesy. But Napoleon was not conciliated. He bided his time, resolved that the cousin who had devised the affront should pay for it. We shall see him presently exacting payment on the fields of Magenta and Solferino; but we must first follow Francis Joseph as he enters upon the path of reconstruction at home. It was the period in which his personality began to count.

He introduced what is called the Bach System—Bach being Schwarzenberg's successor in the Ministry of the Interior, a bureaucrat, who wanted to Germanise everybody and everything, as German bureaucrats always do: a process which pleased the Czechs and Croats as little as the Hungarians. "This is good," chuckled a Hungarian, in conversation with a Croat. "The Austrians give to you as a reward what they give to us as a punishment." That, clearly, was a frame of mind symptomatic of trouble to come; but two things staved off the trouble for the moment. Austria was strong, and Francis Joseph was affable, and could give the impression that his *bonhomie* was his own and that his severities were his ministers'.

He travelled about his dominions, making himself as pleasant as he could; he released two thousand political prisoners, and reduced the sentences of others. The mere possibility of such a magnanimous act shows how terribly cruel the previous repression had been; but the clemency produced a certain effect. No doubt Francis Joseph's reception in Hungary was, to some extent, stage-managed; but it was at least possible to pretend that it had been enthusiastic. The fact that he sat his horse like a centaur and spoke Hungarian like a native produced its effect; and he knew what to ignore, and how to turn a compliment. "I have met many Hungarians," he said on his return from his first journey, "and every one of them was a man of heart." It was what the French call *le mot de la situation*; and it helped.

Another thing which helped was the attempt made on his life at about this time by the journeyman tailor Libenyi, who tried to stab him in the back of the neck while he was walking on the Vienna ramparts, but struck a bone at the base of the skull, which turned the edge of the blade. He bore himself gallantly on the occasion, making light of the wound. "Do not be frightened, dear mother. My neck is merely a little stiff," he said to the Archduchess Sophia. "It is no great matter," he said to his officers. "After all, I was in no greater peril than my brave soldiers in Italy." These, again, were *mots de la situation*, appealing to the imagination. The Hungarians had a chivalry of their own which bade them repudiate the dagger as a weapon. Batthyany's widow and Karolyi's mother—she who had uttered the curse—would no doubt have been equally ready to pray God to smite the Emperor, and to thank God for sparing him, in order that he might suffer; but the Empire as a whole—not the Austrian section of it only—saw him as a gallant young man who had had a fortunate escape. Deputations came from the remotest parts of his dominions to congratulate him.

He was making a good impression, too, on shrewd observers. Bismarck, then a young man, being sent on some mission to him, spoke of "the fire of his twenty years joined to the dignity and thoughtfulness of a riper age," adding: "Were he not an Emperor, he would seem to me almost too grave for his years." The King of the Belgians, a little later, reported very favourably of him to Queen Victoria:—

"The young Emperor" (he wrote), "I confess I like very much, there is much sense and courage in his warm blue eye, and it is not without a very amiable merriment when there is occasion for it. He is slight and very graceful, but even in the mêlée of dancers and Archdukes, he may always be distinguished as the *Chef.*... He keeps everyone in great order without requiring for this an *outré* appearance, merely because he is the master, and there is that about him which gives authority, and which sometimes those *who have the authority cannot succeed in getting accepted or in practising*. I think he may be severe *si l'occasion se présente*: he has something very _muthig_. We were several times surrounded by people of all classes, and he certainly quite at their mercy, but I never saw his little _muthig_ expression changed either by being pleased or alarmed."

Lady Westmorland also wrote, at about the same time, to Mr. Hood:—

"I am very much pleased with the young Emperor, and especially with his tender affection for his mother, and his tender and respectful manner to her. He looks even younger than he is, and is not handsome, but has a well-built, active figure and a most intelligent and expressive face. He has a thoughtful face, and is perfectly unaffected. His mother is a very interesting person, and is wrapped up in this son, who seems likely to justify the pride she takes in him. The father is a very poor creature, who cares for nothing but having his leisure unmolested."

The picture, save for the reference to the inadequate Archduke Francis Charles, is a pleasant one. The portrait of Francis Joseph is the portrait of a man whose personality was already a great asset to his country; not at all the portrait of a man who was conscious of having been cursed by the woman whose son he had slain, and feared that the blows of fate would smite him—blow after blow from youth to age—in untiring fulfilment of that curse. On the contrary, it is the portrait of a fairly strong man who is also a decidedly cheerful man, with a mind conscious of rectitude; and no doubt it is accurate as far as it goes, for one cannot expect portraits to be prophetic. But the years were nevertheless to be full of trouble: political trouble was soon to strip the Habsburgs of treasured territorial possessions; while family troubles were to make their name a by-word as that of the most tragic house in Europe.

The political troubles were to begin with the bungling of Austrian policy in connection with the Crimean war, when Austria tried to run with the hare and hunt with the hounds, and gave offence to both. The Tsar, having saved Francis Joseph's throne in 1849, now thought himself entitled to more gratitude than was shown to him. "The two stupidest Kings of Poland," he said to Valentine Esterhazy, "were John Sobieski and myself"; for both of them had helped Austria in her hour of need, and been deserted by Austria when they were themselves embarrassed. Austro-Russian enmity in the Near East dates from that desertion; but the desertion was not complete enough to gain Austria the compensating friendship of France. So that presently, in 1859, France would help Sardinia to deprive Austria of the province of Lombardy, and Russia would stand by, chuckling at her discomfiture. But that, again, is an anticipation.

For the moment, indeed, all seemed well. Neither the political troubles nor the family troubles were as yet in sight; and it must have appeared, to any who gave a thought to the matter, that the Countess Karolyi had pronounced her curse in vain. Francis Joseph was the most eligible *parti* in Europe; and the time having come for him to seek a wife, he was not to have his marriage arranged for him by statesmen, to suit their policy, but to fall in love, almost as Princes do in fairy tales, in very romantic circumstances, though the romance, unlike so many of the Habsburg romances, was to be consonant with Habsburg dignity and self-respect.

It was not, of course, a Cophetua story. The Habsburgs are very fond of imitating King Cophetua; but they do so to their disgrace, and at their peril. Their names—unless good reason to the contrary can be shown—are changed. They cease to be Archdukes, become mere Orths or Wulflings, or Burgs, and are bowed, or kicked, as the case may be, out of the imperial circle. But a Cinderella story—that is another matter; and the story of Francis Joseph's marriage is one of the most famous Cinderella stories of modern times. Every fresh narrator of it adds some fresh detail, whether romantic or picturesque; but the essential facts in all the versions of the story are the same. It is always a story of a match arranged by a match-making mother, and of Prince Charming himself taking the matter into his hands at the eleventh hour, preferring Cinderella to her sisters, insisting upon his own way, and getting it, amid loud popular acclamations.

The Archduchess Sophia flattered herself that she had settled everything over her son's head. She wished to do a good turn to her poor relations—the Wittelsbachs, Dukes in Bavaria, and cousins of the reigning Bavarian House to which she herself belonged. There was a strain of insanity in the House of Bavaria—in both branches of it, in fact—as well as in the House of Habsburg; but the Archduchess Sophia did not think of that. The eugenists had not yet spoken, and she might not have listened to them if they had. Insanity, in those days, was regarded—especially in royal circles—as the accidental misfortune of the individual. "Tendencies" to insanity did not count; and any royal personage who was not mad enough to be locked up was thought sane enough to be married. Moreover, the Bavarian insanity was not, at the moment, very pronounced. Ludwig I. was not accounted mad because of his subjection to Lola Montez; and the vagaries of Ludwig II. and the raving mania of Otto still belonged to the future. It seemed to the Archduchess Sophia as right and reasonable as anything could be that the House of Bavaria and the House of Habsburg should intermarry yet again.

She talked the matter over with her cousin, Maximilian, Duke in Bavaria. He had a daughter, Princess Helen, of a suitable age—a very beautiful and charming girl; and it was settled between them that Princess Helen should become Empress of Austria. She was trained for that position as carefully as Francis Joseph was trained for the position of Emperor; and Francis Joseph quite approved of the plans which were being made for him—quite understood that his dignity limited his choice—quite believed that all was being contrived for the best by the best of all possible matrimonial agents. It was arranged that Princess Helen should be brought to Ischl to meet him; the subsequent announcement of his betrothal to her was, as it were, on the order of the day.

He went to Ischl, and met Princess Helen. She was very charming, but—still more charming, as it seemed to Francis Joseph, was her younger sister, Princess Elizabeth: the Cinderella who was kept in the background.

Elizabeth had not been trained for any great position. She was only sixteen: a madcap and a child of nature—accustomed, in so far as anyone in her station might be, to the untrammelled freedom of a highlander. She roamed the woods and the mountains—though not, as the author of "The Martyrdom of an Empress" tells us, with a gun in her hand, in pursuit of game. There are stories of her playing the zither, at the doors of cottages in remote Bavarian valleys, while peasant children danced to the music; and she was strangely beautiful, with haunting eyes and a wonderful wealth of hair. Depths of meaning looked out of those eyes: indications of those mysteries of her soul through which she was presently to figure as an unfathomable conundrum challenging a curious world. Francis Joseph—tall, handsome, blond, blue-eyed, a proud soldier and a gallant man, with no mystery or semblance of a mystery about him—looked into the girl's eyes, and was conquered.

Elizabeth was not formally presented—it was almost by accident that Francis Joseph first saw her. He was alone in a room when she entered, in a simple white dress, with flowers in her hair, and greeted him with a "Good morning, cousin." He kept her talking—and, of course, as he was the Emperor, she could not possibly run away and leave him, however shy she felt—for quite a long time; and he ended by saying that he hoped to resume the conversation at dinner, or at the dance which was to follow. But Elizabeth feared not. She was still "in the schoolroom"—not yet "out"—had "nothing to wear." "Still if your Majesty insists ..." she hesitated. "I do insist," said Francis Joseph. "Listen! We'll play a comedy. Say nothing to anyone, but dress for the party, and come down to it." "But I shall be scolded." "No, you won't. I'll see to that—you can trust me."

So the comedy was played; and, of course, when the Emperor expressed his pleasure at seeing the unexpected guest, the scolding flickered out; and, after that, matters progressed at a great pace, to the great chagrin, as one cannot doubt, of Sister Helen. The Emperor outraged all the proprieties by dancing half the night with the school-girl. When the dance was interrupted for tea to be served, he showed her an album containing coloured illustrations of the various national costumes worn in the eighteen States of Austria. "There," he said. "These are my subjects. I wonder if you would like them to be your subjects, too." Then they danced again; and when the cotillon came, he presented his little Cinderella with a bouquet of edelweiss, gathered with his own hands, with the result that everyone except Cinderella herself began to suspect that his intentions were serious.

His Cinderella, indeed, could hardly believe that his intentions were serious, even when her mother told her so. "What! Me an Empress! But I am nobody!" she exclaimed sceptically; but she had not long to wait before the sense of her importance was brought home to her, for at ten o'clock the next morning, Francis Joseph's carriage rattled up to the door of her hotel. "Is the Princess Elizabeth up?" he asked; and the reply was that Princess Elizabeth had not finished dressing. "Then I will see the Duchess," he said; and he went up and made his formal demand for his Cinderella's hand, with the result that, half an hour later, all the members of the Imperial family then in Ischl were summoned to the little parish church, and there, to the strains of the Austrian national anthem, the betrothal was solemnly celebrated. His words to his affianced bride, as he came out of the church, are said to have been:—

"This is the happiest day of my life. I owe my happiness to you, and I thank you for the light which you have brought into my life."

It was very sad, of course, for Sister Helen, who afterwards sought consolation—but perhaps failed to find it—by marrying the Prince of Thurn and Taxis. It was not altogether satisfactory to Duke Maximilian, who raised such objections as Laban raised when Jacob proposed to marry Rachel and leave Leah a spinster. It did not altogether please the Archduchess Sophia, who was a masterful woman, and would rather have got her own way than see her son insist successfully upon his. But it was a love match; and that, after all, is the main thing in royal as in other marriages. There was no need for the Court and Society journalists to rack their brains for reasons for describing the union as "romantic." It was romantic on the face of it—as romantic as anything in any fairy-tale.

And yet——

And yet, as it proved, things were not exactly what they seemed to be; and that marriage, so romantically contrived and concluded, was to be the starting-point of tragedies; the beginning—if one is superstitious and takes that view of things—of the fulfilment of Countess Karolyi's curse.

CHAPTER VIII

The failure of the marriage—Difficulty of explaining it—The two conflicting personalities—Francis Joseph's personality obvious—The Empress Elizabeth's personality mysterious—Her sympathy with the Hungarians, and its political importance—Her confession of melancholy.

The failure of a marriage—of a royal marriage as of any other—is necessarily wrapped in mystery. The full facts are never made known; and one always feels that the facts kept secret were probably more important than the facts disclosed. Moreover, personality—that mysterious thing which none of us ever reveals completely to any one observer—inevitably counts for more than the tangible events on which we can lay our fingers. So with this marriage of Francis Joseph's. The outcome of it—what the world has been allowed to see of its outcome—can only be understood, in so far as it is intelligible at all, if we examine it in the light of a personality which perplexed Europe for a generation, perplexing it more and more as years went on.

Not two personalities, be it observed, but one. There are some personalities which fail to create an atmosphere of mystery even behind an impenetrable screen; and Francis Joseph's personality is of that type. One always feels that, beyond what one knows of him, there is very little to be known. It is characteristic of all the Habsburgs that they cannot cross the road without striking an attitude which shows us exactly where they stand and what they think of things; and it is easy enough to accept the present Emperor as typical of the Habsburgs at their best. He comes before us, frank and brave, adaptable and affable, but, at the same time, proud as Lucifer; infinitely gracious to those who do not presume—readily regarded by such as a gallant soldier who has grown into a genial old gentleman, anxious to make things pleasant for everybody—yet seeming, at some crises of his fate, to mistake himself for God, and the Archdukes for the archangels; not because they behave as such, but because they are Habsburgs and ought to.

That is a perfectly simple type; one does not complicate it when one adds that Francis Joseph has always been a punctual observer of Roman Catholic ritual, and, taking the *métier* of Emperor seriously, has risen early throughout a long life in order to work at it with all the diligence of a devoted civil servant. All that—down to and including the occasional ceremonial washing of the feet of the poor, in imitation of his Master Christ—has been the straightforward fulfilment of an intelligible programme. If Francis Joseph had washed the feet of the poor because he had felt that they needed washing, and would not otherwise get washed, the case would have been different, and one would have suspected subtlety in his character. But he has only washed them gingerly—after servants had seen to it that they were already clean—in the manner of an actor aiming at spectacular display; and one no more finds anything subtle or elusive in that piece of symbolism than in anything else that he has done.

About the Empress, on the other hand, it is impossible to read a page from any pen—whether that page be written by an intimate or by a stranger—without feeling oneself in the presence of a mystery which the most favourably placed chroniclers have failed to penetrate. A novelist of genius might perhaps have invented her—Mr. Maurice Barrès, for one, is a little prone to write as if he had invented her; but she was not to be understood by courtiers, secretaries, and ladies-in-waiting. They recite her traits at great length, but almost in vain; telling us of her kindnesses, her eccentricities, her vanities, but still leaving us at sea—puzzled by the melancholy which preceded the apparent occasions for melancholy, and by the restlessness which chased her, like a gadfly, from the haunts of men, unless it was that she herself pursued—she knew not exactly what—and never found it. Countess Marie Larisch seems to have been more in her confidence than anyone else; but Countess Marie Larisch only saw what she was capable of seeing—which assuredly was not all. One may admit all Countess Marie Larisch's facts, and yet doubt the completeness of her portrait.

And if Elizabeth's confidante, in so far as she had one,

did not understand, how was her husband—a mere man—a mere soldier—a mere Habsburg—to do so? He, being, as the French say, *tout en dehors*, could not possibly comprehend her who was *tout en dedans*. His happiness in marriage—as long as he actually was happy in it—must have depended on the assumption that his wife was as simple and translucent as himself: as simple and translucent as Cinderella or the Sleeping Beauty. He fell in love with her in that belief, as any other gallant young soldier might have done; and there is no doubt whatever that he was very passionately in love. "As much in love as any lieutenant in my army," was his own way of putting it; and when his bride came down the Danube to join him, he ran to greet her on her boat before the gangway was made secure, and very nearly fell into the water.

That, as he did not actually slip in, was an auspicious beginning; and it is on record that Emperor and Empress and everybody else said, and sincerely meant, the right and proper and auspicious things. "The bride," said the Austrian people—and the Hungarian people too—"is the most beautiful woman in all Christendom." "I am glad," Elizabeth wrote in the veteran Radetzky's album, "that I am about to belong to a country which possesses an Emperor who is so great and good, and a hero of Radetzky's valour." "Never before," said Francis Joseph to O'Donnell—the officer who had grappled with the tailor Libenyi, on the day of the attempted assassination—"did I feel so grateful to you for saving my life, for never before did I value my life so much"; and he showed his joy by pardoning prisoners and giving 200,000 florins to the poor; while the sympathies of the whole people followed the young couple when they departed on their honeymoon, and gathered edelweiss together, like any other honeymooning couple:—

"The recollection of that April day," wrote a witness of the scene, "will never be effaced from my mind. The old among us felt themselves young again, the sorrowful became glad, the sick forgot their pains, and the poor their poverty. All alike were eager to see the companion whom the Emperor had chosen as the partner of his life. God only knows how many tears of joy ran down our cheeks, and what ardent prayers were uttered by our lips."

It is easy to say, in the light of subsequent events, that the joy was too bright to last, and that the hope arose, only to be overcast; but it is difficult, setting superstition aside, to say why it was so, though it is not impossible to trace some of the steps by which it came to be so. In this exalted household two factors which are often seen at work in humbler households were presently, though not quite immediately, to play their part: a mother-in-law and an Egeria.

The pity was the greater because, from the point of view of politics and the dynasty, the Emperor's beautiful bride promised to be, and indeed was, an asset of great value. The popularity for which he had to work hard she achieved without an effort by the indefinable charm of her youth and loveliness, especially among the romantic and chivalrous Hungarians, who had not yet forgiven Francis Joseph for the severities of 1849. She had Hungarian blood in her veins, though her Hungarian ancestors were remote; and she had no responsibility for the atrocities of the repression. On the contrary, she made it clear to Hungarians that she sympathised with their sufferings and delighted in their country: its vast spaces and its heroic patriots, indomitable even though conquered.

Amnesties, as we have seen, attended her arrival among them—amnesties which she may or may not have inspired, but of which she certainly got all the credit. Whatever she was or was not, she was, at any rate, tender-hearted and impulsive with the impulsiveness of a generous girl who feels instinctively that all the people who are locked up ought to be let out and given a second chance, unless they are really dangerous criminals. The Hungarians, in consequence, fell in love with her to a man, with a passion different from, but more enduring than, her husband's; and one of them—Count Alexander von Bertha—wrote of her marriage:—

"It was the installation on the throne, under the ægis of beauty and charm, of the guardian angel of the Magyars, to whom the young Empress felt herself specially attracted by the memory of her patron saint who belonged to the House of Arpad."

THE EMPRESS ELIZABETH OF AUSTRIA.

The allusion is, of course, to the Empress's namesake, Saint Elizabeth of Hungary; and the sentiment stirred by the association bore practical political fruit. It is no depreciation of the work done in later years by Deák and Beust to say that their task would have been vastly more difficult if Elizabeth had not charmed the spirits of the Hungarians, and that it was largely owing to the spell which she had thrown upon them that Deák was able to announce, when asked to name his terms after the disasters of 1866, that Hungary demanded no more after Sadowa than she had asked before.

That was a great achievement—not to be made the less of because it was due to no conscious statesmanship, but merely came about through the idealisation of a beautiful and sympathetic woman by a childlike and romantic race, too long accustomed to be treated as pariahs by the domineering Teutons. If the laws of romance had governed the business of the world, it would have set the seal on the happiness of a marriage which had begun so happily; but it seems that, as a matter of fact, the happiness had taken wings and fled long before Elizabeth's charm had conciliated her husband's enemies to this good purpose—long, also, before the occurrence of those specially tragic events which were to make their reign memorable for tragedy.

At first, no doubt, she showed a naïve delight at her sudden elevation to imperial dignity. The dramatic change in her fortunes appealed to her imagination; and it seemed as if all the glories of the world were hers. But—vanity of vanities! The years passed—a few years only—and Elizabeth had learnt the Preacher's lesson. Even then, one suspects, the desires which haunted her were vague. She did not know exactly what it was that she wanted; but she knew only too well that, whatever it was, neither her marriage nor her exalted rank had given it to her; and we soon begin to hear of her long journeys in pursuit of the fugitive shadow, and of the mysterious melancholy which had visibly settled on her. She was still a young woman when she said to a confidante, *apropos* of what one is left to guess: "I feel as if something had died in me." She was not yet thirty when Countess Marie Larisch—a child who had climbed a tree— saw her in tears in circumstances which she has graphically described:—

"I nearly fell out of the tree when I recognised the Empress, who had apparently given up the idea of riding, and was walking quite unattended.... Elizabeth came slowly to my tree, under which was a stone seat. She sat down, clasped her hands in a despairing kind of way, and began to cry silently. I could see that she was greatly distressed, for her face wore a hopeless expression, and occasionally a sob shook her. She then wept unrestrainedly, and at last I wondered whether I dared attempt to comfort her. I bent down, and as the leaves rustled with my sudden movement, the Empress looked up and saw me."

That is, perhaps, the most typical of all the pictures of

her melancholy, though one could take many others from the writings of other chroniclers. She told the child she had been crying because her little daughter had been unwell during the night, but the child did not believe her. She told the child not to tell anyone that she had seen her cry, which she would hardly have troubled to do if her tears had had such a simple source. Some speeches attributed to her at other times would seem to indicate that she cried sometimes for lost illusions, like a child for a broken toy:—

"The happiness which men seek in sincerity and ask from it is controlled by tragic laws. We all live on the edge of an abysm of grief and pain, dug for us by the falsehood of social morality. That is the abysm which separates our actual condition from the condition in which we ought to find ourselves. An abysm is always an abysm. The moment we try to cross it, we fall and break our limbs."

That is her own confession of melancholy; and we must make what we can of it in the light of what we know. It is not, perhaps, a melancholy of which we shall be able to discover all the causes, but we may be able to arrive at some of them. The quest will bring us back to certain matters already touched upon, and lead us on to other matters. We shall have to speak of the Egeria, the mother-in-law, the formal rigidity of Court etiquette, and the way in which Emperor and Empress endeavoured to escape in different directions from what they were both, in their several ways, coming to regard as irksome imprisoning restraints.

CHAPTER IX

Francis Joseph's Egeria—Elizabeth's mother-in-law—Elizabeth's quarrels with etiquette—The beginnings of estrangement—The functions of Countess Marie Larisch in the imperial household—Captain "Bay" Middleton—Nicholas Esterhazy—Elizabeth's fairy story—Her cynical attitude towards life.

Francis Joseph's Egeria was the Archduchess Elizabeth, grandmother of the present King of Spain. It has been written that she "set her cap" at him; but she was a widow, and it was held that a widow was no proper bride for a Habsburg Emperor. So she became his Egeria, and a source of discord. The Empress could not get on with her; nor could the Empress get on with her mother-in-law.

The Archduchess Sophia was jealous to see this chit of a child winning the affection of the very people by whom she had herself been hooted in the streets of Vienna; jealous, too, because the child's influence over the Emperor promised to be greater—as it was indubitably more salutary—than her own. Moreover, she was a woman with many old-fashioned prejudices; and she disapproved of Elizabeth, pretty much in the way in which Victorian mothers disapproved of revolting daughters, and for somewhat the same reasons. She saw this chit of a child—abominably brought up, as it seemed to her, in free-and-easy Bavaria—not only chafing under the fetters of immemorial etiquette, but actually tossing those fetters off with gestures of defiance. War between them was inevitable—war not the less deadly because it was not openly declared, but was waged by means of shuns and slights. Naturally, too, while the common people were in favour of the Empress, the courtiers of the old school sided with the Archduchess. Let us cite a few of the details.

Just as Marie-Antoinette had once scandalised the French Court by riding a donkey, so Elizabeth scandalised the Austrian Court by calling for beer—the excellent beer of Munich—and, according to some chroniclers, also for sausages, at the imperial luncheon table. She scandalised it a second time by refusing to throw her shoes away after she had worn them once; a third time by going shopping on foot, attended only by a single lady-in-waiting; a fourth time by taking off her gloves at a banquet at which etiquette prescribed that gloves should be worn, and laughing at the regulation when her attention was called to it. The anecdotes, thus summarised, seem trivial; but they have an inner significance as a record of an embittered conflict on that eternal theme: Which are the things that matter?

For the Archduchess Sophia the things that mattered were those rites and ceremonies which distinguished Habsburgs from inferior members of the human family. Whatever were the things that mattered to Elizabeth—and she might have found it difficult to say what they were—they certainly were not these things. So that her case which, at the beginning, recalled the story of Cinderella, comes also to remind us, after the lapse of a little time, of the story of that Village Maiden, who was wooed and married by the Lord of Burleigh; and one thinks of the lines which tell us how

> her gentle mind was such
> That she grew a noble lady,
> And the people loved her much.
> But a trouble weighed upon her,
> And perplex'd her, night and morn,
> With the burthen of an honour
> Unto which she was not born.
> Faint she grew, and ever fainter,
> And she murmured, "Oh, that he
> Were once more that landscape painter,
> Who did win my heart from me!"
> So she droop'd and droop'd before him,
> Fading slowly from his side:
> Three fair children first she bore him,
> Then, before her time, she died.

Or rather, as Elizabeth herself put it in the quotation from her table-talk already given, something died within her.

Mme. de Boigne, it will be remembered, commenting on the story of the Lord of Burleigh, said that the fate of the Village Maiden served her right, and was a just and proper vindication of class distinctions. The Archduchess Sophia's attitude towards Elizabeth was very similar. Just as the haughty Windischgraetz laid it down that "mankind begins with the baron," so the Archduchess Sophia would seem to have held that mankind began at the confines of the imperial circle, and that the traditional manners and tone of that circle depended upon first principles and universal laws. So she had no sympathy for Village Maidens who set up their own likes and dislikes against the prescriptions of Habsburg ritual.

Gossip charges her with doing more than scold—of throwing a mistress at the head of her son, and a lover at the head of her daughter-in-law, in order to estrange them from each other; but those who knew her declare her to have been too pious a woman to engage in such intrigues. Mischief-makers are often pious; and pious people are often mischief-makers; so it may have been so. But estrangement nevertheless soon succeeded to enthusiasm; and the present writer has the word of Countess Marie Larisch for the fact that Francis Joseph was the first—whether his mother's promptings had any influence in the matter or not—to feel that the marriage had not yielded all that had been hoped for from it.

He, at any rate, had felt the *coup de foudre*. The Empress had been too young to feel it, and had accepted an offer of marriage very much in the spirit in which she would have accepted an invitation to a ball. So she was not responsive, for they were not born to understand each other; and he, in his disappointment—keenly conscious of the very real, but impalpable, barrier between them—let his fancy stray. Then she, in the course of time, did the same; with the result that, even at the end of their married life, they were "strangers yet," not openly, nor even privately, so far as anyone knows, at variance, but drifting apart, and each ceasing to take an interest in the other's inner life.

The process had already begun when Countess Marie Larisch saw the Empress weeping under a tree in the Bavarian Highlands. It had reached a further stage when the Empress sent for Countess Marie Larisch to live with her and be her confidante, and initiated her into her delicate duties at Gödöllo, her Hungarian hunting-box, with the significant warning:—

"Listen, my child. At Gödöllo there is one thing to remember every hour of the day: You must not speak of anything which you hear or see, and your answers to questions must be 'Yes,' and 'No,' or 'I don't know.'"

The time has since come when it has seemed good to Countess Marie Larisch to disregard that injunction, in her own defence, and to give the world rather a full account—albeit in the form of hints and insinuations—of a good many of the things which she heard and saw. She had, as she admits, her own very definite and somewhat delicate functions at Gödöllo; functions with the performance of which the Crown Prince Rudolph was, some years later, when she quarrelled with him, to reproach her:

"You are a fine one" (Rudolph was to say) "to talk of honour or morality. You have been the go-between for my mother since you were a girl. And yet you dare to mention morality to me, when you have not scrupled to stand by and see my father deceived."

That was the outburst. Of course Countess Marie Larisch protested; but the general trend of her book shows that the protest was due to anger rather than to the indignation of outraged innocence. This being the Life, not of the Empress, but of the Emperor, there is no need to go into the matter at great length; but some of the scenes pictured and some of the facts set forth have a symbolic value, which forbids their omission. Even before Countess Marie was in attendance—as early as Elizabeth's long sojourn in Madeira—people seem to have found occasion to talk:—

"Count Hunyadi" (writes Countess Marie) "was one of her suite, and I do not know what actually happened, but I *do* know that the Chamberlain spied most effectually on my aunt. The Count was recalled to Vienna, and Elizabeth's stay in Madeira came to an abrupt conclusion."

Evidently it was for the purpose of throwing dust in the argus eyes of Chamberlains and the like that Countess Marie was enlisted in the Empress's service. She portrays herself, more than once—though always with apparent care not to say either too little or too much—in the act of throwing the dust. The great occasion was the day on which Captain "Bay" Middleton—sometimes called William Tell because he was something less than a model of reticence—who had been on a visit to the Austrian Court, had to say good-bye. Elizabeth (Countess Marie tells us) "made no attempt to disguise her liking" for the celebrated English sportsman, whose good looks, athletic prowess, and popularity with ladies have furnished the theme of many chapters of many volumes of social gossip.

At all events the Empress's eyes were swollen with weeping on the day of Captain Middleton's departure; and the Emperor came to pay a most inopportune visit to her apartments at the time when the adieux were being said. Elizabeth appealed to Countess Marie to find an excuse to keep him out; and Countess Marie's powers of invention did not fail her:—

"I ran forward. 'Who is there?' I asked. 'The Emperor,' replied a voice; 'can I come in?' 'Oh, Majestat,' I stammered, 'how unfortunate that Aunt Cissi is not able to see you! She is trying on some riding habits.' 'Oh, then I'll return later,' answered Francis Joseph, and I heard the sound of his retreating footsteps in the corridor."

Whereupon Countess Marie was congratulated by the Empress on "unusual tact"; and we encounter, a few pages further on, the following significant paragraph:—

"The Emperor's rooms were far away from Aunt Cissi's, and her doors were always guarded by soldiers. Francis Joseph, who was very much in love with his wife, was often kept at a distance when Elizabeth's love of solitude obsessed her, and then she was never seen by anyone except the members of her immediate *entourage*."

Another passage of a different kind of significance is that in which Countess Marie tells us how she herself received a proposal of marriage from Count Nicholas Esterhazy, and informed the Empress, and subsequently was visited by the Empress in her bedroom at the dead of night:—

"Elizabeth was all in white; her hair was wrapped about her like a heavy mantle, and her eyes shone like a panther's; in fact, she seemed so strange that I was quite frightened, and waited, trembling, for her to speak.

"'Are you awake, Marie?'

"'Yes, Aunt Cissi.'

"'Well, sit up and listen to what I have to say.'

"I sat up obediently, and she continued in cold, decisive tones:

"'It is my duty to tell you that Count Esterhazy has a *liaison* with a married woman, who loves him. After hearing this, will you accept his proposal?'"

What Countess Marie means us to think is clear enough, though she does not tell us; and equally clear is the inner meaning of that Fairy Story which she says that the Empress told her by the side of a mountain tarn at Possenhofen. Countess Marie's reviewers, occupied mainly with her new facts about the Meyerling tragedy, seem to have thought that Fairy Story unworthy of comment; but when one comes to read it carefully, one finds it a consummate example of the art of conveying a suggestion without making a definite statement. Observe: it is Elizabeth who is represented as speaking:—

"Once there was an unhappy young Queen, who had married a King who ruled over two countries. They had one son, but they wanted another to succeed to the other kingdom, which was a lovely land of mountains and forests, where the people were romantic and high-spirited. No child came, and the young Queen used to wander alone in the woods, and sit by just such another lake. One day she suddenly saw the still surface move, the lilies parted, and then a handsome man appeared, who swam towards her, and presently stood by her side."

And now let us see how the dots drop by themselves on to the i's. Austro-Hungary is known to all of us as "the dual monarchy"; and Hungary—or a portion of it—is justly described as "a lovely land of mountains and forests." Elizabeth bore only one son—the Crown Prince Rudolph. The date of Prince Rudolph's birth was 1858; and, for a period of ten years, Elizabeth had no other child. Those indications given, we return to our Fairy Story.

It relates how the stranger—who announced himself as "the spirit of the lake"—carried the young Queen down "a crystal staircase" to a mysterious palace, where she "sat beside her lover on his crystal throne, and slept in his arms on a bed of lily leaves," but afterwards "returned to the King's palace"; and so we are led along the paths of poetry and fantasy to this conclusion:—

"Some months passed, and the Queen knew that she would have a child, and she longed for a son like the Water Spirit, who would reign over the romantic country of mountains and forests which she loved.

"But no son came, for when the child was born, the young Queen pressed to her heart a little daughter, with her Fairy father's large black eyes.

"'Did she ever see him again,' I asked, much interested.

"'I do not think so,' replied the Empress, 'when you have more experience of the world you will realise that a baby is the end of many love-affairs.'

"'What did the King say?' I queried.

"'He had too much vanity to say anything, whatever he may have suspected,' said Elizabeth; she laughed her mocking laugh, and was her cynical self again."

All this, Countess Marie would have us think, is an allegory; but it is safer to leave the veil hanging over the facts, or alleged facts, which she means it to allegorise. Fairy Stories are not evidence—least of all when one only gets them, as in this case, at second hand; but, if this Fairy Story cannot be trusted for facts, at least it can be trusted for atmosphere, and both Elizabeth's and Francis Joseph's attitudes towards life seem to be displayed in it.

Of his attitude we will speak at the appropriate time; hers strikes one as that of a woman who could not escape from her emotions and her longings, and yet never got any lasting satisfaction from the indulgence of them. Her life, on its sentimental side, one feels, was not continuous but episodical; not an epic poem, nor even a drama, but a series of short stories,—each of them ending, as Guy be Maupassant's short stories so often do, in anti-climax. Hence the importance which she attached—and Countess Marie accumulates details about that—to the preservation of her beauty; for the dwindling of beauty necessarily made those "beginnings" which Mme. de Staël tells us "are always happy," more difficult. Hence also those frequent journeys, apparently so meaningless, which give one the impression, not of a cultivated tourist eager to see the world, but of a shadow pursuing shadows, and brought to melancholy by the repeated failure to capture and hold them, and then continuing to travel as a means of escape from herself. Countess Marie quotes a speech which indicates that mood:—

"Marie, sometimes I believe that I'm enchanted, and that after my death I shall turn into a seagull and live on the great spaces of the ocean, or sheltered in the crevice of some frowning rock; then I, the fettered Elizabeth, shall be free at last, for my soul shall have known the way of escape."

Hence, again, the superstition which led her to consult fortune-tellers, and look for omens in glasses of water. Hence finally that cynicism already remarked, and further exemplified in another speech which Countess Marie reports:—

"What *I* do not mind doing, nobody else need cavil at," she often said. "Love is no sin," she would remark. "God created love, and morality is entirely a question for oneself. So long as you do not hurt anyone else through love, no one ought to presume to judge you."

There shall be no attempt to judge her here; the attempt is only to portray.

A good deal would have to be added to make the portrait complete; not merely those details of the toilette which Countess Marie gives in such abundance; not merely particulars of the daring horse-woman's delight in the tricks of the *haute école*—a delight so intense that Elizabeth once followed the circus-rider Elisa to Paris, and brought her back to Austria, paying the forfeit on her broken engagement; but facts which show her compassion with the sufferings of humanity. Sustained philanthropic endeavour was not, indeed, much in her way; but she was easily stirred to those *élans* of sympathy which are far more effective than systematic philanthropy in winning the hearts of the humble. When she visited the hospitals after Sadowa, the wounded blessed her on their deathbeds.

Still, these facts, though necessary to completeness, are not of the essence of the portrait. The essence of the picture lies in Elizabeth's unavailing pursuit of happiness, and her unavailing flight from herself—on horseback as long as her health let her ride, and always with a volume of Heine's poems in her pocket. It was not, perhaps, a very sane proceeding; but she came, as we know, of a family which was not very sane. One of her sisters—the Duchesse d'Alençon—was for some time under observation in a private asylum at Graetz, known as *le rendezvous des Princes*, on account of the number of its royal inmates; and the sister whom Francis Joseph jilted in order to marry her, became, as Princess of Thurn and Taxis, a victim of religious mania. Her own eccentricities must not be estimated without reference to these facts.

Estimate them as we may, however, one thing is certain. Between Elizabeth, with her fancies and vague cravings for she knew not exactly what, and Francis Joseph, with his direct, straightforward, soldierly outlook on life, no enduring bond of sympathy was possible. Fate forbade it, and ordained that they should drift apart; and Fate had its way with its playthings. How Francis Joseph's fancy strayed—and how Elizabeth, instead of opposing its divagations, encouraged them—we shall see in the course of a few pages.

THE COUNTESS MARIE LARISCH AT THE TIME OF HER MARRIAGE.

CHAPTER X

"The Martyrdom of an Empress"—Correction of inaccuracies contained in that popular work—Francis Joseph's friends—"A Polish Countess"—Frau Katti Schratt—Enduring attachment—Rumour of morganatic marriage—Interview with Frau Schratt on that subject—"Darby and Joan."

Of the many Lives of the Empress Elizabeth the most widely circulated has been the one entitled "The Martyrdom of an Empress"—a work which purports to give an authoritative "inside" view of the Habsburg Court. Even M. Jacques La Faye, the author of the very latest of the Lives, appears to have accepted it as a source of trustworthy information. The writer, who is known in America as a journalist, and implies that she was on terms of intimacy with the Empress, has doubtless raked together a good deal of floating Viennese gossip, but she nevertheless makes, on nearly every page, statements which it is hard to believe that she would have made if she had ever conversed with Elizabeth, or even been in the same room with her.

A copy of "The Martyrdom of an Empress," annotated in pencil by a lady once attached to the Austrian Court, is now lying on the writer's table. "To read this book," runs the first note, "is a martyrdom for one who knows"; and corrections of points of detail follow quickly—corrections, in many cases, of statements of little importance in themselves, but none the less completely destructive of the claim of the writer corrected to have studied the life of the Hofburg, or even of Gödöllo, from within. The Empress's eyes, according to the author of "The Martyrdom of an Empress," were "glorious dark blue orbs"—or, in another passage, "luminous sapphire-hued": her eyes were actually brown. The Empress, according to the same authority, stamped "her little foot"; she actually had large feet, as became an energetic pedestrian, and is reputed to have been very jealous of the tiny feet of that rival beauty, the Empress Eugénie. Bismarck's reptile Press, at one time, derided her for the size of her feet.

And so forth. A few further passages of text, with the annotator's gloss appended to each of them, will most effectually show the claim to inside knowledge evaporating under the incisive examination of one whose knowledge was really acquired inside:—

AUTHOR: "The Duke (in Bavaria) was by no means a wealthy man, and all his disposable means were lavished upon the education of his older daughters."

COMMENTATOR: "There was only one older daughter, Helen, Princess of Thurn and Taxis."

AUTHOR: "She hunted and shot with her brothers."

COMMENTATOR: "The Empress never took a gun in her hand—never touched one."

AUTHOR: "All her love became centred upon little Archduchess Gisela, who had made her appearance in the world in 1856."

COMMENTATOR: "She never looked at the baby, and Archduchess Sophia took care of it."

AUTHOR: "A very unpalatable adventure of which her husband was the hero ... broke the last restraint upon her indignation, and, without informing anybody of her intentions, she hurriedly left the imperial palace of Vienna for Trieste, and set sail for the Ionian Islands on board her yacht, fully resolved never to allow her husband to approach her or to speak to her again."

COMMENTATOR: "She had no yacht of her own at that time, and travelled with the consent of the Emperor. Her brother accompanied her to Trieste."

AUTHOR: "In the summer following Baby Valérie's birth, the Empress spent several months with the Crown Prince and his two sisters."

COMMENTATOR: "Baby Valérie was quite separated from the others, the Empress being very jealous about Valérie. Gisela and Rudolph were mostly kept in Laxenburg."

AUTHOR: "Elizabeth walked over to a large harmonium which stood near the open window. She sat down before it, and after striking a few chords which echoed through the stillness of the chamber, she sang Schubert's 'Serenade.' She was a great musician."

COMMENTATOR: "The Empress never touched a harmonium nor a piano. She was not a bit musical, and *never* sang."

AUTHOR: "'Rudi,' who was watching them, said suddenly——"

COMMENTATOR: "The Crown Prince was never called 'Rudi,' always 'Rudolph.' His pet name was 'Nazi.'"

AUTHOR: "'Mutzerl,' as Baby Valérie was called——"

COMMENTATOR: "Valérie was never called 'Mutzerl,' but 'Shedvesen,' by her mother. It means 'darling.'"

AUTHOR: "Valérie ... swam like an otter, rode almost as well as her mother, fenced and shot with great skill."

COMMENTATOR: "Valérie never learnt to ride, as the Empress would not allow it, and never fenced or shot."

AUTHOR: "She was riding alone on that day."

COMMENTATOR: "The Empress *never* went out riding alone."

AUTHOR: "'My poor boy! my poor boy!' she kept repeating. 'I am afraid you do not realise what misery such a marriage as that which you are about to make can bring about!'"

COMMENTATOR: "To *me* the Empress said, 'Let him marry whom he likes. I don't mix myself up in Rudolph's affairs.'"

AUTHOR: "That Rudolph met Marie Vetsera and her mother in London and called upon them several times is quite certain."

COMMENTATOR: "Rudolph never met the Vetseras in London."

AUTHOR: "Mademoiselle Ferenzy read to her from English, French, and Hungarian books."

COMMENTATOR: "Mademoiselle Ferenzy could only read Hungarian."

That may suffice; but any reader who has skipped the quotations should turn back to them. They may not matter very much in themselves—except to those to whom everything connected with royalty matters; but they do show us how Court history is sometimes written by journalists, and what is the historical value of the "revelations" of anonymous pretenders to the intimacy of Sovereigns. It was worth while, as the opportunity offered, to elaborate the demonstration, because the book containing the statements confuted— together with many others of an equally untrustworthy character—was for a time accepted as authoritative by the readers of two continents, and passed through several editions, on the assumption that it presented the authentic depositions of one who had really been behind the scenes.

The author was, in fact, so little behind the scenes—and so little qualified in other respects for her task—that she did not even know her way through the Almanach de Gotha, or remember elementary facts which anyone without special sources of information could easily ascertain. She places the scene of the imperial betrothal at Possenhofen, whereas it actually occurred at Ischl; and she states that the Empress was not of "royal" birth, whereas she was the granddaughter of a King. These things being so, it obviously is not to her writings that one must turn for details of the secret history of the estrangement between the Empress and the Emperor. That secret history, in so far as the Emperor's flirtations are concerned, would not, in the opinion of those who are nearest to knowing it, make a very startling tale even if one could know it all.

It is not the rule, of course, for Emperors in the prime of life, estranged from their consorts, to deny themselves, on principle, all alternative attachments; and there is no reason to suppose that Francis Joseph did so. But his volatility was only comparative, and did not last long. The witnesses who attest the volatility also assure us that, taking his imperial grandeur as seriously as it deserved to be taken, he soon "settled down" and became, in the language of less exalted circles, "steady." There was a certain Polish Countess; but that is too old and unimportant a story to be revived. The one lady whose name it is imperative to mention in connection with this branch of the subject is, of course, Frau Katti Schratt; and the circumstances in which the Emperor made Frau Schratt's acquaintance shed an illuminating light upon the terms on which he and the Empress came to live.

It was in 1885, when the Empress was about to depart upon one of her frequent journeys. "Her kind heart," writes Countess Marie Larisch, "reproached her when she thought that her husband would perhaps be lonely during her absence." So she inquired whether any of the ladies about her knew of any other lady who would be willing to "entertain" the Emperor while she was away, but could be trusted not to exercise any undue influence over him:—

"I mentioned several ladies" (Countess Marie continues) "who, I felt sure, would only be too delighted to console the imperial grass widower, but Aunt Cissi did not approve of them, and the matter dropped until she suddenly told me one day that she had discovered the right person in the actress Katrina Schratt, who was always considered to be more interesting off the Burg Theatre than on it.... People rather disapproved of Elizabeth's attitude, but she was quite right in thinking well of the actress, who has, since the death of my aunt, proved herself to be a devoted friend to Francis Joseph."

That, assuredly, sounds as improbable as anything in "The Martyrdom of an Empress." An Empress sallying into the highways and byways to seek a guardian angel for the Emperor, and finally extracting one from the *coulisses*, and presenting her, with the result that she becomes the friend of the family as well as the Emperor, and the Emperor takes a continual delight in her society for thirty years—that, indeed, is an amazing picture, not to be accepted, even on Countess Marie Larisch's authority, without corroborative evidence. But the story seems, nevertheless, to be literally true. The corroborative testimony is available, and shall be produced.

In the main, indeed, the Emperor's attachment is as

notorious as his marriage, and stands in as little need of proof. Frau Schratt at once became, and has ever since remained, a national institution—related to Court circles, though not exactly of them. It became the recognised thing that, when the Emperor went to Ischl, she should go to Ischl too; that she should have a cottage there, and that the Emperor should take tea at that cottage daily—entertained by Frau Schratt, but not by her husband, of whom one hears little, though it is understood that he was given an appointment which kept him usefully and profitably occupied at a distance from the tea-parties.

Nor was it at tea-time only that Francis Joseph was to be heard of at Frau Schratt's domicile. He was occasionally an evening visitor as well; and one of his evening visits concluded with a dramatic incident. He had stayed into the small hours, and desired, in consideration for the feelings of others, to depart without disturbing the household. Being unaccustomed, however, to stealthy movements, he stumbled over the furniture and disturbed the cook, who, suspecting that a burglar had intruded, came courageously downstairs, attired in her nightgown, and carrying a bedroom candle. Her impulse was to scream, but Francis Joseph checked it. "Don't you see that I'm the Emperor, you silly woman?" he said in a stage whisper. Whereupon the cook, profoundly loyal, but not knowing exactly what course of conduct a manual of etiquette would prescribe in the situation, fell on her knees at her Sovereign's feet, and began to sing at the top of her voice: *Gott erhalte Franz den Kaiser!*

Such was life in the early days of this interesting relationship, which settled down, as the years passed, into a very peaceable and comfortable domestic alliance. That there have never been any unfavourable comments is more, of course, than can truthfully be said. Rebellious members of the House of Habsburg, anxious to go their own amorous ways without reference to the Habsburg rules, have sometimes felt that the state of the affections of the head of the house gave them a handle, and have sometimes pulled that handle. If the Emperor flaunted his attachment to Frau Schratt, why should not the Archduke Leopold permit himself to love Fräulein Adamovics, and the Archduke John permit himself to love Fräulein Stübel—these ladies, at any rate, not being married women? So they have argued; and the former Archduke once, on a very dramatic occasion, brought the vials of the Emperor's wrath down upon his head by calling him "Herr Schratt" to his face.

But Francis Joseph, being a strong man and a loyal friend, was not to be moved by such affronts, or turned from the path which he chose to pursue, by the fear of scandal; and presently there was a battle royal on the subject in the House of Habsburg. The Emperor's daughters—the Archduchesses Valérie and Gisela—expressed themselves as scandalised and shocked, and conceived it to be their duty to wean their aged father, who was now more than seventy years of age, from the society which gave him so much pleasure. They so far succeeded that Frau Schratt left Ischl in a hurry for Brussels, and a wag braved the perils of *lèse-majesté* by inserting in the "agony colum" of the *Neue Freie Presse* an advertisement in conspicuous type, running: *Katti, come back to your sorrowing Franz.*

And she came back, albeit by a circuitous route, honourably attended, and in triumph. The first hint that she was about to do so appeared as exclusive information in the Paris *Le Siècle*:—

"Everyone in Austria knows of the affectionate relations which bind Frau Schratt, formerly of the Burg Theatre, to the Imperial Family. Some time ago Vienna learned with surprise that she was about to retire, and make a journey from Bavaria that would end in Rome. The journals soon after announced that she had come back from Rome, and that the Pope had given her a lasting benediction. Now it appears, though the affair is not yet wholly unveiled, that the Pope not only vouchsafed to Frau Schratt, who was accompanied by the Comtesse de Trani, sister of the late Empress, a paternal reception, but even yielded to pressing instances, supported by diplomatic action, in granting her prayer to declare the nullity of her marriage with Baron Kisch, by whom she has a son."

Rumour added that these proceedings were only preliminary to the celebration of a morganatic marriage between the Emperor and the actress; morganatic marriages being, as is well known, contrivances for reconciling the human passion which over-rides the barriers of rank with that family pride which does not over-ride them. But rumour, for once, was wrong. A Berlin paper—the *Lokal Anzeiger*—sent its representative to ascertain what Frau Schratt had to say on the subject; and Frau Schratt opened her heart freely to the reporter, and, in doing so, supplied the confirmation of the story which we have quoted, with provisional scepticism, from Countess Marie Larisch. All this talk about her marriage with the Emperor, she said, was "nonsense." Those who engaged in such talk knew neither her nor the Emperor. And then came the allusion, for which we have been looking, to the part played in the matter by the Empress:—

"That high-minded and noble lady was my most gracious patroness and friend. In the unrest caused by the mental and bodily pains which drove her from one place to another, it was a comfort to her to know that a good-tempered, light-hearted woman cheered up her husband, and gave him many a pleasant, harmless hour by chatting with him and relating all sorts of anecdotes and stories; attending him in his morning walks in the Schönbrunn Gardens whilst he was taking his Carlsbad water, and never abusing her extraordinary position for intrigues or to push *protégés*. It was the Empress herself who, hating the stiff Court life and Court dignitaries and ladies-in-waiting, had created my position, which I then maintained owing to the gracious confidence and gratitude of the Emperor.

Every spring I was the first to bring the late Empress, wherever she was staying, the first violets, and I always spent a few days with her. An Empress, however magnanimous and high-minded she may be, remains in certain questions above everything a woman. And is it, therefore, really possible to believe that the Empress would have honoured me with her grace and confidence in such an extraordinary way if even the possibility had existed in her thoughts that, after her death, I might marry the Emperor?"

It is really a remarkable interview. One is not, of course, entitled to say that the whole of Mme. Katti Schratt's soul is revealed in it. One may take the liberty of doubting whether her respect for the memory of her friend, the Empress, was the sole reason why the proposed morganatic marriage was not concluded. There must also have been representations from many quarters—from the Emperor's Ministers as well as from his daughters—that while such a marriage would cause a public and family scandal, it would hardly, in the circumstances, add anything appreciable to the happiness and privileges of either party. On that point one is certainly entitled to prefer one's own judgment to the lady's account of the self-denying ordinance. But Frau Schratt's tacit assumption that the society of frivolous actresses is, of all kinds of society, the most agreeable to men, is a very delightful trait, and, though not a universal truth, does appear to have been supported by the facts of the particular case she was discussing. The assumption, too, that she was, naturally and necessarily, a good deal more to the Emperor than the Emperor could ever hope to be to her, is a pleasing example of the proper pride of the ladies who achieve distinction on the stage and leave it because they are even more admirable off the stage than on it.

On the episode of the divorce—and perhaps even on the whole story—a stern, unbending moralist might have something to say. Such a one might even contend that the Pope himself does not come out of the story very well. But then Popes have almost invariably, throughout the course of history, proceeded on the assumption that the ordinary rules of morality may properly be waived in favour of Catholic potentates; and a distinguished French moralist has laid down the rule that a *liaison* may acquire the dignity of marriage if it lasts long enough.

And this particular alliance has certainly endured for an extraordinary length of time. It still endures at the time at which these lines are written; and when one contemplates it, one finds oneself thinking, not of frivolous gallantries or passionate romances, but of domestic idylls, such as those of Darby and Joan, Philemon and Baucis, and John Anderson, my Jo.

One does not know, of course, whether Frau Katti Schratt ever, at any of her *tête-à-tête* tea-parties, sings the Emperor the sentimental ballads which consecrate those legends, but there is no reason why she should not—unless it be that she does not know them—and there are many reasons why she should. An unruffled fidelity extending over a period of nearly thirty years, and lasting until extreme old age, has surely earned both him and her a full title to the enjoyment of the emotions which they express.

CHAPTER XI

Francis Joseph's passion for field sports—Enthusiasm of a nation of sportsmen for a sportsman Emperor—Anecdotes of sport—Estrangement of the Emperor and the Empress—The Empress's departure for Madeira—Her *wanderjahre*—Her attitude towards life—The keeping up of appearances.

It seemed better to defy chronology, and speak of Frau Schratt at once. We do not want her continually flitting across the stage, to the interruption of grave historical discourses; but we do want to realise that she is there—a fixed domestic institution, bringing Francis Joseph, in a sense, into line even with the Habsburgs whose vagaries have caused him consternation. If she had predecessors, she has had no rivals; and no story arises out of the invitations to the imperial alcove of which certain other theatrical ladies used to boast in the earlier years of the reign. We will leave those matters, therefore, and next give the necessary passing glance at the Emperor's notorious passion for field sports—a passion which has contributed more than a little towards his popularity.

It often is so; such tastes being held to contribute the touch of nature which makes the whole world kin, and the belief that a good shot is sure to be a good fellow being deeply rooted in the human breast—especially if the sportsman respects the rights of property, and compensates agriculturists for damage done in the pursuit of game. To some extent, indeed, the mere fact that an Emperor does not go shooting in his crown and royal robes, but in a costume similar to that worn by the peasants themselves, conveys to the bucolic mind a pleasant impression of condescending affability. Moreover, rustics like to be employed as beaters, and enjoy hearing and handing on stories of imperial sportsmen wandering, and losing themselves, and being mistaken for other people, and keeping up the illusion, and laughing at the mistake.

There has been a good deal of that sort of thing in Francis

Joseph's reign; and his most popular portraits are those which exhibit him, alike as a young man, an old man, and a man of middle age, attired in knickerbockers, heavily nailed boots, and a picturesquely plumed Tyrolese hat. A certain *rapport* seems to be established by those portraits between a sportsman Emperor and a nation of sportsmen. Habited in the costume indicated, Francis Joseph has sometimes in the mountains, and even in his own parks, played the part of Haroun-al-Raschid; and many anecdotes are told about his adventures in that character.

Not all of them, of course, are true; and we will hope that the more malicious stories are false. The story, for instance, that Francis Joseph, taking part in a *battue* in the midst of the troubles of 1866, asked an aged peasant for a light for his pipe, and was told the aged peasant's candid opinion of Emperors who amused themselves by pursuing game when their subjects were dying for them on the stricken field, is probably the invention of a political malcontent. A more agreeable story—and one at which the Emperor himself may chuckle—is that of his encounter with the farmer who took him for an ordinary trespasser and threatened that, if he did not clear off his land at once, he would first shoot him in the posterior parts as a mark of identification and then inform the police; and he is, no doubt, as pleased as his people are to remember how he once arrested poachers with his own hand in one of his own parks, and having satisfied himself of the truth of their representation that they were honest old soldiers who had come to poverty through no fault of their own, gave orders that they should be given appointments as gamekeepers. A ruler of whom stories of that last kind are told never fails to be popular with the sporting classes of the community; and the parade of gamekeepers from all parts of the Empire, which was one of the most picturesque features of Francis Joseph's Jubilee celebrations, impresses one as a most proper sequel thereto. These stories, however, though necessary to atmosphere, are only incidental. It is enough to glance at them, just as it is enough to glance at the story of those world-wide wanderings of the Empress which began, long before she had provided Frau Schratt to "entertain" the Emperor during her absence, with her sudden departure for

Madeira, in 1860.

Legend has crystallised round that departure: it has been called a "flight," and attributed to the cumulative effect of three distinct domestic disturbances. First of all, we are told, there was a disturbance caused by the terrible Archduchess Sophia, who would not allow the Empress to bring up the infant Crown Prince in her own way: a trouble which may have been bitter at the time, in spite of Countess Marie Larisch's assurance that the matter presently became one of absolute indifference to her. In the second place, we are informed, there was a disturbance because Francis Joseph made too public a display of his affectionate regard for a certain Fräulein Roll, of one of the Viennese theatres; and finally, if the reports may be trusted, the quarrel reached its climax because Francis Joseph suffered himself to be fascinated by a peasant girl whom he met when out shooting.

Francis Joseph, on that occasion, according to the story which was current, stayed out all night after dismissing his retainers; and one of the retainers told his wife what had happened; and the lady repeated the story to other ladies of the Court at one of Elizabeth's receptions; and Elizabeth overheard, and acted on the impulse of the moment. She dismissed her ladies, and called her maid, announcing her intention of setting out at once, secretly, for a long journey. The maid did her bidding; and she got as far as Trieste, where a functionary, sent in pursuit, overtook her and induced her to return—a course to which she consented only on the understanding that, after appearances had been saved, she should be allowed to set out again, with the Emperor's express approval.

Whether things really happened just like that; whether it is true that the flight was only hindered by the discretion of the captain of the yacht, who opportunely discovered that his engines were out of repair; whether it is also true that Francis Joseph threw himself at Elizabeth's feet, confessing his fault, imploring her pardon, and ascribing the blame to his mother—all these are points on which a conscientious investigator would hesitate to commit himself. The story— given in M. Weindel's *François-Joseph Intime*—is more than fifty years old; and no authoritative correspondence or *procès verbal* relating to it has been published. All that is positively established is that the doctor was called in, and certified that Elizabeth was suffering from a pulmonary weakness which necessitated her removal to a warmer climate. So she set out for Madeira; and Francis Joseph accompanied her a part of the way. How she left Madeira in a hurry, in consequence of reports sent home concerning her manner of life there, has already been set forth on the authority of Countess Marie Larisch.

That was the beginning of her *wanderjahre*; and there was to be no end to them until her death. Elizabeth had learnt the importance of keeping up appearances; and she did not forget it. Francis Joseph did not need to learn it; for he has always stood out among the backsliding Habsburgs as a great actor-manager, so to say, keeping up the imperilled dignity of the House by playing a great part on a great stage in a manner worthy of the great traditions to which so many members of his family have proved unfaithful. *Noblesse oblige* has been his motto, though not theirs—though he may only have given it a limited, spectacular application; and, if Elizabeth did not meet him half way in the matter, at least she went a part of the way to meet him.

The result is known. On great ceremonial occasions Elizabeth consented to appear, as she put it, "in harness," and performed imperial functions with splendid, though perhaps absent-minded, dignity. She was as beautiful as the Empress Eugénie. She had a grander—a less skittish—manner; and she quite understood that the frame in which her beauty and grandeur were set at Schönbrunn and the Hofburg threw a halo of glory about her head, quite different from that which adorned the rival beauty who was Queen of the Revels at the Tuileries, Fontainebleau, Saint-Cloud, and Compiègne. But she was, nevertheless, always glad when the functions were over and the harness could be taken off. She was like Little Nell's grandfather, whose one desire was to be "further away." She never lost that impulse; and, if it ever slackened, something was always sure to happen to renew it. It received a great impetus from the Tragedy of Meyerling; perhaps—it is hardly doubtful—an earlier impetus from the incident which drew from her the bitter remark that "a baby is the end of many love affairs."

So she wandered as much as she could—though she returned to Vienna when she felt that she must—and a detailed relation of her wanderings would almost read like a chapter from a road-book. She saw the Isles of Greece and the Norwegian Fiords. She bathed on the coast of Norfolk, and hunted in Ireland and in the Shires. She sojourned, for a season, at Steephill Castle near Ventnor in the Isle of Wight— the present dwelling of an American gentleman who sells medicines reputed to be beneficial to the liver; and a red-brick house in which she passed another season is pointed out at Cromer. She also went to Amsterdam for massage, and to Cap Martin to sit in the sun; and she visited her home in Bavaria, and her sisters' homes in Paris, and stayed at Claridge's in London, and drank the waters at Kissingen. It was sometimes thought that she deliberately courted death by her daring feats of horsemanship. Her manner became that of a woman for whom life had nothing left, except what converse with Nature could offer. She even spoke of Nature as her "sole mediator with God"; and the scattered fragments of her table talk which those who knew her have preserved, are full of detached sentiments of a kind of poetic pessimism:

"We must try to make islands of ourselves."

"When we cannot be happy in the way that we desire, there is nothing for it but to fall in love with our sorrows."

"In the life of every man there comes a time when his inner life becomes extinct."

"I know that he who revolts suffers a hundred times more than he who is resigned; but resignation is a thing of which I am not capable."

"I should like to be buried near the sea, so that the waves might beat against my coffin. Then all the stars in Heaven would shine on me, and the cypresses would lament for me far longer than either men or women."

Such phrases sound, as it were, the *leit motif* of the mystery of Elizabeth's life. She seems to have thrown them out, without telling anyone what sorrow or disappointment had inspired them. Each reporter who tries to guess at their meaning offers a different conjecture. The unkindness of Francis Joseph, who was not unkind—the unkindness of some lover, who was—the tragic deaths of her son, her cousin, her brother-in-law, and her sister—all these things have been cited, by one chronicler or another, as explanations of her funereal gloom. But, as she confided in no one, no one need pretend to know, or to do more than draw the picture of a woman as unhappy as she was beautiful—clinging to her unhappiness as she clung to her beauty—wandering restlessly through Europe like a shadow pursuing shadows, but running home from time to time to keep up appearances.

And the picture, to be complete, should also show the figure of Francis Joseph, doing his full share in the keeping up of those appearances, and taking long journeys in order to pay periodical visits to the Empress, who was making it so clear, to all who cared to look, that she was happiest away from home, and always wearing on his countenance that look of bland and imperturbable serenity with which his innumerable portraits have made Europe familiar. It is a picture full of lights and shadows and strange contrasts; but we must not dwell upon it any more. Our attention is claimed by the supplementary spectacle of the Emperor at odds with fate, confronting the difficulties which threatened to tear his Empire to tatters, and gradually getting that Empire into some sort of order.

CHAPTER XII

Francis Joseph's snub to Napoleon III.—Proposal to address him as "Sir" instead of "Brother"—The consequences—Napoleon asks: "What can one do for Italy?"—Austria at war with France and Italy—The crimes committed by Austria in Italy—Battles of Magenta and Solferino—Francis Joseph compelled to surrender Lombardy, but allowed to retain Venetia.

Other things besides his wife's secret sorrows—or even his own—claimed Francis Joseph's attention through the 'fifties, 'sixties, and 'seventies. The hour for the fulfilment of Countess Karolyi's curse had not yet sounded; but it did seem as if that "break-up" of Austria which statesmen think about when they lie awake at night was imminent. Hungary was sullen; Prussia was ambitious and jealous; the Italian subjects of the Habsburgs hated them. It was the Italians who were destined to speak first.

They had already spoken in 1848; but then they had been silenced, because Radetzky had been a good general, and Charles Albert a bad one. But Victor Emmanuel was a greater man than Charles Albert, and he had Cavour to guide him. *Italia fara da se*—Italy will work out her own destiny—had been Charles Albert's motto. Victor Emmanuel and Cavour played a more subtle game, and looked out for allies; and in Napoleon III. they found an ally who was quite willing to help them; a sympathetic man who had once been involved in the Carbonari movement; a sensitive man whom the head of the House of Habsburg had snubbed as a *parvenu* by proposing to address him as "Sir" instead of "Brother."

So Napoleon's sympathies were worked upon, and the wires were pulled. It is said that the beautiful Countess Castiglioni helped to pull them, adding the influence of her charms to that of her arguments; and the statement is probable enough, for the Emperor of the French was susceptible. At any rate, he presently asked Cavour the point-blank question: "What can one do for Italy?" and a little later, in July, 1858, he had a quiet talk with Cavour at the Baths of Plombières, and arranged what should be done, and what should be his own share of the plunder.

Francis Joseph may have guessed what was coming when he read the reports of Victor Emmanuel's speech at the opening of his Parliament, in January, 1859, containing the pregnant declaration that, "while respecting treaties, we cannot disregard the cry of grief which rises to us from so many parts of Italy." His guesses must have become certainties when, at the New Year's reception of the *corps diplomatique*, Napoleon remarked, with chilly politeness, to Hübner, now Austrian Ambassador, in the hearing of all the other Ambassadors:—

"I regret that our relations with your Government are not so good as they have been; but I beg you to assure your Emperor that my personal sentiments towards him have undergone no change."

A double-edged saying; for his feelings were hardly likely to be friendly towards the originator of the scheme for snubbing him as "Sir" instead of saluting him as "Brother." In any case it was a saying which meant war; and war was not long delayed. Francis Joseph, in fact, anticipated the inevitable by summoning Sardinia to disarm within three days; but Sardinia refused to disarm, and the French came over the Alps, beat Francis Joseph at Magenta and Solferino, and turned him out of Lombardy, though allowing him to retain Venetia.

That was the beginning of the end; and the event contains an important moral,—the moral that the one permanent peril to European peace arises out of the hatred invariably felt for persons of German nationality by the races subjected to their rule.

The trouble with the German, whether of the North or of the South, is always this: that he regards himself as a heaven-sent ruler of men, but can, as a matter of fact, only govern in a state of siege. He can win battles, and organise a civil service; but he can neither conciliate nor assimilate his subjects. The German Empire is sometimes compared (by Germans) to the Roman Empire; but the difference between the two things is wide. The Romans, when they conquered the world, made it contentedly Roman. The French, similarly, when they took over Savoy from Italy, made it contentedly

French. But no German dependency is ever contentedly German. Alsace is not; nor is Schleswig-Holstein, or Prussian Poland. In all these places, the German, in his jack-boots, strides about among a people who find his language barbarous, his culture ridiculous, and himself an odious interloper. And it has been the same thing in Austrian Italy, where, even to this day, the few Italians who remain "unredeemed" refuse so much as to join the Austrian Alpine Club, but have preferred to form a smaller Alpine Club of their own.

In the days of which we are speaking, Austria ruled Lombardy and Venetia as subject provinces. At the same time, other Habsburgs reigned in Modena and Tuscany, while the abominable Bomba of Naples was the Empress Elizabeth's brother-in-law. Not in his own provinces only, but throughout Italy, popular representation was roughly refused. Italy, it was held, was "a geographical expression," and must behave as such. If it did not, then leading Italian citizens must be hanged; and, if there were any difficulty in getting evidence to hang them on, it must be obtained by torture.

It is a fact, incredible as it may seem, that the Austrians used, in the 'fifties, to torture their Italian subjects in prison. It is a fact that they flogged, and sometimes executed, Italian civilians for "failing in outward respect" towards the Austrian soldiery. It is a fact that they flogged women for the comments which they passed on such proceedings. It is a fact that they shot a butcher, found in possession of a butcher's knife, for carrying forbidden arms, and a lunatic for going through the motions of drill in a public thoroughfare. It is a fact, finally, that, exasperated at the manner in which every official Austrian institution was boycotted, they notified the public that "if anybody by criminal political obstinacy persisted in not frequenting the theatre, such conduct would be regarded as the silent demonstration of a criminal disposition, which merited to be sought out and punished." The policy was as childish as it was savage, and as savage as it was childish. Gladstone had it in mind when he made his famous remark that nowhere on the map of Europe could one lay one's finger and say: "Here Austria has done good." His mistake lay not in offering that criticism, but in afterwards apologising for having offered it. What the Italians themselves thought of the matter is best shown by the written declaration which one of their victims handed in to his judges after his condemnation to death:—

"I declare" (he said) "that, rather than deny the sacred principles on which the cause of Italian liberty and independence repose, rather than adhere to the rapacious policy of Austria, rather than sanction its claims by any act which might seem to concede them, or by any submission to its authority, I, Pietro Fortunato Calvi, once officer of the Austrian Army, and late Colonel of the Italian Army during the War of Independence, now condemned to death for the crime of high treason, go joyfully to this death, declaring from the scaffold that what I have done I have done knowingly, and that I would be ready to do it again in order to drive the Austrians out of the States which they have infamously usurped."

His judges asked him, in their arrogance, whether he would ask the pardon of the Austrians for his disloyalty to them. His reply was that he desired neither their pardon nor any other favour:

"I hate, and will always hate, the Austrians, until the end of my life, for all the ill they have done to Italy."

The Austrians, that is to say, behaved as shamefully in Italy as in Hungary; and this time Francis Joseph was held responsible. When he took his bride to pay his Italian dominions a ceremonial visit, the Italians made it clear to him, as they subsequently made it clear to the Archduke Maximilian and the Archduchess Charlotte, that what was desired was not his condescension, or that of any member of his family, but both his and their ejection.

They made it clear in various ingeniously offensive ways. When the Archduke Maximilian appeared, with the Archduchess, in the Piazza at Venice, the whole population withdrew, leaving them alone there, as if they were lepers who might spread contamination. When Francis Joseph, accompanied by the Empress Elizabeth, drove through the streets of Milan, not a head was uncovered, and not a cheer was heard; all the acclamations being pointedly reserved for the Italian Syndic, who was compelled, as an official, to follow in the procession. The Italian ladies, at the same time, dressed so as to display, by a cunning arrangement of stuffs, the colours of the Italian flag; and, when the "Guerra, guerra" chorus, from *Norma*, was sung in the Scala, the audience applauded it as if they would never stop.

It seemed, therefore, to be Victor Emmanuel's clear mission to help the Italians to fulfil an obvious destiny; and Victor Emmanuel's mission was Napoleon's opportunity to show Francis Joseph, as he had already shown the Tsar, that Emperors who treated him as a *parvenu* did so at their peril. So he and Victor Emmanuel fought shoulder to shoulder, and made a typical little bit of Austrian history: typical because, as we shall see when we proceed, Italia Irredenta is only one of many districts whose inhabitants regard themselves as "unredeemed," and desire to work out their salvation with the help of their "nationals" over the border. There is also, as we shall note presently, a Servia Irredenta and a Roumania Irredenta, of which we are likely to hear a good deal in the immediate future, though this is not the place for speaking of them. Here we will merely note that Francis Joseph himself took part in the Italian campaign, heading a charge with the cry: "Forward, my lads! I, too, am a married man with a family!"—an exclamation not without its irony for those, if there were any, among his hearers who knew the particulars of his married life.

Though a brave soldier, however, he was by no means a soldier of genius. Apparently, indeed, it is only as a linguist and a figure-head—the sublime figure-head of the Habsburgs who need a figure-head so badly—that he possesses genius; in other respects he seems to have been, as Herr Wulfling was, at a later date, to the Princess Louisa of Tuscany, "a very ordinary man." In any case, he proved himself a very ordinary general, whom very ordinary generals were able to defeat— partly, perhaps, because his Hungarian soldiers showed great alacrity in deserting him; but he sulked, with characteristic Habsburg sullenness, over the terms of peace. In particular, he sulked over the following article:—

"The Emperor of Austria cedes his rights over Lombardy to the Emperor of the French, who, in accordance with the wishes of the population, will hand them over to the King of

Sardinia."

What, he asked Prince Napoleon, who was charged with the negotiations, was the meaning of that odd expression—"the wishes of the population"? Prince Napoleon replied that it meant just what it seemed to mean—that there was not an Italian in Lombardy who was not eager to see the Austrians turned out of that province. Whereupon Francis Joseph smote the table and raised his voice:

"For my own part" (he said) "I recognise no rights except those which are incorporated in treaties. According to the treaties, Lombardy belongs to me. My arms having been unfortunate, I am quite willing to cede the territory to the Emperor Napoleon; but I cannot recognise the wishes of the population, for that is only another phrase for the right of revolution. Use the phrase if you must in your treaty with the King of Sardinia, and in your proclamations to the Italian people—that is no business of mine; but you must clearly understand that I, the Emperor of Austria, emphatically refuse to put my signature to such a form of words."

It did not matter; so Napoleon did not insist. The Head of the Habsburgs was quite welcome to make the gestures of pride while munching the pie of humility—a way of keeping up their dignity in depressing circumstances in which the Habsburgs are the worthy rivals of the Bourbons, and Francis Joseph in particular is the worthy rival of Louis XVIII., who treated the allied sovereigns as his lackeys when they restored him to his throne. A more important matter was that, though Francis Joseph had been given his lesson, he had not learnt it, and that Napoleon, owing to dangers near home, had not been able to make the lesson as complete as he would have liked.

Napoleon had promised that Italy should be free "from the Alps to the Adriatic"; but he heard that Prussia was mobilising on the Rhine, and left his work unfinished. Not only was Venetia left to Austria; but Habsburg Dukes of Tuscany and Modena were also restored to the States from which their subjects had expelled them, though the latter had actually shot his political prisoners, after first flogging them, before taking to flight. Whence, of course, two consequences followed. In the first place Francis Joseph was confirmed in his stubborn view that he did really possess the right of ruling over Italians who loathed him. In the second place, the Italians continued to loathe him; and it was as certain as anything could be that, when his struggle with Prussia for the German hegemony came to a head, he would have to face a second day of reckoning with Victor Emmanuel.

CHAPTER XIII

An interval of peace—Beginnings of trouble with Prussia—Habsburg pride precedes a Habsburg fall—Refusal to sell Venetia to Italy—Italy joins Prussia—The war of 1866—The disaster of Sadowa—Benedek's failure—Shameful treatment of Benedek by the Empire—Vain attempts to conciliate him—His widow's comments.

Between 1859 and 1866 Francis Joseph had a seven years' respite in which to solve his problems; but 1866 found them still unsolved. At home he had advanced a little way towards Liberalism, and then withdrawn; abroad, he had let himself become entangled in the net spread by Bismarck. Nor can the two mistakes be separated; for it was largely because he had failed to conciliate his subjects that he could not face his enemies. The fact that the Hungarians were still sullen made it comparatively easy for Prussia to turn Austria out of the German Confederation.

Space forbids one to say more of the difficulty between Austria and Prussia than that it was the difficulty which arises when two men have to ride the same horse, and both of them want to ride in front. It was brought to a head by dissensions over the settlement of that complicated Schleswig-Holstein question concerning which a British statesman once remarked that only two men had ever understood it, and that one of the two was dead and the other in a lunatic asylum. An agreement on the question, concluded at a personal interview between Francis Joseph and the King of Prussia, was described by Bismarck as "no better than a piece of sticking plaster"; and no doubt Bismarck made it his business to see that the sticking-plaster did not stick. He first secured French neutrality at a famous interview at Biarritz; and then he proceeded to negotiate with Italy.

Here again we see an instructive example of Habsburg pride preceding a Habsburg fall. Italy had recently proposed to buy Venetia from Austria. Francis Joseph, knowing that the Venetians loathed him to a man, had nevertheless replied, in a scornful communication, that Austria's military honour and dignity as a first-class Power required him to retain them as his subjects:—

"She would be unaffected by an offer of money or by any kind of moral pressure. She could only abandon the territory of her own free will in the event, not specially desired by her, of a war which terminated gloriously for Austrian arms, and facilitated the extension of the Austrian Empire in the direction of Germany."

In one and the same despatch, that is to say, Austria insulted Italy, and invited Italy to help her in despoiling Prussia. That was a rash temptation of Providence; and the result of it was that an Italian envoy went to Berlin to negotiate a treaty. Then Austria was frightened, and offered to eat her words and cede Venetia, if only Italy would leave her free to deal separately with Prussia. It was a tardy and clumsy piece of suppleness, and it did not answer. Victor Emmanuel liked fighting, had promised to fight, and fought.

We all know what happened: how the defeat of the Italians at Custozza by the Archduke Albert was more than counterbalanced by the defeat of the Austrians at Sadowa; and how Austria had to accept her humiliation, submit to be turned out of the German Federation, and surrender Venetia to Italy, after a *plébiscite* had been taken to ascertain those "wishes of the population" which Francis Joseph had so haughtily refused to recognise. The figures give eloquent evidence of the feelings of alien races towards Austrian rule. They were as follows:

For annexation	640,000
Against	40
Majority for	639,960

The result, one may be sure, would have been pretty much the same if a *plébiscite* had been taken in the Trentino, and South Tyrol. There also Austrian rule was unsympathetic; and that sore still remains open, with the result that, though Austria and Italy are now nominally allied, they are very far from being friends, and Italy still awaits her chance of responding to the lamentations which continue to reach her from the Purgatory of the Unredeemed. We shall see what we shall see in this connection when Austria is next embarrassed; but meanwhile we must return to Francis Joseph's part in this great drama of 1866. His sphere of action was not the battlefield, but the council chamber; but there his prestige was felt, even in the hour of his discomfiture. Europe was still, to some extent, a family party in which the sentiment prevailed that Kings and Emperors must not be too hard on each other; and German Europe, at any rate, was still fascinated by the spectacle of the magnificent façade of the House of Habsburg, and reluctant to damage it in the spirit of Goths and Vandals. Even Bismarck's "realistic politics" had to allow for that sentiment; and it was a sentiment of which Francis Joseph, on his part, instinctively perceived the value. His perception of it is the solid fact at the back of the strange story of his shameful behaviour towards General Benedek: a story in which he figures as the Jesuit convinced that the end justifies the means and that individuals must be sacrificed ruthlessly to the interests of the Order.

"One cannot expect much of a man who has been educated by the Jesuits," said the late Prince Consort, summing him up with curt scorn; and there will be no pleasant disappointment of expectations in the story which is to follow.

The interest of the Order, in this instance, meant the interest of the dynasty: whatever happened to Austria, the House of Habsburg must not suffer. Francis Joseph did not enter upon the struggle in a spirit of blind confidence: the Prussians, he knew, were armed with the new needle-gun, which might work surprising wonders. Defeat was possible; and if defeat occurred, a scapegoat would be wanted. Francis Joseph, as a young soldier, had been ready to take risks, and had gallantly assured Radetzky that "Austria had no lack of Archdukes." But Francis Joseph in his maturity did not want it to be possible for anyone to say that an Archduke had led the Austrian army to disaster, lest his subjects should lose their illusions about his House, and the revolutionary spirit should revive.

His best general was the Archduke Albert; and he dared not risk him in conflict with Von Moltke. That Archduke had played an odious part, not yet forgotten, in the street fighting at Vienna. His men might follow him with reluctance; his defeat would disgust Austria with the dynasty itself; and the interest of the dynasty was, in Francis Joseph's view, "the thing." So the Archduke was given a comparatively easy task in Italy, and the really difficult work in Bohemia was forced upon General Benedek, who knew that he was unfit for it, and said so. He was too old, he pleaded; he did not know the country in which he would have to fight. As the Prussian General von Schlictling afterwards put it:—

"His experience was like that of a pilot who has all his life guided small boats over the shallows and by the rocks of his native bay with unsurpassable skill and knowledge of the locality, and has now for the first time to take a warship of the first class across strange seas and through cyclones of which he has no experience."

It was a perilous, and almost a hopeless attempt; but Francis Joseph insisted upon his making it. He wanted to be sure, in case of disaster, of a scapegoat, who could be sent out into the wilderness, leaving the honour and dignity of the Habsburgs intact. So he sent Benedek a message through Adjutant-General Count Crenneville, begging him to accept the command as a personal favour, saying that, if he refused it, and the war turned out badly, his own abdication would probably be forced upon him. "In such circumstances," wrote Benedek, "I should have acted very wrongly if I had refused the command"; and no doubt the dictates of discipline did necessitate his acceptance of it.

So Benedek marched to Sadowa: the battle which hit Austria as hard as Sedan was afterwards to hit France. His losses there were 7 flags, 160 guns, 4,861 killed, 13,920 wounded, and about 20,000 prisoners. He was "broken like an old sword," and there was nothing for him to say, except:—

"How could we face the Prussians? They are men of study, and we have learned little."

Or rather, though there was a good deal more which he

might have said, he was persuaded not to say it either before the Military Court which reviewed his conduct, or elsewhere. As Adjutant-General Count Crenneville had been sent to him before, so the Archduke Albert was sent to him now, at Graetz, in Styria, whither he had retired after being deprived of his command. He was asked to give a written promise that he would not publish any of the correspondence which had passed between himself and his generals or himself and the Emperor, or publicly vindicate himself in any way. He gave that promise; and the proceedings begun against him were suspended. But then—we come to Francis Joseph's perfidy.

Francis Joseph wanted a scapegoat badly; and he paid Benedek the compliment of believing him to be a more honourable man than himself. He acted indirectly instead of directly—semi-officially instead of officially; hitting at the man who was down, and had promised to make no attempt to rise, by means of an article in the *Wiener Zeitung*. The article began by stating that there was no law in Austria which punished incompetence; and it continued:—

"For the rest, the loss of the confidence of his imperial master, the destruction of his military reputation before the world of to-day and of the future, the recognition of the immeasurable misfortune that, under his command, has befallen the army, and, through its defect, has befallen the whole monarchy, must be a heavier penalty for the high-minded man that Benedek always was, than any punishment that could have come upon him by the continuation of legal proceedings."

One can imagine Benedek's anger at this black treachery; but he did not allow it to sting him into the retractation of his pledged word. He maintained to the end the attitude of an honourable man whom a dishonourable Emperor had tricked; and he bore contumely in silence. It was only in his will that he spoke out; but then he gave full vent to the indignation which he had so long suppressed. This is his last word on the matter:—

"That the Austrian Government, having in its hand my promise of silence (given to the Archduke Albert on November 19, 1866) and believing in the honourableness of my promise, should publish this strange article, in which my whole past was ignored, and that this Government article, which it is impossible to qualify, was conceived in the presidential chancellery of the General Staff, corrected and improved by Field-Marshal Lieutenant Baron John, Field-Marshal Archduke Albert and others, and finally published by order of the Government in all its peculiar features—all this surpasses my ideas of right, decency, and propriety. I suffered it in silence, and I have now, for seven years, borne my hard lot as a soldier with philosophy and self-denial. I take credit to myself that, in spite of it all, I feel no anger against anybody and am not soured. I am at peace with myself and the whole world and have a clear conscience; but it has cost me all my poetic feeling for soldiering. I should like to be borne to my grave with the utmost simplicity and without any military honours. A plain stone, or an iron cross, without any epitaph, must be put over my grave."

Meanwhile Benedek refused ever again to put on his uniform, and lived as a lodger in a boarding-house at Graetz. Francis Joseph did not like it—it was a reflection on him, especially after Von Moltke had complimented Benedek as a commander of courage and merit; but all the overtures which Francis Joseph's pride permitted him to make were met in a spirit of sullen resentment. When the Archduke Albert was directed to write to Benedek as to an "old campaigner and a brother-in-arms," he replied "with cold respect." The Crown Prince Rudolph was then directed to write to him; but he neither asked for an audience, as he was expected to do, nor even answered the letter, merely permitting the Crown Prince's military tutor to fabricate and carry a message, thanking the Emperor "for the graceful way in which he has remembered me."

"I am an isolated man" (he then said). "I need no external honour, and I feel that my internal honour is unstained. In this matter I acknowledge no earthly judge."

Not long afterwards he died of cancer of the larynx; and even then the memory of the wrong lingered. This is what his widow wrote to her nephew in reference to the letters of condolence which she had received:—

"Bismarck's letter, written throughout with his own hand, was the only one from a high personage which touched me; the telegrams from the Emperor and the Archduke left me very cold. When the Emperor sent the Crown Prince to us in 1873 as an apostle of conciliation, Benedek had suffered so much during the seven years that he refused everything and begged that they would not disturb the repose he had at last attained. The Emperor, always generous, had at least the goodness to ask if there was nothing he could do for me. He is generous. I thanked him sincerely: I need nothing."

So the story ends; and it has been necessary to tell it at some length because of the luminous light which it throws on Francis Joseph's character. Some historians have spoken of it as an isolated stain upon an otherwise blameless personality; but it is, in fact, of a piece with the whole personality, though the occasions which have called for such disagreeable manifestations of the personality have happily been rare. Francis Joseph was always able to give his equals, and has gradually learnt to be able to give his inferiors, the impression that he is genial affability incarnate. It is not natural to him to be mean or paltry—he very much prefers to be splendid. But there is, and has always been, at the bottom of his mind, a certain confusion of thought. If he has not mistaken himself for God, at least he has mistaken the interests of the House of Habsburg for that Higher Law to which the ordinary laws of honour and morality which bind ordinary men must be subordinated.

In the case under review the interests of the House of Habsburg needed a scapegoat; and therefore Benedek had to go out into the wilderness. He did not go out of his own accord; he was not driven out; he was tricked out by false pretences, and then pointed at with the finger of scorn. His widow's letter, which we have just read, reads like a quiet, measured echo of Countess Karolyi's curse, to the various fulfilments of which we shall come in the course of a few chapters. If she had less reason than Countess Karolyi to curse Francis Joseph, at least she had reason enough.

CHAPTER XIV

Francis Joseph comes to terms with Hungary—His famous interview with Francis Deák—"Well, Deák, what does Hungary demand?"—Dualism—The objection of the Slavs to Dualism—Coronation at Buda—Andrassy, whom he had hanged in effigy, becomes his Prime Minister.

Defeated by the Prussians, Francis Joseph felt that he must come to terms with the Hungarians. Their sullen and enduring disaffection had been one of the causes of his discomfiture. They seemed to be looking on, rather pleased than otherwise, at the spectacle of the Habsburg Empire in the melting-pot, and there were even Hungarian exiles helping the enemies of the Habsburgs. It was necessary to win them over, even at the cost of giving them what they wanted.

The popularity of the Empress helped to make them approachable. It would be an exaggeration to say that the Hungarians loved the Emperor because they had first loved the Empress, and loved the Empress because of her friendship for Nicholas Esterhazy; but that, nevertheless, was the trend of Hungarian sentiment. Elizabeth was, at all events, a friend at Court, and since she had been Empress there had been far more Hungarians about the Court than previously. So now, after Sadowa, but before his acceptance of the Prussian terms, Francis Joseph sent for the Hungarian leader, Francis Deák: a stubborn man, but moderate, and with a statesman's eye for the practical.

Deák obeyed the summons, and was ushered into a room in which he saw the Emperor alone, absorbed in thought. After a short silence, a short dialogue passed between them:—

"Well, Deák, what does Hungary demand?"

"No more than she demanded before Sadowa—but no less."

"And what have I to do now?"

"Your Majesty must first make peace, and then give Hungary her rights."

"If I give Hungary a constitution at once, will the Hungarian Parliament vote me money to carry on this war?"

"No, your Majesty, the Hungarian Parliament will do nothing of the kind."

For two reasons: because Hungary had no quarrel with Prussia, and because the hour of Francis Joseph's embarrassment was the hour in which it would be easiest to bargain with him. So Francis Joseph realised that Deák had him at an advantage. He remained silent for a few moments, and then said simply: "Very well. I suppose it must be as you insist."

That was the quiet origin of the present Austro-Hungarian constitution—the system known as Dualism. It solved one Austrian problem with a stroke of the pen; but there were a good many other problems which it left unsolved. Notably it left unsolved the pressing problem of the Slavs, whom the Hungarians, no less than the Austrians, regarded as inferior people, only fit to be oppressed. What the Hungarians had wanted—and now obtained—was not equal rights all round, but an invitation to go into partnership with the oppressors, and Magyarise one-half of the Empire while the Austrians were Germanising the other half. Whereupon there came a furious protest from a Slav historian:—

"If it is decided" (wrote Palacky) "to reverse the natural policy of Austria; if this Empire, composed of a medley of different nationalities, refuses to accord equal rights to all, and organises the supremacy of certain races over the others; if the Slavs are to be treated as an inferior people, and handed over to two dominant peoples as mere material to be governed by them; then Nature will assert herself and resume her rights. An inflexible resistance will transform hope into despair, and a peaceful into a warlike spirit; and there will be a series of conflicts and struggles of which it will be impossible to foresee the end. We Slavs existed before Austria; and we shall continue to exist after Austria has disappeared."

That is hardly doubtful. "Imprison a Slav idea," it has been written, "in the deepest dungeon of a fortress, and it will blow up the fortress in order to get out." But that peril belonged to the future. For the moment Austria was once more saved; and the Emperor's coronation in the cathedral, in 1867, was a magnificent ceremony, every detail of it fraught with significance to those who knew their history. We have to picture Francis Joseph, mounted on a snow-white horse, ascending the ancient hill, and brandishing his sword to the four points of Heaven as a sign that he would confound his subjects' enemies, whether they came from north, south, east, or west; a very different experience truly from that of the days when Milan had received him and the Empress, with their heads covered, in stony silence, and the people of Venice had shunned the Archduke Maximilian and the Archduchess Charlotte as if they were lepers who had escaped from quarantine. A part of the ceremony consisted in the presentation to him of a purse of money, and he ordered its contents to be distributed among the families of those who had fallen fighting against him in 1849. It was one of those magnificent gestures which, like kind words, are worth much and cost little.

So that Francis Joseph, having turned a rebuff to his advantage, was stronger after Sadowa than before it; and he soon showed his skill in conciliating individuals by bestowing the office of Prime Minister upon the Count Andrassy who had been condemned to death, and hanged in effigy, for his share in the Hungarian rebellion. "I am so glad I didn't really hang you," he said genially, "for, in that case, I should have deprived myself of the most capable and amiable of my Prime Ministers"; and he did as good a day's work when he said that as when he promoted the old soldiers whom he had caught poaching to be game-keepers. Moreover, he displayed a similar readiness to let bygones be bygones and to fight shoulder to shoulder with his old enemies when Prussia fell out with France in 1870.

That, however, is an intricate story, and demands a separate chapter.

CHAPTER XV

Attitude of Austria in the Franco-German War—Proposed alliance of France, Italy, and Austria against Prussia—General Türr's interview with Francis Joseph—Victor Emmanuel's conditions—The bargain concluded—The French plan of campaign drafted by the Archduke Albert—Beust's letter to Richard Metternich—Reasons why the Austrian promises were not fulfilled.

What was Austria doing in 1870? What did she mean to do? What did she promise to do? Was there a sudden right-about face? And, if so, why? Those are our problems, and the solution of them is supposed to be one of the secrets of the political *coulisses*. Doors and windows have been opened here and there, however, affording peeps at the mystery; and enough can be seen to make it clear that, just as Austria astonished the world with her ingratitude in 1854, so, if the full truth had been made known, she would have astonished the world with her perfidy in 1870.

There is, of course, an official Austrian version of the events: that any promises made were contingent upon conditions which were not fulfilled. There is also an official French version: that France was lured on, and treacherously left in the lurch. By no means all the documents bearing on the matter have been made public,—there may still be surprises in store for us; but future revelations are likely to throw light upon motives rather than facts. This much, at any rate, is certain: that an Austrian Archduke—Archduke Albert, the victor of Custozza—drafted the French plan of campaign against Prussia for the French War Office, on the assumption that Austria would take part in that campaign, and that the Austrian pledge of assistance was only withdrawn at the eleventh hour.

Now let us go back and note the circumstances and atmosphere in which the plot was laid.

Long before the Franco-Prussian War came, the feeling that it was bound to come was in the air. It was understood that Prussia, having fought Austria for the hegemony of Germany, would fight France for the hegemony of Europe.

What the pretext would be was doubtful, but it was certain that a pretext would be found. The quarrel about Luxembourg was a symptom of a deeply-seated rivalry. Napoleon foresaw the peril, and determined to anticipate it by forming an irresistible Triple Alliance with Italy and Austria for his partners. The story of that alliance—and of its failure—can be pieced together from the "indiscretions" of various persons charged with the negotiations.

It was in 1869 that Napoleon began to negotiate with both Victor Emmanuel and Francis Joseph; and Francis Joseph and Victor Emmanuel, either simultaneously or soon afterwards, entered into negotiations with each other. The actual phrase Triple Alliance occurs in this connection in a letter from Victor Emmanuel to Napoleon, first printed in the *Giornale d'Italia*. This is the essential passage:—

"I cannot possibly refuse to give my adherence to the idea of a Triple Alliance between France, Austria, and Italy; for the union of these Powers will present a strong barrier against unjust pretensions, and so help to establish the peace of Europe on a more solid basis."

Peace, of course, is always the ostensible object of alliances of the kind. It is very seldom their real object; and it was not in this case. Victor Emmanuel desired as little as Napoleon to limit it in that way. What was at the back of Victor Emmanuel's mind appears from his negotiations with Francis Joseph—negotiations which he entrusted to General Türr, a Hungarian officer in the Italian service. General Türr is one of those who have been indiscreet. He eventually told the correspondent of a German newspaper what had passed between him and Francis Joseph, and how, after reviewing the subject in its general aspects, he went into details from the Italian point of view, and raised the inevitable question of Italia Irredenta:—

"I mentioned the Trentino to Francis Joseph, and he interrupted me.

"'Ah!' he objected, 'it is always I who am expected to give something up.'

"'Naturally,' I replied. 'But it is also clearly understood that your Majesty will obtain compensation for the surrender in some other quarter.'"

It was a proposal by which Francis Joseph might very well have been tempted, especially as he had not yet realised that the future of Austria was in the Balkans. We have already seen him hinting that he might be able to give up Venetia if he could obtain "an extension of the Empire in the direction of Germany"; and the same bribe might very well have induced him to part with the Trentino. Of course, too, the memory of Sadowa rankled; and, with the French and the Italians for his allies, he could hardly fail to avenge that humiliation. The chance of thus playing off his various enemies against each other was not one to be scoffed at.

He did not scoff at it, but the three-cornered bargain was too intricate to be settled in a hurry. In particular, Victor Emmanuel was in no hurry, but was hanging back in order to make conditions with France as well as with Austria. With him, the position of the Pope was the obstacle. He wanted the Pope's temporal dominions in order that he might fix his capital at Rome; and the Pope was protected in those temporal dominions by French bayonets. Victor Emmanuel, therefore, stipulated that the French troops should be withdrawn from Rome.

Napoleon himself was willing enough to withdraw them, but the Clericals, with the Empress Eugénie at their head, objected. He was afraid of the Clericals; and so the negotiations hung fire. When he did recall his troops, because he wanted them in the field, it was too late. Victor Emmanuel had heard the news of the French defeat at Wörth, and he uttered the memorable words:—

"The poor Emperor! I am very sorry for him; but I have had a narrow escape."

Even so, however, Victor Emmanuel would have signed the proposed treaty if his Ministers would have let him, as he told the German Emperor frankly when he met him in 1873:—

"Your Majesty knows, no doubt, that if it had not been for these gentlemen (Minghetti and Visconti-Venosta) I should have declared war on you in 1870."

But "these gentlemen" had only held Victor Emmanuel back because they were themselves held back by the counsels of the Austrian Cabinet. "Too late!" was their verdict; for they, too, had heard of Wörth. But if they drew back when Victor Emmanuel was willing to go on, they could also be reproached for having pledged themselves more deeply than he: a piece of secret history which those who held the secret have only recently revealed.

The essential "new fact" is that already set forth in this chapter: that on the eve of the declaration of war the Archduke Albert, whose success at Custozza had gained him the reputation of a great strategist, was sent to Paris by Francis Joseph to concert a joint plan of campaign against Prussia. He conferred there with Lebœuf, Lebrun, Frossard, Jarras, and other leading French soldiers, and Lebrun was sent off to pursue the negotiations at Vienna.

France, it transpired in the course of the discussions, was much readier to take the field than either of her allies. She claimed to be able to mobilise in a fortnight, whereas it was admitted that it would take both Austria and Italy about six weeks to mobilise. The Archduke proposed, therefore, that the three Powers should begin their mobilisation simultaneously, but that Austria, instead of declaring war before she was ready, should affect neutrality while concentrating two army corps at Pilsen and Olmütz. Lebrun did not altogether like the arrangement. He smelt a rat, and suspected a disposition on the part of the Austrians to wait and see which way the cat would jump. Still, there was something to be said for it; for it could be no advantage to France that her ally should be crushed while in the act of mobilising. So a formal agreement between France and Austria was concluded on June 13th, 1870.

That was the occasion on which the Archduke Albert drafted the plan of campaign: not merely a general scheme of joint action between the two Powers, but a detailed plan of campaign for the distribution and employment of the French army. His draft still lies in the archives of the French War Office, though naturally it is not shown to everyone; and the plan itself conforms in almost every particular to the plan which Napoleon adopted. The criticism passed on it by the few military experts who have since reviewed it is this: that it was an excellent plan on paper—excellent on the assumption that the French generals could direct the enemy's movements as well as their own, but that it was composed without regard to the actual conditions of the case, allowing nothing for independent Prussian initiative, and therefore was, on the whole, a bad plan.

The premature attack on Saarbrücken—the first skirmish of the war—was undertaken in accordance with the plan. It was a good move on the assumption that the French were ready to follow it up; but they were not ready to follow it up, and therefore it was a bad move. The failure to follow it up was as fatal in the diplomatic as in the military sense, for it gave point to the Archduke Albert's report that the French army did not seem to him as strong as he had been led to expect. It served, consequently, as a starting-point for hesitations; but Austria was nevertheless committed, though she drew back from her commitments; and the Archduke's visit to Paris and his proceedings there give special point to Grammont's grandiloquent words, addressed on July 15th to the Finance Commission, which he had kept waiting:—

"If I have kept the members of the Commission waiting, my excuse is that I had with me, at the Ministry for Foreign Affairs, the Austrian Ambassador and the Italian Minister. I am confident that the Commission will not require me to say any more."

Grammont, when he spoke thus, believed, and had reason to believe, that the proposed Triple Alliance was a real thing. The Austrian contention is that he had mistaken courteous expressions of sympathy for specific pledges; but that view can hardly be maintained in the face of the facts disclosed as to the Archduke Albert's mission; and other correspondence which has been published is equally at variance with it.

Only two days after his speech to the Finance Commission, Grammont wrote a request to Austria for the help promised. He asked that 70,000 or 80,000 Italian troops should be allowed to march through Austria to Bavaria, and that Austria should herself send 150,000 men to Bohemia. If that were done, he said, the peace would be signed in Berlin, and the memories of 1866 would be effaced. But everything depended upon promptitude:—

"Never again" (Grammont concluded) "will such an

opportunity present itself. Never again will you obtain such effective support. Never will France be so strong as she is to-day, or better armed and equipped, or animated by a more intense enthusiasm."

Whereto Beust replied in a letter addressed to Count Richard Metternich, the Austrian Ambassador, in Paris:—

"Be so good as to assure the Emperor and his Ministers once again that, faithful to the engagements defined in the letters exchanged by the two Sovereigns at the end of last year, we consider the cause of France our own, and shall contribute in every way possible to the success of French arms. Our neutrality is only a means towards the true end of our policy: the sole means of completing our armaments without exposing ourselves to a premature attack on the part of Prussia or Russia."

"Or Russia": those are the words which hold the key to the position.

Austria, acting in conjunction with France and Italy, had no reason to be afraid of Prussia; but if Russia should side with Prussia, she might have a good deal to be afraid of. Count Nigra has specifically stated that Russia intimated her intention of doing so, and that it was by that intimation that the Triple Alliance was brought to nothing. Its collapse, it must be added, was a triumph not only for Prussia, but also for Hungary. Up to the last hour Austria was willing to take the risks, but Hungary declined them. An extension of the Austrian Empire in the direction of Germany was the last thing which the Hungarians desired, for its result would obviously be to increase German, at the expense of Magyar, influence in the dual monarchy. Moreover, the Hungarians, owing to their geographical position, had more to fear than the Austrians from a Russian invasion.

So Andrássy argued, putting his foot down, and Francis Joseph gave way to him. Our chapter, therefore, concludes with the ironical spectacle of Francis Joseph reversing his foreign policy and breaking his word to a friendly Power in deference to the wishes of a rebel whom he had hanged in effigy: a spectacle which we may view as a humiliation or a proof of sagacious flexibility, as we prefer.

CHAPTER XVI

Austrian expansion in the Balkans—Occupation of Bosnia—Problem of Servia Irredenta—Postponement of the day of reckoning—Luck of the Habsburgs in public life—Calamities dog them in private life—List of Habsburg fatalities during Francis Joseph's reign.

The four great dates in modern Austrian history are 1859, 1866, 1870, and 1878—the year of the Russo-Turkish war. The events of those years gradually made it clear that the future of Austria was not in Italy, nor in Germany, but in the Balkans: that the real rival of Austria was Russia, and that the real contest would be for the hegemony, not of Germany, but of the Slav subjects of the Sultan of Turkey. Thenceforward the central principle of Austrian foreign policy was that, for every step which Russia took towards Constantinople, Austria should take a corresponding step towards Salonica; and its first tangible expression was the secret treaty which, in 1878, allowed Austria to occupy Bosnia as the price of her neutrality.

It took an army of 200,000 men, with 480 guns, to pacify that little strip of land; and the occupation, and the subsequent events in the peninsula, have brought Austria up against another problem, uncommonly like the old one which disturbed the beginning of Francis Joseph's reign. For the inhabitants of Bosnia are of Servian race; and there are many other Servians in other parts of the Austrian dominions; and there is a Kingdom of Servia, full of fiercely patriotic men, from whom the cry of Servia Irredenta is going up. Austria once despised them, as she once despised the Italians; but they have proved, like the Italians, that they can fight; and they demand, as loudly as the Italians, to be taken seriously. So that Austria, in spite of her losses and gains, retains her essential character as the Purgatory of the Unredeemed.

It is not a quiet purgatory—perhaps no purgatory is ever quiet—but a purgatory in which order is only kept by the strenuousness of the police, and the frequent declaration of martial law. Consequently it is a purgatory in which startling things may happen at any time; but speculation as to what will happen there may be deferred until a later chapter. Probably nothing in particular will happen during Francis Joseph's lifetime; but the matter needs nevertheless to be mentioned here as a part of the spectacle of trouble perpetually dogging Francis Joseph's footsteps alike in public and in private life. People speak of him as a lover of peace; and it is likely enough that he has learnt to love peace through sheer weariness of war and rumours of war. But it is none the less true that, whenever he has sought to extend his paternal sway, he has not brought peace but a sword; and it was mainly with reference to the events of his reign that Gladstone said: "Nowhere on the map of Europe can you lay your finger and say: 'Here Austria has done good.'" It has already been demonstrated to him, more than once, that the Servians are of Gladstone's opinion; and the demonstration will not become less emphatic with the lapse of time.

We must let that pass, however, though we shall have to return to it. The day of reckoning is not yet; and it will not come in Francis Joseph's life-time if either he or his Ministers can help it. One's continual impression, when reading modern Austrian history, is of a day of reckoning always imminent, yet repeatedly by some happy hazard adjourned.

In public affairs, that is to say, Francis Joseph has enjoyed, and continues to enjoy, a luck like that which is said to attend the British Army and save it from the consequences of its blunders. It is only in his private life that misfortune has pursued him so closely and incessantly that, when the news of the assassination of the Empress Elizabeth was broken to him, he covered his face with his hands and broke down, exclaiming: "What! Is there no sorrow possible to man which I am to be spared?"

The time has come to speak of these sorrows; and the black series began, curiously enough, in the very year in which Francis Joseph achieved his most signal triumph as a ruler. It was in 1867, as we have seen, that he pulled his Empire out of the fire after the disaster of Sadowa, conciliated Hungary, and was crowned with gorgeous and impressive ceremony in the Buda Cathedral. It was also in

1867 that his brother, the Archduke Maximilian, was shot for pretending to be Emperor of Mexico; and that execution was the first of the series of tragedies which never fail to strike one as due to happen in fulfilment of Countess Károlyi's curse. Since we have come to the theme, we must have the text of that curse before us once again: the curse of a mother whose son had forfeited his life as a rebel:—

"=May Heaven and Hell blast his happiness! May his family be exterminated! May he be smitten in the persons of those he loves! May his life be wrecked, and may his children be brought to ruin!="

And now let us set beside that curse a newspaper cutting, taken from one of the Vienna journals at the time of the assassination of the Empress Elizabeth. It is a bald summary, headed "The Sorrows of the House of Habsburg," and it runs thus:—

"On January 30, 1889, Crown Prince Rudolph took his own life in his hunting-box at Meyerling. In May, 1897, Sophie, Duchess d'Alençon, at one time the affianced bride of Ludwig II. of Bavaria, was burnt to death, in Paris. On June 16, 1867, the Emperor Maximilian of Mexico, the Empress's brother-in-law, was shot by a firing-party at Queretaro. His consort, the Belgian Princess Marie-Charlotte, lost her reason, and has been, for the last thirty years, under restraint at the Château of Bouchout. Archduke William Francis Charles died, in the summer of 1894, at Baden near Vienna, from injuries sustained through a fall from his horse. Archduke John of Tuscany, who had resigned his rank and taken the name of John Orth, disappeared on the high seas off the coast of South America. King Ludwig II. of Bavaria, the Empress's cousin, committed suicide on June 13, 1886, drowning himself in the Lake of Starnberg in a fit of insanity. Count Ludwig of Trani, Prince of the Two Sicilies, husband of Duchess Matilda in Bavaria, and sister of the Empress, committed suicide at Zurich. Archduchess Matilda, daughter of Field-Marshal Archduke Albert, was burnt to death in her father's palace as the result of a blazing log from the fire having set alight to her ball dress. Archduke Ladislas, son of the Archduke Joseph, came to grief while hunting by an accidental discharge of his gun. And now we learn that the

Empress Elizabeth has been murdered."

A mere list, it will be seen, eloquent in his simplicity: a list which takes cognisance of nothing except violent deaths, but enumerates ten such deaths among the near relatives of the Emperor and Empress. It is a list which we shall have to lengthen by the inclusion of calamities of other kinds: scandals due to the proceedings of those whom Bismarck styled "Austria's idiot Archdukes," and of more than one Archduchess; and outrageous marriages, as they generally seemed to Francis Joseph, on the part of scions of his house— some of them quite close to the throne—who made light jests about his agreeable relations with Katti Schratt, and left him alone in his glory, turning their backs upon the exclusive magnificence which seemed to him essential to the time-honoured grandeur of the House of Habsburg, and quitting imperial for theatrical and bourgeois circles, not reluctantly, but with an eagerness which suggested a hurried flight from a plague-stricken city.

All these catastrophes will have to be reviewed; and we will speak first of the bitter fate of that young Archduke Maximilian, who, at the very time when his brother was adding a kingdom to an Empire in Europe, was led out into the Square of Queretaro and shot for pretending to be an Emperor in Mexico.

CHAPTER XVII

Francis Joseph's brother Maximilian—Invited to be Emperor of Mexico—Hesitates, but consents to please his wife—Resignation of his rights as a Habsburg—The *Pacte de Famille* and the quarrel about it—The compromise—The last meeting of the brothers—Maximilian's melancholy—He composes poetry—He receives the benediction of the Pope and departs for his Empire.

The tragic circumstances of the death of the Emperor Maximilian—pulled off his imperial pinnacle to be shot to death in a public square—have encircled his memory with a halo to which the bald facts of his case do not entitle him. The word "martyr" has even been used in the connection; and a letter has been published in which his wife, quoting Scripture, compares him to "the Good Shepherd who lays down his life for the sheep." He was, in truth, if metaphor be wanted, merely the titular leader of a pack of wolves who came to a violent end in conflict with another pack of wolves; and, if metaphor be dropped, the best that can be said for him is that he was a weak and vain man who allowed himself to be fooled into undertaking a task for which he had no qualifications except an agreeable manner and an historic name.

If an ornamental Emperor had been all that Mexico wanted, Maximilian might have filled the post and shone in it; but he was grossly unfit, both intellectually and temperamentally, to be an Emperor of any other kind. He seems to have felt that, and to have tried to turn back before even setting his hand to the plough; but various considerations impelled him to the hopeless enterprise. He was jealous of Francis Joseph, who had snubbed him in Italy, and made his position in Austria unpleasant. His wife, the Archduchess Charlotte, daughter of the King of the Belgians, was ambitious, and urged him on. Napoleon, and the Mexican exiles of the clerical party, flattered him; and he allowed himself to be made their tool. He did not understand that Napoleon himself had only interfered in Mexico as the tool of unscrupulous cosmopolitan financiers—notably the notorious Baron Jecker, who had bribed de Morny—and was now chiefly anxious to build a golden bridge over which he could withdraw from an untenable position.

We have met Maximilian already as Francis Joseph's Viceroy in Lombardy and Venetia. We have seen the Italians turning their backs on him, and leaving him and the Archduchess to stand alone, like lepers, in the Square of Saint Mark at Venice; and we have seen Francis Joseph dismissing him from his governorship, because, trying to be sympathetic towards the Italians, he did not govern with a sufficiently high hand. He felt his disgrace, and retired to sulk on his estate, at Miramar, on the Adriatic, where, like so many of the Austrian Arch-dukes, he abandoned himself to the composition of poetry and political pamphlets. He was far more a dreamer than a man of action; but action—or, at least, the attempt at action—was the inevitable outcome of his dreams. The Archduchess Charlotte, being vain and ambitious, saw to that.

Legend—for she has passed into legend, though she is still alive—represents Charlotte as Maximilian's superior in energy and capacity,—the sort of woman who is resolved to keep her husband up to the mark and make a man of him; but it is hard to see upon what evidence that estimate of her rests. Assuredly, she was more anxious to be an Empress than Maximilian was to be an Emperor; but that proves nothing. She merely egged her husband on in the spirit in which the wife of a city magnate urges her husband to accept a knighthood which he does not particularly want. She foresaw the glory; she did not foresee the responsibilities and the danger. When she did perceive the danger it frightened her, quite literally, out of her wits whereas Maximilian, however incompetent, at least contrived to be calm and dignified in the extreme hour when the penalty of his error was exacted. Then, though hardly till then, he showed himself worthy of the great House which, when it does not defy appearances, keeps them up with admirable magnificence.

There is no need to relate the story of his many interviews with the Mexican delegates who, at Napoleon's instance, lured him from his retreat at Miramar. It is merely, in brief, the story of Maximilian's "I dare not" overcome by

Charlotte's "I would." In the first place, he said that he would go to Mexico if it were the unanimous wish of the Mexicans that he should do so, but not otherwise. In the second place, he accepted ridiculously inadequate evidence of Mexican unanimity. The pressure of Charlotte, who appears to have desired an Imperial crown as ardently as humbler women desire gorgeous hats, had evidently intervened. So Maximilian learnt Spanish, and toured Europe, to ascertain what potentates thought of his enterprise, and concluded a treaty with Napoleon, and entered into negotiations with Francis Joseph with regard to his future status as a Habsburg.

The text of his Treaty with Napoleon is sufficient proof of Maximilian's knowledge that he was called to the throne by a faction, and not by a nation. He stipulated for the support of French bayonets, which he obviously would not have needed if the Mexicans had been unanimous in their desire that he should rule over them: a fact which it will be important to bear in mind when the question whether he should be regarded as a usurper or a rightful sovereign, dethroned by murderous rebels, comes to be considered. Meanwhile, his negotiations with his brother resulted in something uncommonly like a family quarrel. It was a question there of the text of the Family Compact which he should be required to sign, before he could be allowed to set out for Mexico with his brother's blessing.

They were not brothers between whom there had latterly been any superfluity of affection. On the contrary, Maximilian had been making himself popular at Francis Joseph's expense in Austria as well as Italy. The citizens who cried "Hurrah for Maximilian!" were taken to mean "Down with Francis Joseph!"; and if the Crown Prince Rudolph, who was a delicate child, had died, Maximilian would have been Francis Joseph's heir. It suited Francis Joseph perfectly, therefore, that Maximilian's name should be erased from the list of members of the royal family. The Family Compact was drafted so as to erase it, depriving Maximilian of all his rights as an agnate of the House of Habsburg; and the matter was debated with great heat and violence—to the amazement of the Mexican delegates, who protested that what they required was a permanent Emperor, not an Emperor leased to them for a term of years.

Never, said Maximilian, would he put his signature to that degrading document. Very well, replied Francis Joseph. Maximilian could sign it or leave it unsigned as he preferred; but, if he did not sign it, then he would not receive the sanction of his sovereign to go to Mexico. In that case, rejoined Maximilian, he should dispense with his sovereign's sanction, and start from Antwerp on a French boat. The answer to that, retorted Francis Joseph, would be a message to the Austrian Parliament, charging him with disloyalty, and formally depriving him of all the rights which he now declined to renounce.

So the domestic battle raged: and various people were dragged into it. Maximilian complained to his mother, who took his side; but the Archduchess Sophia, once so influential, could obtain no concession from the Emperor, and left his cabinet, slamming the door behind her. Maximilian threatened to appeal to the Pope; and the Archduchess Charlotte appealed to Napoleon, who sent General Frossard to Vienna with an autograph letter for Francis Joseph. Then Charlotte went to Vienna, saw Francis Joseph, herself, and arranged something which could be called a compromise. The Pact must be signed—there could be no question of that; but Francis Joseph consented to express his regret for the necessity which compelled him to insist upon its signature, and proposed that the ceremony should take place at Miramar, "where the Emperor of Austria would only be the guest of the Emperor of Mexico." Those were the terms which Maximilian and Charlotte accepted.

Maximilian did not really care, and made no secret of his indifference. The dream of Empire had dazzled him; but the prospect of the realisation of that dream alarmed him. While his wife rushed to and fro, sending off and receiving telegrams, negotiating with feverish excitement, he, on his part, sat at Miramar, writing poetry which gave eloquent utterance to his apprehensions and regrets:—

What! Must I quit my fatherland for ever,—
The country where my first delights were seen?
Those sacred ties am I condemned to sever,
Which link the present with the might-have-been?

And so on and so forth through six stanzas, in which Maximilian expresses deep disdain for sceptres and crowns and palaces, and a marked preference for the tranquil paths of literature, science, and art. It is not a mood in which a man enters with much prospect of success upon such an enterprise as that of founding a European Empire in Central America, in the face of opposition from blood-thirsty Republicans; and it is to be noted that what Maximilian said to himself in verse he also said to his intimates in prose:—

"For my own part," he is reported to have told one of them, "if anyone came and told me that the negotiations had been broken off, I should lock myself up in my room and dance with joy. But Charlotte...?"

It is his admission that he was accepting the Empire, as men profess to accept knighthoods, for his wife's sake, rather than his own. Charlotte had made up her mind that the Imperial crown would suit her, and she meant to wear it. She stirred Maximilian up, if not to enthusiasm, at least to the point of saying:—

"The establishment of an Empire in Mexico is an enterprise which may possibly fail; but the experiment is one worth trying."

So the die was cast; and Francis Joseph fulfilled his promise with the affability which distinguishes him when he has got his own way in essentials. He repaired to Miramar with Archdukes, Ministers, Chancellors, Vice-Chancellors, Chamberlains, Vice-Chamberlains, Aides-de-camp, Field-Marshals, Governors, Lieutenant-Governors—all the *dramatis personæ* of ceremony. After the Pact had been signed, the lunch was served; and then the two Emperors parted in the dignified manner of Emperors, neither embracing nor shaking hands, but merely exchanging military salutes—albeit, it is said, with the red eyes of men who found it difficult to pay their tribute to appearances, and whose hearts harboured dark forebodings.

Maximilian's heart, at all events, harboured them. At the very time when the Mexican flag was flying from the topmost tower of Miramar, his emotions proved too much for him, and he broke down. His emotions prevented him from appearing at the lunch which he gave to his Mexican supporters; and the Empress had to preside at it in his place, while he paced moodily up and down an arbour in the remotest corner of the garden. A congratulatory telegram from Napoleon which Charlotte brought to him was the cause of a nervous explosion. "I forbid you to speak to me of Mexico," he snapped out; and the date of his departure had to be postponed, to give him time to recover his composure. Even so, he wept as the coast of Austria sank out of sight, first weeping in public on the deck, and then retiring to his cabin to weep unobserved. Assuredly Maximilian had his full share—if not more than his full share—of that neurosis which the Habsburgs inherit.

And so, in the first instance, to Rome, where Pius IX. bestowed a benediction on his enterprise: a benediction which has an ominous ring in the ears of those who read it in the light of subsequent events:—

"Behold the Lamb of God, who taketh away the sins of the world! It is through Him that Kings reign and govern. It is through Him that Kings do justice; and if He sometimes permits Kings to pass through sore trials, He is the source of their power.

"I recommend to you in His name the happiness of the Catholic peoples who are confided to you. Great are the rights of peoples, and they should be satisfied, but greater and far more sacred are the rights of the Church, the immaculate bride of Jesus Christ, who has redeemed us with His precious blood."

An exhortation, it will be observed, to Maximilian to go to Mexico as the elect, not of the nation, but of the clericals: those clericals whose prevailing principle of conduct was that money ought to be taken away from laymen and given to clergymen; who had introduced ridiculous laws to the effect that no one must work on a Sunday without the permission of a priest, and that, when the Host was carried through the streets, everyone must kneel, and remain kneeling until the clerical procession was out of sight, and the tinkling of the clerical bell could no longer be heard. A prediction, further, that the clerical policy which the Pope pressed upon the Emperor might get the Emperor into trouble; so that Maximilian went to his mission with shaky nerves, and in the spirit of a missionary who fears that his cross will prove too heavy for him.

Charlotte, it seems, kept up his spirits during the voyage. She was going to be an Empress—that was enough for her. She knew nothing about Mexico, except that El Dorado lay thereabouts—nothing of the imperial status, except that it was outwardly splendid. She believed the people who told her that she was going to lie in a bed of roses in a gold mine. The things to which she looked forward were the banquets, the levées, the drawing-rooms, and the Court balls. Her talk—and Maximilian's talk also when she launched him on the subject—was of rules of precedence, the creation of new Orders of Nobility, and new and lucrative offices for the benefit of personal friends. In short, as Emmanuel Domenech puts it in his History of Mexico:—

"One saw renewed on the *Novara* the story of the Frenchman who, having decided to open up trade with the Redskins of North America, stocked his shop with ostrich feathers, the most delicate linen of Belfast, and a number of costly porcelain tea-services."

But the reality was widely different from the dreams; and disillusion followed quickly. Maximilian, like Charlotte, was puffed up with pride. He was even proud at Charlotte's expense, and told her that, now that he was an Emperor, it would be unbecoming for her to enter his presence, without first asking permission, unless he sent for her; but that regulation was of no service to him in the practical conduct of Mexican affairs. His actual business as an Emperor consisted, and had to consist, in the waging of a civil war. So long as he had Bazaine and the French Army of Occupation to help him, he was able to wage his civil war successfully; but it was not long before Napoleon heard the voice of the President of the United States drawing his attention to the Monroe doctrine. Breaking his word to Maximilian, he withdrew his troops; and, after that, Maximilian's position was hopeless.

So that we see misfortune and peril assailing the two Emperors of the House of Habsburg simultaneously: Maximilian fighting for his throne in every corner of his Empire in the very year in which Francis Joseph had to fight for his throne at Sadowa and Custozza. Only there was an important difference between the two cases. Francis Joseph's enemies wished him no particular harm. They had certain affairs of honour and precedence to settle with him, and they meant to settle them; but, when those affairs were settled, they meant to shake hands and be friends. They did not thirst for his blood, but regarded his position as rather a convenience to Europe than otherwise, provided that he did not presume on it. He might suffer, but he would be left strong, and—above all—safe.

His brother Maximilian, on the contrary, was in personal peril, and knew it. Civil wars in Mexico were waged in a very different spirit from dynastic wars in Europe. There had once before been an Emperor of Mexico—the adventurer Iturbide—and he had been shot. There was a large party in Mexico—the party of Benito Juarez and Porfirio Diaz— which refused to recognise Maximilian, declaring that he was only pretending to be an Emperor, and that the real Government of the country was still Republican. The French had never quite subdued that party; and it began to lift its head again as fast as the French retired. If Maximilian was a nervous man, he had every reason to feel frightened.

He was a nervous man, and he did feel frightened. Charlotte was a nervous woman, and she was frightened too. It does not seem to have occurred to either of them that, if they could not maintain themselves in Mexico without French bayonets, they had no business there—ideas of that sort do not occur to Habsburgs who have tasted power: their accumulated pride—which is their substitute for strength— forbids. The idea was rather that, if they could not maintain themselves without French bayonets, those bayonets must be supplied; and it was agreed that Charlotte should go to Europe and lay that view of the matter before the Emperor of the French.

Her journey, in the year of Sadowa, was the occasion of the first of those blows which have since fallen, almost without cessation, on Francis Joseph's head.

CHAPTER XVIII

Vanity and nervousness of the Empress Charlotte—Evil omens which frightened—Her journey to Europe to seek help for Maximilian—Her cold reception by Napoleon III.—Symptoms of approaching insanity—Her madness—Maximilian abandoned by the French—Attacked by the Republicans—Captured at Queretaro—Francis Joseph's vain attempt to save him—His trial and execution.

It must be repeated that the common view of the Empress Charlotte as a valiant woman who took matters into her own hands when the Emperor Maximilian was timorous and hesitating cannot stand. She was, in the first place, a vain woman who took purely frivolous views of Imperial responsibilities; in the second place, a woman who lost her mental balance when she discovered that the position for which she had longed had its duties as well as its pleasures, and its perils as well as its privileges.

The legend has grown up that she came to Europe to plead for the life of a husband who was in the hands of his enemies, and lost her reason in despair at Napoleon's decision to leave him to his fate; but that is not the case. At the time when she started for Europe, Maximilian was still free to walk out of Mexico at any moment; and her purpose in coming to Europe was to ask Napoleon for more soldiers to keep him there against the will of the majority of the Mexican people. Moreover, the first signs of insanity had already shown themselves before her embarkation at Puebla, where, no one could imagine why, she woke up the whole of her escort in the middle of the night and insisted upon their all going with her to call upon the Prefect. That assuredly was the action of a woman whose wits were already taking flight through terror!

It used to be whispered that her Mexican enemies tried to poison her, and that the drug, though it failed to kill, drove her mad; but that is another story unsupported by any shred of evidence. Charlotte was simply scared; one needs—and one can find—no other explanation. Warnings to which she attached no importance at the time now rang like alarm-bells in her ear. There was the warning of Louis-Philippe's consort, Queen Marie-Amélie, who was Charlotte's grandmother. "They will be assassinated," Marie-Amélie had said, and repeated daily to her little Court, when she heard of her granddaughter's adventure. There was the warning of the Archduchess Sophia. "Remember, my son," she had said to Maximilian—forgetting what she had previously said to the Emperor Ferdinand—when bidding him farewell, "one does not descend from a throne except to mount a scaffold."

Charlotte remembered these things, and remembered also the stories she had heard of the savage temper of the Mexicans: Indians and half-breeds who had no bowels of compassion, but were capable of torture as well as murder. Those memories, and the apprehensions roused by them, were so many haunting phantoms; and the news which Charlotte heard when she landed at St. Nazaire, and the circumstances of her reception at Paris, were like a further series of evil omens. At Saint-Nazaire she was told of the catastrophe of Sadowa; and at Saint-Lazare she found no representative of the French Court awaiting her on the platform—an omission not the less painful because it was due to a misunderstanding. There would have been no such misunderstanding if Napoleon had not been indifferent. An Empress whose regard Napoleon valued would not have been left to drive to the Grand Hotel and ask for a bed in that great caravanserai.

The Empress Eugénie, hearing of her arrival, hurried to see her at the Grand Hotel, and the two women cried together. General Castelnau, who was in attendance on the Empress, tells us that when she left Charlotte's apartment her eyes were red. The interview with Napoleon himself followed; but, though he kissed Charlotte's hand with proper gallantry, he would do nothing for her. He was "gentle but obstinate," as his mother, Queen Hortense, had always declared him to be. When Charlotte knelt at his feet, sobbing and supplicating, he was moved to kind words, but he would make no promises. The Mexican expedition, he pointed out, had become unpopular in France. It had already cost him too much money and too many men. He must get out of it—as he probably had always meant to do from the hour at which he had inveigled Maximilian and Charlotte into their false position:—

"Then we shall abdicate," said Charlotte, believing that this menace would intimidate the Emperor.

"Yes, I suppose you had better abdicate," was Napoleon's polite reply.

That was all she could get out of him; and she got still less out of his Ministers. One of these, indeed, begged her to grant him permission to retire, "lest your Majesty's eloquence should induce me to make promises incompatible with my position as a Cabinet Minister." It was Maximilian's sentence of death if he still insisted upon obeying his mother's injunction: never to descend from his throne unless pulled off it to mount a scaffold. Charlotte, in full flight from her terror, hurried to her old home at Miramar; and Miramar was only a halting-place on the road to Rome.

What comfort she expected to find at Rome it might be difficult to say. The Pope, so far as his temporal power went, was the mere creature of Napoleon; even more dependent on the support of Napoleon's bayonets than Maximilian himself. Perhaps Charlotte expected him to intercede with Napoleon; perhaps she expected him to work a miracle—she was quite mad enough by this time to take the pastoral staff for a magician's wand. At Miramar, as at Puebla, her proceedings betokened irresponsible frivolity. She paused there to give a *fête* in celebration of the anniversary of Mexican independence: that independence for which the Mexicans were, at that very hour, fighting against her husband. She told the President of the Trieste Chamber of Commerce that Maximilian might, in the course of the next year, "take a little trip to Europe," in which case he would not fail to pay a visit to Trieste. Francis Joseph sent his brother, the Archduke Louis Victor, to see her there; but sympathy was all that he could offer. He lay at the proud foot of the Prussian conqueror, and was helpless.

So Charlotte at last went on to Rome, and there the crisis came. There was no lack of ceremony, no lack of consideration. The Pope received her in a manner befitting her rank, and went to her hotel to return her visit. She went to see him again, and then, in a Vatican ante-chamber, broke out into a violence of word and action which permitted of no doubt as to her mental state, though the attempt was made to mask the truth:—

"The words 'mental alienation,'" wrote an official, "have been pronounced. The truth is that the Empress is in a state of excitement which indicates serious nervous agitation, but does not preclude the exercise of her reasoning faculties. This excitement is specially remarked whenever Mexico and the Mexicans are mentioned in her presence."

CHARLOTTE, WIFE OF MAXIMILIAN, EMPEROR OF MEXICO.

"The crisis demands rest—mental as well as bodily; and the Pope has, for that reason, assigned the Empress an apartment in the Vatican, close to his own, while awaiting the arrival of the Comte de Flandre, who will conduct his august sister to Miramar."

But rest was of no avail. Charlotte was not only mad, but a monomaniac. She had the delusion that there was a conspiracy to poison her; she was insisting upon trying all her food on the cat before she would touch it. A telegram had to be sent to Maximilian:—

"Her Majesty the Empress Charlotte was seized, on October 4th, at Rome, by a cerebral congestion of the gravest character. The august Princess has been taken back to Miramar."

That was the end of Charlotte's tragical odyssey; and Maximilian's struggle was also nearing its close. No one wanted to prevent him from abdicating, and one may fairly say that nothing but Habsburg pride stood in the way of his abdication. He had all that pride without any of the strength of character which ought to go with it. It was the creed of the family—the creed, in particular, as we have seen, of the Archduchess Sophia—that a Habsburg might yield his throne of his own free will to another Habsburg, but must on no account resign it for the paltry reason that his people did not want him to rule over them. Maximilian decided to be true to the tradition—to throw himself into the arms of the Clericals, and with their help, and in conformity with the simple Papal doctrine that the rights of the Church were more sacred than the rights of peoples, make a fight for it.

So long as the French were with him, he could not do everything that the Clericals would have liked him to do; for France, while remaining Catholic, had ceased to be ultramontane and obscurantist. Now he could embrace them, and even restore the Inquisition if he chose—on the one condition that he defeated the Republicans. On the day of the departure of the French from the city of Mexico he shut himself up in his Palace, with all the blinds drawn, peeping out from behind the blinds to watch them march away, while remaining himself unseen. When the last of them had gone, he reopened the blinds and the windows, exclaiming dramatically:

"Now at last I am free!"

Free to do what?

Free to give orders that if Benito Juarez and certain other Republican leaders were caught in arms against him, a court-martial should sentence them to be shot; but not free to carry out his threat, for the order never reached General Miramon, to whom it was addressed, but fell into the hands of Juarez himself, to be produced against Maximilian at his own trial by court-martial. Free to march, with his Clerical host, into Queretaro, but not free to get out again; for it was on Queretaro that Juarez, and Diaz, and Escobedo, and Corona, and Regules, and Riva Palacio converged to take him prisoner, and bring him to judgment in the Theatre of Iturbide—that name of evil omen—on the charge of pretending to be an Emperor.

It all happened quickly—almost in the twinkling of an eye. The date of the departure of the last French detachment was February 5th, 1867; and it was on the following day that Maximilian dispatched his letter instructing Miramon to condemn Juarez to death. On February 13th, he left the city of Mexico, and on February 17 he entered Queretaro amid the acclamations of the Clerical inhabitants. On February 26th he decreed a forced loan, and actually got the money; but on March 2nd his enemies began to arrive. Roughly speaking, there were 40,000 Republicans against 7,000 Imperialists; and, after sustaining a siege of rather more than two months' duration, Maximilian had to surrender in the early morning of May 15th.

The news came to Europe. A Habsburg—the brother of the head of the House of Habsburg—was in the hands of Indians and half-breeds, who threatened to treat him as he himself had threatened to treat their leaders, under that notorious Black Decree which his own hand had signed. It was an urgent question for Francis Joseph what steps, if any, he should take in order to try to save his brother's life.

He could have made excuses to himself if he had decided to take no steps at all; for he, no less than the Mexicans, had his grievances against Maximilian. At a time when Francis Joseph seemed to have been compromised by disaster,

Maximilian had been cheered in the streets of Vienna. There had been a party in Vienna which had entertained the idea of putting Maximilian on Francis Joseph's throne. Maximilian had himself spoken imprudent words on that occasion; and the imprudent words had been reported. Moreover, even after Maximilian's elevation to the throne of Mexico there had been stormy diplomatic passages-at-arms between the brothers.

Maximilian had resented Francis Joseph's allusion, in his speech at the opening of the Reichsrath, to his resignation of his Austrian privileges, and had addressed an indignant protest to his diplomatic representative at Vienna: a protest in which he set forth that he had consulted the most eminent jurists of the day about the Family Compact which he had been induced to sign, and that they had unanimously advised him to treat it as null and void. The protest had been published in the Viennese newspapers, but had not been formally presented at the Austrian Foreign Office. The Austrian Foreign Minister, taking unofficial cognisance of it, had unofficially intimated that if it were so presented, the Mexican Minister would be conducted to the frontier. It would have been easy, therefore, for Francis Joseph to excuse himself for bearing malice and leaving Maximilian to his fate.

He bore no malice, and he did what he could. The Austrian Minister at Washington was instantly instructed to solicit the intercession of the Government of the United States. As a guarantee that, if Maximilian were spared, he would definitely abandon his ambitions, it was proposed to offer formally to restore him to his old status as a Habsburg, and a family council was convoked for that purpose. One of the Archdukes present raised objections, recalling Maximilian's ambitions as an Austrian Pretender, and predicting trouble; but Francis Joseph would not listen. "That question," he said, "is not before us. Our only question is: how to save human life."

But Maximilian's life was not to be saved. The man who had him in his power was a man whose life he had threatened. Juarez might play with Maximilian as a cat with a mouse, but he would not let go. He used fine phrases about it—"high considerations of justice," and the like; he most punctiliously accorded Maximilian the benefit of all the forms of law. But the law was against Maximilian; there was no way through that Black Decree which he himself had promulgated. Legally and morally alike, Juarez had as good a title to execute him as he had ever had to execute Juarez; and Juarez stood upon his rights. He laughed—or rather the President of the court-martial laughed on his behalf—at Maximilian's naïve invocation of "the immunities and privileges which appertain in all circumstances to an Austrian Archduke." The Indians and half-breeds knew nothing and cared nothing for those privileges and immunities. The Austrian Archduke had pretended to be their Emperor, and had killed some of them and threatened to kill others, and for those offences he should be shot. They shot him in the early morning of June 19th, 1867. For Charlotte, who still had occasional glimmerings of sanity, he was "the good Shepherd who gave his life for the sheep"; but for his Mexican subjects he was merely the foreigner who had presumed to come among them and pretend to be an Emperor.

Such was the first of the long series of tragedies which were to punctuate Francis Joseph's personal life; and there is a moving irony in the fact of its occurrence in the very year of his first great political triumph. One can imagine that the shame of it was an even heavier blow to him than the sorrow. A Habsburg, close to the Habsburg throne, tried like a criminal and shot like a dog by Indians and half-breeds; the head of the House of Habsburg unable to help him, and curtly told, almost without the formula of politeness, that his attempt to interfere was an outrage on "high considerations of justice"! Truly Francis Joseph must have felt in that hour that the curse of Countess Karolyi, called forth because he too had tried his enemies like criminals and shot them like dogs, had not been unavailing.

CHAPTER XIX

Habsburgs and Wittelsbachs—Which is the madder House?—
Insanity of the Empress Elizabeth's cousin, Ludwig II. of Bavaria—
His eccentricities—His tragic death—Grief of the Empress—
Suicide of Elizabeth's brother-in-law, the Comte de Trani—Tragic
death of the Archduchess Elizabeth.

Archduke Maximilian was dead, and Francis Joseph had
to humble himself to the Indians and half-breeds, and beg
their permission to fetch his brother's body to Europe and
bury it in the tombs of the Habsburgs. Archduchess Charlotte
was stark, staring mad, and all hope of the restoration of her
reason had been abandoned. There was to be no other tragedy
quite so tragic, or quite so intimate, until that of Meyerling,
to which we shall quickly come; but there were intervening
tragedies, tragic and intimate enough, which hit Francis
Joseph through his cousins of Bavaria. Notably there was the
tragedy of Elizabeth's cousin—who was also Francis
Joseph's cousin—King Ludwig II.

It is a question sometimes debated by the members of the
two families, whether the Wittelsbachs are madder than the
Habsburgs, or the Habsburgs madder than the Wittelsbachs.
According to Countess Marie Larisch, who speaks for the
Wittelsbachs, the difference is that "with the Habsburgs
insanity usually shows itself in depravity, self-effacement,
and common marriages, while, in the case of the
Wittelsbachs, it transforms the sufferer into a romantic being
who is quite above the banalities of everyday life, but who
occasionally deteriorates and becomes a gross feeder"; but
that is not quite a true antithesis. Common marriages, as
Countess Marie calls them—and the marriage of her own
father, the brother of the Empress Elizabeth, to the actress,
Henrietta Mendel, falls in the category—are not necessarily
unromantic; and Wittelsbachs, as well as Habsburgs, have
contracted them. Still, as an introduction to the story of the
career of Ludwig II., the contrast is not without its point.
Ludwig was as mad as a hatter; and he has also been spoken

of as "the last of the Romantics"—the last, at all events, of the Romantics who have sat on thrones.

The beginning of his tragedy was the breaking off of his engagement to the Empress Elizabeth's sister, Sophie; and the ease with which he was manœuvred out of that engagement, as the result of a Court intrigue, is, in itself, a sufficient proof that his intelligence was none too strong. It was represented to him, quite untruly, that his affianced bride had been flirting with his Master of the Horse, Count Holnstein. The Count and the Princess were inveigled into being photographed together; and this testimony of "the camera which cannot lie" was brought to Ludwig's notice. There was also some story of a ring which Count Holnstein was observed to be wearing, and which was believed to have been given him by the Princess, though, as a matter of fact, it had been given to him by an actress who had stolen it from the Princess.

That was the bait; and Ludwig walked into the trap and took it. He made no inquiries, and asked for no explanations. Instead of doing so, he made unsatisfactory excuses for postponing his wedding-day; and when Duke Maximilian charged him with trifling with his affianced bride's affections, he lost his temper, smashed Sophie's bust, tore up Sophie's portraits, and declared that Sophie was welcome to marry anyone she liked provided that she did not marry him. So all was over, and they were both unhappy; and it does not seem that Sophie found perfect bliss in her subsequent union to the Duc d'Alençon. The day came when Sophie clamoured for a divorce: not because she had any tangible grievances, but because she had conceived the idea that she would like to marry a doctor in practice at Munich, and devote herself to philanthropic activities. She had to be kept under restraint for a season at a private asylum at Graetz, already referred to as "the rendezvous of princes," because of the large number of august lunatics whom it harboured: among others, the Duchess of Augustenburg, Pedro of Saxe-Coburg, whose mania was a dread of poison, and Charles of Lichtenstein, who had gone mad on account of his failure to meet the woman of his dreams.

And Ludwig, meanwhile, was so mad that there could be no mistake about his madness, though it was a kind of madness which gained him, as has been said, the title of the Last of the Romantics. He lived, like William Beckford, in a solitude of fantastic splendour. He had the table laid, in an empty banqueting hall, for ghostly guests, and fancied that he was entertaining Marie-Antoinette, and Catherine of Russia, and Hamlet, and Julius Cæsar. He caused command performances of the best operas to be given to himself alone in an empty theatre. He sailed about the Starnberg Lake in a gondola, towed by a swan. He caused eminent actors to recite to him while he ate, and he went on eating, and kept them reciting, until five o'clock in the morning. He outraged the feelings of the Court by bestowing titles of nobility on his tailor and his barber; and the end of it all was that keepers took the place of courtiers, and a Regent was appointed.

The story goes that Elizabeth refused to believe that he was mad, and, after vainly imploring Francis Joseph to insist upon his release, engaged in a plot to rescue him. The King was to dive into the lake, and swim across it, and a carriage, with swift horses, ready harnessed, was to be waiting to carry him far away from his keepers to a place of safety. It sounds like a story built on a foundation of careless emotional talk; and the end, at any rate, came differently, and somewhat mysteriously. Ludwig persuaded his doctor to send the keepers away, declaring that their presence worried him; and the doctor was a muscular man who believed that he could trust himself to cope with any emergency. Strong as he was, however, Ludwig was still stronger; and when the keepers returned, they found that both the King and the physician had been drowned, after a struggle, of which there was abundant evidence. Whether the King had murdered his physician, in order that he might be free to escape, or the physician had perished in attempting to frustrate the King's attempt at suicide, remains to this hour uncertain.

There is a further story to the effect that the Empress Elizabeth saw the tragedy in a dream, and awoke, screaming, to learn that her dream was a true vision; but though the dream itself is well accredited, one may suspect that legend has taken a liberty with the date. There is something characteristic, however, and therefore probably true, in the report of the words which the Empress is declared to have spoken as she bent over her cousin's corpse:

"Leave the King here! Leave him in his mortuary chapel! He is not dead. He is only pretending to be dead, in order that he may be left in peace, and that no one may be able to torture him any more."

The conception of life as a torture which must be stoically endured had, by that time, grown upon the Empress;

and there were still other trials in store for her, which were to confirm it, even before the tragic day on which her sister was to meet her death in the fire at the Bazaar de la Charité at Paris. There was to be another suicide in the family, that of the Comte de Trani, at Geneva. The Archduke Joseph's son, Archduke Ladislas, was to be killed, accidentally, while shooting. The Archduchess Elizabeth, daughter of the Archduke Albert, and granddaughter of the Archduke Charles, who had fought so well against Napoleon, was to perish in a still more tragic accident.

She was in her ball-dress of lace and muslin, leaning out of one of the windows at Schönnbrunn, smoking a cigarette. It was a forbidden pleasure; and hearing her father's footstep, she made haste to hide the cigarette, first covering it with her hand, and placing it behind her. The Archduke stopped to talk to her, and a moment later the ball-dress was in flames. He could not reach her, and so could do nothing to help her. She ran, shrieking, down the corridor, and the draught fanned the flames. Before they could be extinguished, she was burnt almost to death; and though they placed her in a bath of oil, and took her to Vienna, the best physicians could do nothing for her, and she died in agony a few days later.

There we have another example of the poignant sorrows to which Francis Joseph has been condemned through the sufferings of members of his family; and now we come to the greatest tragedy of all—the tragedy which was to deprive him of his only son, the Crown Prince Rudolph.

CHAPTER XX

The Crown Prince Rudolph—His quarrel with the German Emperor—His affability and his hauteur—A spoiled child—His search for a wife—Marriage to Princess Stéphanie—Disappointment and disillusion—Stéphanie's book—"A long, long, terrible night has gone by for me"—Mary Vetsera and her family—How Mary Vetsera was taken first to the Hofburg and thence to Meyerling.

The name Rudolph had not been borne by a Habsburg ruler for five hundred years. A curious fatality seemed to attach to it, and probably had inspired a superstitious fear of it. Rudolph II. had died mad. Rudolph III. and Rudolph IV. had died young—the one at twenty-seven and the other at twenty-six. But people had ceased, as it seemed with good reason, to think of such ominous things; and the Crown Prince Rudolph inspired great hopes as well as great affection.

That he was really a degenerate, touched by the hereditary taint, is hardly, indeed, to be doubted; but the symptoms of degeneracy were not conspicuous, and, on the whole, passed unobserved. He must be classed with the brilliant Habsburgs, or, at least, among those who had literary and artistic tastes, which they cultivated, and were proud of. He travelled, and wrote a book about his travels; he edited a monumental work on the scenic beauties of the Austrian Empire; he consorted, on very affable terms, with artists and men of letters. He was also one of the friends of the late King Edward, who remarked of him that he was a good German—"at all events in the sense of being anti-Prussian"; and he showed character in a passage-at-arms with the German Emperor, who spoke contemptuously of his preoccupation with the fine arts:

"Nonsense of that sort," the Emperor is reported to have said, "is unworthy of a soldier and a Crown Prince."

"There is only one thing," Rudolph is reported to have replied, "which is unworthy of a Crown Prince, and that is to aspire to the throne during his father's life-time."

And yet, when Countess Marie Larisch came to tell what she knew of the Meyerling tragedy, her "secret" was to the effect that Rudolph himself had not only aspired to, but also conspired for, the throne of Hungary during Francis Joseph's life-time. But neither story can be said to disprove the other; for one can discover no grounds for crediting Rudolph with firm and consistent principles.

He was capable of affability; but he was also capable of *hauteur*. One might compare him, as one might compare a good many of the Habsburgs, to a poker which will unbend itself, but declines to be unbent by others. Some workmen employed in the Palace discovered that, when he came among them, as a child, and talked to them while they were engaged in decorations and repairs. "Well, what is your name, young fellow?" they presumed to ask him; and the little boy drew himself up. "Papa and mamma call me Rudolph," he answered. "Other people call me Monseigneur." He was young enough for the snub to amuse without giving pain. Most likely the workmen declared him to be whatever is the German for "a chip off the old block." At any rate he grew up to be popular with people who did not know him, or only knew him slightly. He was "unser Rudi," just as the German Emperor Frederick was "unser Fritz."

Still, he was a spoiled child, and precociously cynical; and perhaps, in view of the way in which he was brought up, it would have been hard for him to be anything else. The legend of his mother's devotion to him is found at the circumference of his circle, but cannot be traced to its centre. From an early age, he saw and understood too much for innocence. Among other things he saw the "go-between," and knew for what purpose she went between. There was no example before his eyes to lead him to look upon happiness in marriage as an easily attainable ideal; and he held women cheap, because so many of them made themselves cheap with him. One of Countess Marie's stories is to the effect that she boxed his ears for laughing at "love-sick girls," and boasting of his conquests, and saying of a certain Elizabeth T——: "The silly goose thinks I adore her, and so I can do anything I like with her."

THE CROWN PRINCE RUDOLPH.

It was, therefore, as a young man who had already lost his illusions that Rudolph set out in search of a wife. The story has been told that another lady travelled with him as a provisional companion while he was looking for a wife, and was, at least once, caught in his company in compromising circumstances by his prospective mother-in-law. He was too eligible a *parti* for any prospective mother-in-law to attach more importance than she could help to such a *contretemps*; and after Rudolph had rejected the suit of Princess Mathilde of Saxony, on the ground that her style of beauty was of too luxuriant an effulgence, then, "weary," to quote Countess Marie, "of a choice of many evils, he decided to take the least of them, as represented by the Princess Stéphanie of Belgium." And Stéphanie said, or is said to have said, "He asked me for my hand so prettily that I could not possibly refuse it to him."

That in spite of the compromising discovery of the provisional lady companion in his rooms. His manner must indeed have been charming if it removed the impression of that surprise; but Rudolph could be fascinating when he chose, and his ready wit may have prompted a plausible explanation. Moreover, Stéphanie was little more than a child—too young to understand; and her father, Leopold II., was not a man into whose calculations either sentiment or morality entered. We all know him as the King who neglected the Austrian Archduchess to whom he was married for such persons as Cléo de Mérode and the Baroness Vaughan; and he may well have said to himself that he saw no reason why his daughter should expect to be any happier in her marriage than his wife, or why his younger daughter should expect to be any happier in her marriage than her elder sister.

It is notorious, at any rate, that no love was ever lost between Leopold and either of his daughters. The marriages of both of them were failures; and anyone who has ever lived in Brussels knows how many stories are current there as to his callous indifference to their matrimonial calamities. Again and again the story ran round Brussels that Princess Louise of Saxe-Coburg had run away from her husband and taken refuge at Laeken, and that her eyes were not only red but black: that Philip of Saxe-Coburg, in fact, had been knocking her about, and that she had vowed, with tears streaming down her cheeks, that nothing would induce her to return to him. But Leopold always sent her back; for why— one pictures him asking—should his daughter Louise expect to be any happier than his wife Henrietta, and why should his son-in-law be expected to behave any better than he himself behaved? No doubt there was logic of a kind—though not of the best kind—in the argument. No doubt, too, the same logic was brought into play when Stéphanie's marriage was arranged.

Countess Marie protests that Stéphanie was plain, and had no style. She speaks of her red arms, her deplorable figure, her unbecomingly dressed hair; but that is not the verdict of contemporary Brussels, where she was to be seen daily in the Park and the streets. What Brussels remembers is a little girl—a "flapper," as people say nowadays—simple and exceedingly attractive: a little girl who reminded Brussels of a Dresden china statuette; a little girl in short frocks, with her hair hanging down her back. She was not grown up, Brussels declares, when she was married; she was only dressed to look as if she were grown up. She was put into long skirts, and her hair was done up, *du jour au lendemain*, before the proper time, because this chance of a brilliant marriage had suddenly come her way.

Presumably there was something of the gawkiness of the schoolgirl about her when she was thus first dressed as a woman. Presumably that gawkiness did not entirely vanish in the course of the journey from Brussels to Vienna, where she was certain, as a foreigner, to encounter far more captious criticism; Vienna being nearly as *chic* as Paris, quite as quizzical in a heavier way, and decidedly less disposed to make smooth the path of the stranger. Stéphanie, in short, must at first have seemed a little "provincial" to the Viennese; and there were plenty of Viennese ladies—Palast Damen and others—whose cue it was to make the worst of her, and to rejoice that, as Rudolph had married such a wife, "there was no possibility," to quote Countess Marie, "of his ever becoming a model husband."

Assuredly he did not become one, and there does not even seem to have been an interlude of sunshine before the gathering of the clouds. Even the daughter presently born to the Archduke and the Archduchess is said to have been a cause of contention between them; and Stéphanie, with that passion for self-expression which she shared with almost every member of the House of Habsburg except Francis Joseph, has written out and published a confession of the emotions which her experiences of marriage brought her, and the lessons which she drew from them. This is the essential passage:—

"Two quite young persons see each other for the first time, know each other a quarter of an hour, and speak the binding word which death alone can untie.

"If there is something beautiful in the thought that two human beings who love and respect one another are joined before God in holy matrimony, so there is something uncommonly repulsive in the idea that such a union can be formed without any preparation and remain a lie from the altar to the grave.

"I regret I was not born in humble circumstances in some fisherman's hamlet on the seashore. There one is nearer to happiness and peace than in our high positions and in our complex society. Happiness depends on living naturally, and what increases our distance from nature decreases our happiness.

"Is it possible? A long, long, terrible night has gone by for me, and I see a rosy dawn of hope on the clouded sky, a ray of light which tells of the rising sun of joy. Will the sun rise in full glory? Will he warm me with his rays, and dry the tears from my cheeks? Come, my sun, come! You find a poor faded flower whose freshness has been destroyed by the hard frost of fate."

So Stéphanie wrote, after the tragedy had set her free, and at the hour when she was about to make use of her freedom and seek in a marriage of her own choice the happiness of which she had not enjoyed even the illusory semblance in the marriage into which she was hurried "without any preparation"—suddenly transformed from a schoolgirl into a grown woman—by a father to whom no sacrifice was too precious to be offered up on the altar of the Mammon of Unrighteousness. She was too young and innocent—too *bourgeoise*, perhaps—to enter into the spirit of the sacrifice. It was idle for anyone to tell her that Crown Princes would be Crown Princes, and that Crown Princesses who raised jealous objections to their doing so only made themselves ridiculous; that her splendid position was the substance, and love only the shadow. Taught by instinct, she knew better. She was too simple to wear a mask—or, if she did sometimes wear one, it was continually falling off; and she was too proud to pretend not to see the things which were happening under her nose. Moreover, just as there were women whose cue it was to make her feel provincial, so there were women—in many cases the same women—whose cue it was to make her feel neglected.

The list of the women for whom Rudolph neglected Stéphanie would be long and difficult to make out; but Mary Vetsera is the only one who matters. All the world knows—and knew at the time—that Mary Vetsera died with Rudolph on the day of the mysterious Meyerling tragedy; but there was a good deal of unnecessary reticence about her in the narratives written at the time. She figured as "Marie V——," as "a beautiful Jewess," etc., etc.; but she was, as a matter of fact, a well-known member of a family which was at that time very well known indeed in Vienna.

Her mother, the Baroness Vetsera, was *née* Baltazzi; and the Baltazzis were people who were in Viennese society without being of it. Their precise position in that society may be fixed by the fact that they received invitations to the *bal beim Hof*, but not to the more intimate and exclusive *bal am Hof*. The people who did not like them called them "rastas," meaning that they cut a dash, but that the account which they gave of their antecedents was not quite satisfactory to inquisitive aristocrats. They came from Constantinople by way of London, and they threw their money about. One always finds such people even in the most exclusive societies: people whom Society accepts, without taking them to its bosom.

Some of the brothers were—and still are—tolerably well known in England, as well as in their own country. Alexander Baltazzi won the Derby with the Hungarian horse Kisber in 1876. Hector Baltazzi is now connected with the picture-dealing business, and is sometimes to be met at the Ritz Hotel in London—a dapper little man, standing with his hands in his pockets. One of the brothers is prosperously engaged in some mercantile undertaking in Roumania; and both the sisters made good marriages. Evelyn married Count George Stockau; and Helen, with whom we are more immediately concerned, married Baron Vetsera. But the reputation of Helen, Baroness Vetsera, was not without its flaws; and Viennese society did not always exercise charity in determining its attitude towards her. It frequented her entertainments; but it also called her *la Baronne Cardinal*.

Readers of Halévy's *M. et Madame Cardinal* and *Les petites Cardinal* will understand the significance of that *sobriquet*. The Madame Cardinal of fiction was the typical *mère d'actrice*: a well-known French type, distinguished by taking a purely business-like view of a daughter's attraction for wealthy patrons of the drama. Countess Marie Larisch, who was everybody's confidante in the matter, depicts the Baroness Vetsera as a woman of exactly that character—albeit, of course, on a more exalted plane. She was not rich, she says, but was living on her capital, relying on her daughters as her assets. They must make wealthy marriages, or failing that——

"Will you," she asked Countess Marie, "undertake a very difficult mission for me? I want you to talk plainly to the Prince about Mary. You might even give him a hint that matters might be arranged if he is really desperately in love with her. At any rate, I've no objection to discussing the matter with the Crown Prince."

There we have the dots on the i's in so far as Mary's mother is concerned. Mary, for her, was an article of merchandise; and Countess Marie was, for her as for the Empress, a heaven-sent "go-between." Unfortunately, however, from the mother's point of view, Mary was not an ideal daughter. It is not impossible, Countess Marie thinks, that she might, in cold blood, have fallen in with her mother's plans. It is certainly not by considerations of morality, Countess Marie maintains, that she would have been restrained from doing so; for those considerations had already gone by the board in the course of an "affair" with an English cavalry officer in Cairo. But Mary's blood was, at the moment, anything but cold. She was at once infatuated, and vain, and wilful; and all three emotions—wilfulness, and vanity, and infatuation—had combined to prompt her to the same rash course of action. She had a chance—or, at all events, believed that she had one—of marrying Miguel of

Braganza; but she preferred Rudolph. She threw herself at Rudolph's head, and stuck to him like a leech. Rudolph himself declared that she was not like the others—she could not be shaken off.

She had begun by writing to Rudolph, imploring him to see her; and he had plunged into the adventure, as he had plunged into so many previous adventures, with a light heart, not guessing whither it would lead him. She had gone on to insult the Crown Princess—staring her full in the face, and not recognising her presence in a ball-room. Her mother, crimson with anger—for her own social position was obviously imperilled by such behaviour on her daughter's part—had hurried her off and locked her up in her room; and then Rudolph, hearing what had happened, went to see Countess Marie, and required a service of her:

"Listen. I want you to bring Mary to me at the Hofburg."

"I assure you it is necessary for me to see Mary. Besides, I myself am in great danger."

"I must speak to Mary *alone*; it may possibly help me to escape the trouble which threatens me."

Those are the essential sentences; and they strike one as madly inconsequent. For why should a private interview with Mary be necessitated by the fact that Rudolph was "in danger"? How could such an interview help him to escape the trouble which threatened him,—that trouble being, as he went on to explain to Countess Marie, political? Countess Marie does not answer these questions; she writes as if she did not even perceive them to be questions which a sceptical critic of her narrative would inevitably ask. She goes on, instead, to speak of Rudolph's political troubles, and of the part which he called upon her to play in covering them up:

"'Listen!' he said. 'If I were to confide in the Emperor, *I should sign my own death warrant.*' My heart nearly stopped beating at this dreadful disclosure, and I could say nothing."

Then Rudolph handed Countess Marie a steel casket which he asked her to take charge of, saying:

"It is imperative that it should not be found in my possession, for at any moment the Emperor may order my personal belongings to be seized."

And then:—

The Hofburg, Vienna.

"How long am I to keep this dreadful thing in my possession?"

"Until I ask for it," answered Rudolph, "or until someone else asks for it. If it should come to that," he added gravely, "you must know how to act. There is one person who knows the secret of this casket, and he alone has the right (failing me) to ask for its return."

"His name?"

"Never mind his name. You can deliver it to the person who can tell you four letters. Write them down now, and repeat them after me. Listen: R.I.U.O."

It is as mysterious, and apparently as meaningless, as any conspiracy in a melodrama or a comic opera; and it may be permissible to mention here that Countess Marie was warned, before her story was printed, that nobody would believe it. She nevertheless insisted. She could not be positive that the casket was of steel, because it was wrapped up in a covering which she did not undo. But it was a casket—or at any rate a box of some kind; and it was heavy. She afterwards handed it over, in circumstances to which we shall come, to the mysterious person who gave the mysterious password; and she related all this in London in a very matter-of-fact manner, which gave her interlocutors the impression that, if her story were not true, it would have been absolutely beyond her capacity to invent it. But, true or false, what relation did it bear to the necessity for a private interview with Mary at the Hofburg?

That is what Countess Marie does not explain; and her failure to see that any explanation is required and will be demanded may perhaps be taken as an indirect proof of her *bona fides*. An inventor would not have failed to supply the missing link, which neither a criminal investigator nor a sensational novelist would have any difficulty in conjecturing. Granted that Rudolph had involved himself in a political plot—whether to get himself crowned King of Hungary or for any other purpose—then the whole of the evidence relating to the plot cannot have been contained in the mysterious steel casket. Some further evidence—a letter or some other scrap of paper—must have been in Mary Vetsera's possession. She must have been holding it over Rudolph's head as an instrument of blackmail—demanding, perhaps, that he should divorce his wife and marry her; or, at all events, he must have suspected her of the intention to do so, and have wanted to get the document back from her. On that assumption—but on no other—the political necessity of the interview on which Rudolph insisted is clear.

In any case, he did insist; and Countess Marie yielded to his entreaties. The allegation has been made that he offered her a pecuniary inducement to do so; but there is no reason for believing that. It would have been worth his while; but it can hardly have been necessary. So she found a pretext, drove Mary to the Hofburg, and left her there. "I want," Rudolph said, "to keep Mary with me for two days, in order to come to an easy understanding with the Baroness over her." He also said, alluding to the political trouble: "A great deal may happen in two days, and I want Mary to be with me"—for what reason (seeing that, according to the same narrator, he had spoken of Mary as a woman who refused to be shaken off) we are left to guess.

And so Mary was whisked away to Meyerling; whence the telegraph presently sped the first intimation of the famous and mysterious tragedy.

CHAPTER XXI

What the Archduchess Stéphanie knew—What Rudolph knew that she knew—The search for Mary Vetsera by her relatives—The news of the Meyerling tragedy—The two official versions—The many unofficial versions—The attempt to hush the matter up—Mary Vetsera's letter to Countess Marie Larisch.

Meyerling was Rudolph's hunting-box in the forest, not many miles from Vienna: a hunting-box not used for purposes of sport alone. The Crown Prince had his boon companions, as well as his artistic and intellectual friends; and he used to revel and drink deep with them in this secluded and beautiful resort. It was also whispered that his hunting-box was his Parc-aux-Cerfs: the place, at all events, at which he made romantic assignations. Rumour credited him with a good many of these: assignations with society ladies, assignations with gamekeepers' daughters, &c., &c. It may be, of course, that rumour exaggerated, but there certainly was fire as well as smoke.

Stéphanie had been taken to Meyerling, and had admired its beauties. "What a lovely place to live in!" she had exclaimed. "Yes, and what a lovely place to die in!" Rudolph had replied, speaking morbidly, but without any deliberately ominous intention. That in the course of the honeymoon, and before estrangement had begun; but estrangement had come quickly, and had continued without intermission. Rudolph complained that the love-light had never shone in Stéphanie's eyes; but it does not seem that he tried very hard or very long to kindle it. Those eyes, he confided to a friend, "seemed incapable of expressing any feelings save those of wariness and suspicion"; and the time came when Stéphanie, as little in love with him as he with her, but more obedient to duty, not only suspected, but knew.

And Rudolph knew that she knew. The ball-room scene, described in the last chapter, would have proved that to him, even if there had been no other evidence; but he was aware, as a matter of fact, that Stéphanie had been not only watching him, but following him. There was a day when Rudolph went to visit Mary Vetsera in a hired carriage, and Stéphanie drove behind him, but unseen by him, in a carriage from the Imperial stables. She stopped outside the house which he had entered, and there changed carriages, returning to the Palace in his hired conveyance, and instructing the driver of the Imperial carriage to wait for him. It was quite impossible for Rudolph, after that, to flatter himself that his wife was ignorant of his proceedings; but there is no reason for supposing that he cared very much whether she was ignorant of them or not.

People have said that he wanted Stéphanie to divorce him in order that he might be free to marry Mary Vetsera. The story is also told—we have already spoken of it—that he was plotting for the throne of Hungary in the belief that the Hungarians, who loved him, would have been willing to accept Mary Vetsera as their Queen; but Countess Marie Larisch, who is our sole first-hand authority for the plot, disclaims all personal knowledge of it. She was pressed on the point before her much-discussed book appeared, and her replies to the questions put to her were explicit. "No," she said, "I have no first-hand knowledge of the matter. I only repeat what I was told—what I heard from the Archduke John Salvator—what Julius Andrassy hinted—what was current among those who were in a position to know. The existence of a plot to seize the throne of Hungary was the only possible inference from their confidences."

That is very indirect evidence, and, in the strict sense of the word, it is not evidence at all; but we shall have to return to the story when the Archduke John Salvator comes upon the scene. Most likely there was, at any rate, some loose talk on the subject; most likely Mary Vetsera herself had heard the talk and been impressed by it. A man will sometimes, as we all know, confide to a slip of a girl secrets which he jealously withholds from his most intimate male friends; and such a girl is very prone to believe anything which she wishes to believe—her imagination quickly transforming a vague possibility into a precise certainty. There is nothing, therefore, absurd on the face of it in the theory that Mary Vetsera went to Meyerling in the belief that she would presently leave Meyerling to be crowned at Buda. Nor is it unlikely—for reasons given in the last chapter—that her hopes, and her disposition to chatter about them, made it urgently necessary for Rudolph to see her on the subject and find a means of putting a bridle on her tongue.

THE CROWN PRINCESS STÉPHANIE.

At any rate, Mary Vetsera did go to Meyerling; and Countess Marie Larisch, who had taken her to the Hofburg and lost her there, had to explain her disappearance to the members of her family, and see if she could put them in the way of finding her. She describes a family gathering at which the Baroness Vetsera, justifying the sobriquet of Baronne Cardinal, displayed complete indifference to her daughter's adventures, but her brother, Alexander Baltazzi, was furious, and insisted that Countess Marie should accompany him to the prefecture of police. She complied; and she describes that interview too: a remarkable interview at which Alexander Baltazzi inquired indignantly whether the Habsburgs were to be "allowed to behave like common ravishers," and the Chief of the Secret Police replied that it was no part of his constabulary duty to interfere with the Crown Prince's amours. And then:—

"But perhaps you don't realise," said I, "that this young lady belongs to the aristocracy?"

"Then it's not one of the *bourgeoisie*? Oh, that's quite another story," replied the functionary. "Very well, I will see what I can do."

For the policeman, as for Windischgraetz, mankind evidently began with the baron; and he gave the information. "His Imperial Highness is at Alland,"[3] he announced; but the announcement came too late. It had hardly been made—and no action had yet been taken on account of it—when the telegraph flashed its startling news from Meyerling to Vienna. The Crown Prince had died suddenly at Meyerling—of apoplexy.

That was the first story, officially given out; but it was found that it could not be maintained. People did not believe it—naturally enough, seeing that it is almost an unknown thing for a man of Rudolph's age to die of apoplexy. It might have obtained credence—or, at all events, it might have been upheld in the face of scepticism—if it could have been substantiated by a medical certificate; but that certificate could not be procured. The doctors were asked to draft and sign it; but they refused to do so. They were then asked at least to give a certificate of death from heart failure on the ground that failure of the heart's action played its part in every death; but they would not do that either. So that

---

[3] Alland is quite close to Meyerling.

violence had to be admitted; and an amended official version of the story was issued to the effect that the Crown Prince had committed suicide by shooting himself.

Even so, public opinion was not satisfied. The medical certificates were called for; and when they were published they were severely criticised. There were two such certificates, and they contradicted each other; and neither of them would have been accepted in an English criminal court as compatible with the theory of suicide. According to one certificate, the bullet entered the head behind the ear and carried off the top part of the skull; according to the other, it had entered by the left temple and issued by the right temple. The critics pointed out that Rudolph was most unlikely to have shot himself in the left temple, because he was not left-handed, and that it was materially impossible for him to have shot himself from behind.

The inference was clear. If Rudolph had been shot, and had not shot himself, then he must have been shot by some other person. That is to say, either there had been an accident or he had been murdered. But if there had been an accident, there would have been no need to envelop it in mystery or tell certificated lies about it; so the hypothesis of murder held the field. But who could have murdered him, and why should he have been murdered? Conjecture fastened itself on those problems, and found solution for them: solutions which varied accordingly, as the speculators knew, or did not know, that Mary Vetsera, as well as the Crown Prince, was involved in the tragedy, and that her death, as well as his, had to be accounted for. The theories which obtained the widest credence were the following:—

1. Rudolph had been killed in the course of a drunken quarrel by one of his boon companions.

2. Rudolph had been pursuing the daughter of a gamekeeper with his attentions. The gamekeeper had caught him *in flagrante delicto*, and had shot him without waiting to ascertain who he was. His body had been carried into his bedroom in the hunting-box, and the suicide *tableau* had been arranged in order to cover up the scandal.

3. One of the Baltazzis, jealous of his niece's honour, had tracked Mary Vetsera to Meyerling, and had there committed

the double murder.

Not one of these three theories will hold water, in view of the facts which have since been brought to light. The first and second may be set aside on the ground that there is nothing in either of them to account for the death of Mary Vetsera. The third theory is incompatible with statements, the truth of which there is no reason to doubt, made by Countess Marie Larisch in "My Past."

That, in Countess Marie's book, we have "the secret of Meyerling disclosed" is an exaggerated claim; and there are weak points in her narrative which it is important to enumerate. She was not at Meyerling at the time of the tragedy, nor was she present when the dead bodies were discovered. All that she tells us on that branch of the subject is second-hand evidence, derived from Count George Stockau and the Court physician, Dr. Wiederhofer. But there were two things, not known to the general public, which she did know. She knew:—

1. That the Baltazzis had tried in vain to discover Mary Vetsera's whereabouts.

2. That they knew nothing of the tragedy until Alexander Baltazzi and his brother-in-law, Count George Stockau, were ordered to proceed to Meyerling, in a closed carriage, accompanied by a member of the secret police, and remove Mary Vetsera's body for secret burial in the cemetery of the Cistercian Abbey of Heiligenkreuz.

"And," said the policeman, "you are to support the body between you in such a way as to make it appear that the Baroness still lives."

The purpose of that order was clear enough. The matter was to be hushed up and the truth to be concealed, no matter whose feelings suffered in the process, in order that scandal might be avoided and the remnants of the Crown Prince's reputation be preserved. Mary Vetsera's name was not to be mentioned in connection with the Meyerling affair, but it was to be given out—all her relatives being parties to the deception—that she had died a natural death elsewhere. But that end was not achieved. It leaked out—as such things do leak out—that Mary Vetsera and the Crown Prince had died together; and the next thing to be done was to get rid of the theory of murder, and produce evidence in support of the theory of suicide. And here it is important to note that we are faced by a direct conflict of testimony.

The medical certificates, as we have seen, demonstrate that Rudolph did not shoot himself, but was shot; but the inference which they compel was never formally drawn from them in any court of investigation; and presently letters were handed to the Press, in which both Rudolph and Mary Vetsera appeared to have announced their intention of taking their own lives. The first letter was from Rudolph to the Duke of Braganza:—

"DEAR FRIEND,

"It is necessary that I should die. No other course is open to me. I hope you are well.

> "I remain,
> At your service,
> RUDOLPH."

The other letter was from Mary Vetsera to her mother:—

"DEAR MOTHER,

"I am going to die with Rudolph. We love each other too much. I ask your forgiveness and say farewell.

> "Your very unhappy
> MARY."

Nobody has ever regarded those letters—or other similar letters which have been circulated—as anything but forgeries. They impress one, indeed, not only as forgeries, but as clumsy forgeries. But here again Countess Marie Larisch makes a new contribution to the inquiry. Three weeks after Mary Vetsera's death, she says, she received the following letter, found on the bedside table at Meyerling, but held back by the police:—

"DEAR MARIE,

"Forgive me all the trouble I have caused. I thank you so much for everything you have done for me. If life becomes hard for you, and I fear it will after what we have done, follow us. It is the best thing you can do.

"Your
MARY."

It is a thousand pities that Countess Marie Larisch did not reproduce that letter in facsimile; for that is clearly the manner in which such documents should be put in evidence. Had that course been adopted, the critic, in attempting to reconstruct the story, would have been able to treat the scrap of manuscript as the sole authoritative deposition. As it has not been adopted, other critics would be entitled to deny his right to do so; and he can only give it its due place together with other evidence derived from other sources. Perhaps the ultimate result will be pretty much the same; but we will see.

Chapter XXII

Fantastic legends of the Meyerling tragedy—Talks with the Crown Prince's valet—Foolish story given by *Berliner Lokal Anzeiger*—What the Grand Duke of Tuscany knew—What Count Nigra knew—What Countess Marie Larisch tells—Her story confirmed from a contemporary source—Doubts which remain in spite of it—Was it suicide or murder?

There are, as has been said, innumerable Meyerling legends, most of them fantastic, and not all of them of contemporaneous origin. The mystery has continued to fascinate the world; fresh solutions of it are continually turning up. In every newspaper office some stranger presents himself, from time to time, offering to tell the truth, as he has heard it from one of the very few who knew it; now and again the stranger's offer is accepted. But, as a matter of fact, all the queer stories thus circulated can be traced to one of two sources,—neither of them sources in which any confidence can be placed.

The boon companions who were with Rudolph at Meyerling were Prince Philip of Saxe-Coburg, Count Hoyos, and Count Bombelles; and they, at any rate, have never taken the newspapers into their confidence. There were also present the Crown Prince's confidential valet, Loschek, and the coachman nicknamed Bratfisch (or Fried Fish), who had endeared himself to the Crown Prince by his talents as a whistler. It has been stated that Bratfisch was sent to America, and died in a lunatic asylum in New York; but, as a matter of fact, he died of pneumonia in Vienna, in 1892. It is possible that he talked; but no specific statement can be traced to him. The case of Loschek is different.

Loschek was indubitably a babbler. The world is full of men who claim to have heard the truth about the Meyerling tragedy from Loschek. The late Robert Barr, the novelist, told the present writer that he had heard the truth about Meyerling from Loschek while walking over an Alpine pass with him. The happy thought has often occurred to journalists of all nations that, if they could make Loschek drunk, they might extract the truth from him. But Loschek was wise in his generation, and discreet in a manner of his own. He knew that he could not trust himself to hold his tongue under the combined influence of good cheer and genial company; so he adopted the alternative policy of telling a different story to every interlocutor. It is possible that one of his stories may have been true; but it naturally passed the wit of journalists to decide which of them to credit. The testimony of Loschek, therefore, may be dismissed.

One story in particular in which Loschek's name appears may be dismissed with Countess Marie Larisch's assistance. It was telegraphed from Vienna to the *Berliner Lokal Anzeiger*, and purported to be based upon statements contained in a letter received from "Baron Louis Vetsera, brother of Mary Vetsera, who recently died in Venezuela." This Louis Vetsera, it was set forth, was one of those who forced the door, and discovered the dead bodies. The newspaper cutting was shown to Countess Marie, who courteously supplied the following comment:—

"Mary Vetsera's brother was not called Louis, but Ferenz (Ferry). Her eldest brother, Laszlo, was one of those burnt, many years ago, in the Ring Theatre. Ferry Vetsera was, at the time of the tragedy, only a boy of fourteen or fifteen years of age. He was not at Meyerling, nor was he one of those summoned there afterwards."

That is conclusive, and shows us how history is sometimes made. Our other sources of information— trustworthy as far as they go—are in the so-called "confidences" of Count Nigra, the Italian Ambassador at Vienna, and Princess Louisa of Tuscany's father, the Grand Duke Ferdinand. They both saw Rudolph's body when laid out for burial; and they both brought from the spectacle, if not a story, at least a theory, and the material for a story.

"Papa said" (writes Princess Louisa), "that when he arrived at Vienna, Rudolph had been dead barely eight hours. He went into the room at the Hofburg where the body lay, and was horrified to see that the skull was smashed in, and that pieces of broken bottle-glass protruded from it."

With which account we may compare the longer and more detailed story of Count Nigra, communicated to a representative of the Italian *Corriera della Sera*:—

"He was killed—and in the most awful manner. I had the good or bad fortune—I do not know which to call it—to be the first of the ambassadors to arrive at Meyerling on that fatal morning. The Emperor was not yet there. The Prince was laid out on his bed; a large white bandage covered his forehead and temples. At the sound of my footsteps, his valet Loschek ran up and led me close to the dead body. With looks rather than with words, I interrogated him as to the cause of this tragedy; and the faithful servant, in order to give the lie to the rumour of suicide which had already been spread, lifted up the bandage. Inside either the right or the left temple—my recollection on that point is vague—there was a hole so large that you could have thrust your fist into it.

"The skull appeared to be smashed—shattered as if from a blow of a bottle or a big stick. It was horrible. The hair, the fragments of bone, had been driven into the brain. The wound gaped open beneath and behind the ear in such a fashion that it seemed materially impossible that it could have been self-inflicted. A suicide? Surely not! It was an assassination—I am absolutely positive of that."

Count Nigra, it will be observed, confirms the medical certificate with regard to the position of the wound, but does not confirm the Grand Duke's statement that broken bottle-glass protruded from it. Yet Count Nigra could hardly have failed to mention the bottle-glass if he had seen it. Probably it was not there; probably the reference to it is due to Princess Louisa's conjectural emendation of her father's story—or it may be that her father came to believe that he had seen it, because it fitted in with the popular legend which had become current.

That legend was, as is well known, that Rudolph had been killed with a blow from a champagne bottle in a quarrel which broke out in the course of a drunken orgy. According to some witnesses—if one can call them witnesses—the blow was struck by one of the boon companions. According to others, it was struck by Mary Vetsera herself, after a scene of jealousy; and the part which the boon companions played in the drama was to shoot Mary Vetsera. It cannot be said that Count Nigra's description of the wound really confirms either version of the story. He made no scientific examination of the skull, but only glanced at it hurriedly; and the inferences which he drew from his hurried inspection may very well have been mistaken. But he talked; and his talk was obviously the ultimate source of all the various versions of the champagne bottle legend. They are all based upon that talk; and one can find no corroborative evidence of any one of them.

There is, in particular, no evidence that there was any drunken orgy whatsoever at Meyerling, or that, if there was, either Rudolph or Mary Vetsera took part in it. On the contrary, it was alleged by the boon companions, and assumed by the physicians, that the tragedy took place behind closed doors: that Rudolph, declaring himself to be fatigued, retired early to the apartment in which Mary—of whose presence at Meyerling the boon companions were unaware—was awaiting him. That is what Countess Marie Larisch says—her informant being Professor Wiederhofer; and her narrative corresponds, in all essentials, with the story told by the special investigator of the French paper *L'Eclair*. This is what the latter inquirer tells us:—

"The guests came home late from shooting, and soon retired to their several rooms, the Crown Prince having complained of fatigue. He left them to go to his own room, where Mary Vetsera had been brought, without their knowledge, by the coachman Bratfisch. The party did not sup together, and no one else was at Meyerling that night.

"In the morning the Duke and the Count, astonished that the Archduke did not come down, and feeling uneasy because there was no response when they knocked at his door, caused the door to be forced. They saw the two corpses lying on the bed. The double suicide was evident. In their amazement, and in the hope of avoiding scandal, they wished to hush the matter up. They wished it to be believed that there had been an accident in the hunting field; so they spread a report to that effect, and, in order to gain credence for it, they caused Mary Vetsera's body, fully dressed, to be removed in circumstances of mystery."

The differences between this narrative and that of Countess Marie Larisch are of minor importance; the resemblances are striking. In particular it is to be noted that we get from the French journalist a contemporary confirmation of Countess Marie's account of the mysterious disposal and burial of Mary Vetsera's body.[4] Countess Marie adds many gruesome details; but the story which she supports is one which had already been published, albeit in an obscure quarter and without attracting attention. Even the detail that the body was dressed for removal was, as we have seen, in the Frenchman's narrative.

We may take it as established, therefore, that the tragedy—whether murder or suicide—did, in fact, take place behind closed doors. There were no witnesses of what happened there; and the circumstantial evidence is, as we have seen, conflicting—the considerations which have to be balanced against each other being these:—

1. Both Rudolph and Mary Vetsera are said to have written letters announcing their intention of dying together.

2. The description of Rudolph's wound, given in the medical certificates, indicates that it could not have been self-inflicted; and this view is confirmed by the testimony of Count Nigra.

On the whole it is the medical testimony which inspires the greater confidence. The certificates were challenged at the time; and the doctors then pledged their professional honour that they had signed nothing which was not in accordance with the facts—though they had no responsibility for the inferences drawn from the facts. The letters, on the other hand, are not all genuine; and even Countess Marie Larisch's letter is, at the most, only evidence of what the lovers intended, or of what Mary Vetsera wished to be believed, but not conclusive proof of the way in which things actually happened. So that we are obliged to consider a possible alternative to the theory of double suicide. Did Mary Vetsera kill her lover and then take her own life—after first writing a letter to throw dust in the eyes of the world? Can we find any motive which might have induced her to do so?

---

[4] The same story was also told, long ago, in Paris, to Mrs. Clarence Andrews, by Alexander Baltazzi.

THE BARONESS MARY VETSERA.

A motive can be found; and it is in Countess Marie Larisch's narrative that one finds it. That story which she tells of a conspiracy to usurp the throne of Hungary may perhaps supply the clue.

Suppose there had been, if not a plot in the full sense of the word, at least some loose talk and some compromising correspondence. Suppose Mary was "in it," and really believed what she wished to believe—that the conspirators meant business, and that Rudolph was really working to have her crowned Queen of Hungary. Suppose Rudolph had said things—and written things—which gave some encouragement to that belief. Suppose Rudolph had realised the impossibility of the enterprise before finally embarking on it, and had contrived this secret interview for the purpose of telling Mary that he could not keep his promise—that she could only be his mistress on the same footing as any other mistress—and of recovering from her any documentary proof of his disloyal designs which she may have held.

If we may make those suppositions—and we need them all if we are to attach any meaning to Rudolph's representation to Countess Marie that an interview with Mary might help him to avoid a mysterious peril—then we have all the material for a credible reconstruction of the drama. We picture Mary going to the *rendez-vous* with gloriously ambitious hopes, only to find the promised cup of happiness dashed from her lips; and we picture love momentarily turned to hate by the bitter blow of the disappointment. We see her pleading with Rudolph and reproaching him, and Rudolph, on his part, protesting his affection, but nevertheless opposing a sullen resistance to her entreaties. The rest of the scene proceeds as in a melodrama.

On the table by the bedside lies Rudolph's pistol—the pistol which Rudolph always carried. Mary picks it up in an access of frenzy—or possibly of jealousy, for it is quite possible that she, as well as Stéphanie, had grounds for jealousy—vows that she will be avenged, and pulls the trigger. Rudolph falls, and she is horrified at the spectacle of her crime. She had forgotten—but now she realises—all that it means and all the consequences which it must entail for her. Love and fear impel her in the same direction, and drive her to the same act. She feels that she has no choice but to follow Rudolph into eternity, whether by firing a second shot or by swallowing a dose of poison. That assuredly is how a *Juge d'Instruction*, given the facts which we have had before us, would be tempted to "reconstitute the crime"—and also to explain the letter.

A melodramatic reconstitution doubtless; but that fact does not deprive it of credibility. Melodramas do happen, in real life as well as on the stage. We read of them in newspapers nearly as often as we witness them in theatres. Moreover, in this case, the whole story is melodramatic, and no interpretation of it is so improbable that it must necessarily be rejected. There are, of course, alternative possibilities. The first shot *may* have been fired by accident; and Mary Vetsera *may* have fired it as the first act in a concerted double suicide. But that she did fire it—whether by accident or by design—whether in a fit of passion or deliberately by agreement—seems as certain, if we believe the medical *procès-verbaux*, as anything connected with the mystery can ever be.

That is all that there is to be said about it; and perhaps it is all that can ever be known about it. What happened behind closed doors can, in the nature of the case, only be a matter of inference; and one is bound to come back to the fact that all the documentary evidence indirectly bearing on the tragedy is open to suspicion. The evidential difficulties, in short, may be summed up thus:—

1. Two medical certificates give two different descriptions of the wound.

2. The description of the wound given in both medical certificates differs from the description of it by Count Nigra, who, at any rate, had no motive for deceiving anyone.

3. While the descriptions of the wound are incompatible with the theory of suicide, correspondence in which the intention to commit suicide is clearly set forth has been published; but

4. The only one of those letters of the authenticity of which there is any evidence, may have been written with deliberate intent to deceive.

5. There is no agreement among those who quote the letters as to their exact text. The versions of the letters given in these pages are by no means the only versions which have been current. There are other longer versions, and versions which differ from those here preferred in various particulars. Even, therefore, if we could be sure that we had to do with genuine documents, the question would still remain whether

the documents had not been doctored.

So we must leave the mystery, offering our own reconstruction of the drama for what it may be worth, but, at the same time, declining to accept without reserve the story currently told that the full and final solution of the secret is locked up, at the Hofburg, in an iron chest, which is to be opened after the lapse of fifty years. And yet even that story is not quite impossible; for there are two secrets, indicated by rumour, which may conceivably be guarded thus, with a view to disclosure at a time when the events to which they relate are remote enough to be treated as history:—

1. It was whispered, at one time, that the tragedy of Meyerling was due to the discovery that Rudolph and Mary were really brother and sister: that is to say, that Francis Joseph was really Mary's father. The alleged iron chest might conceivably contain Francis Joseph's acknowledgment of that relationship/

2. There is the rumour of which Countess Marie Larisch makes so much, of the plot to seize the Hungarian throne; and it is not inconceivable that the alleged iron chest may contain some secret police report bearing upon that subject.

Those are the possibilities—one can think of no others; and they are, both of them, exceedingly remote. The former of the two rumours, which is not, in any case, at all well accredited, strikes one as incompatible with the Baroness Vetsera's alleged willingness that a *liaison* between her daughter and the Crown Prince should be "arranged." Not only might the idea of such a thing have been expected to revolt her, she would also have felt that she had "claims" on the Emperor which dispensed her from the necessity of exploiting her daughter by such means. The latter rumour must be regarded as improbable on the ground that, if the alleged conspiracy had really existed, the secret would hardly have been so well kept for so long.

And yet the suggestion, though improbable, is not quite impossible. The secret police of Vienna are very suspicious and acute; and they are also as unscrupulous as they are polite. The idea that there ever was an actual plot worthy to be called a plot must indeed be discarded for the reasons already set forth; but the idea that there was loose talk and compromising correspondence of a quasi-seditious character is not so fantastic. The secret police may have opened letters, or overheard conversations, or even received information. If they had done so, they would naturally have reported their discoveries, even if these were rather intangible; and if it be true that there is, at the Hofburg, an iron chest, to be opened in the fulness of time, bearing upon the Meyerling affair, a report of the kind indicated is, after all, the thing most likely to be found in it.

The blow, however—whatever he knew or did not know—was bound, in any case to be a terrible one to Francis Joseph. When Count Hoyos drove up in a sleigh in the early morning with the news, he broke down and sobbed. Then he mastered himself, and gave the necessary orders, and presently issued this proclamation to his people:—

"Deeply moved by a sorrow too profound for words, I humbly bow before the inscrutable decrees of a Providence which has chosen to afflict myself and my people, and I pray to Almighty God to grant to us all the courage to bear the load of our irreparable loss."

And to his Hungarian Prime Minister Tisza, he wrote:—

"I have lost everything. I had placed my hope and my faith in my son. There remains to me now nothing but the sentiment of duty, to which I hope to remain faithful as long as my aged bones support me."

He must have thought, indeed, at that hour, that the cup of his sorrows was full, and that the curse at last had done with him. But it was not so. In spite of that devotion to duty to which he had pledged himself, calamity after calamity was still to be heaped upon his head. Our story of the Tragedy of Meyerling has to be followed by the story of the tragic disappearance of John Orth.

CHAPTER XXIII

The Archduke John Salvator—His many accomplishments—His criticisms of his superiors—His disgrace at Court—His love affair with an English lady—"Your darling Archduckling"—His proposal to abandon his rank and earn his living as a teacher of languages—His love affair with Milly Stübel—He quarrels with Francis Joseph, takes the name of John Orth, and leaves Austria.

"John Orth," as we shall have to call him, was the Archduke John Salvator: the brother of the Grand Duke of Tuscany—the uncle of the Archduke who was to become "Herr Wulfling," and of the Princess who was to marry Signor Toselli. This is the branch of the House of Habsburg which has been most conspicuous in its revolt against the Habsburg traditions; and the Archduke John Salvator's place among them is that of the first of the family rebels. He was not only a rebel in love; he also caused trouble, and got into trouble, as soldier and politician.

He was a man of many accomplishments: one who "fancied himself," not only as a soldier, and a sailor, and a pamphleteer, but also as a musical composer. He composed a waltz, which enjoyed a great vogue, not only in Vienna; and then, suspecting that its popularity might be due to his rank, he decided to compose something more ambitious, and produce it anonymously. The great work was a ballet—*Les Assassins*—which was duly staged at the Vienna Opera as the production of a new and unknown man. Its anonymity would not have impaired its prospects if the Vienna Opera had had a Press agent who knew his business as the modern Press agents know theirs. Dark hints, mysteriously whispered, would then have stimulated the curiosity of the public and invited the applause of the connoisseurs and leaders of opinion. But the Press agents did not know their business— perhaps there were no Press agents in those days; and the ballet itself, though pretty good for an Archduke, did not come up to the standard of professional musicians. Its reception was chilly, and its run was short; so the Archduke John Salvator turned his activity into other channels.

While little more than a boy he became a military critic and a political agitator, publishing his first pamphlet on the organisation of the Austrian army when he was no more than twenty-one. The gist of his remarks was that the Austrian military system had got into a rut, and that the Austrian artillery was defective. Incidentally, too, he criticised the conduct of the Austrian Foreign Office; and the Foreign Minister made representations, with the result that the Archduke was sent to Cracow, to be out of the way. In his exile, however, he wrote more pamphlets, setting forth that the frontier fortifications were valueless, and that the War Minister did not know his business. He also lectured at the Military Club on the Austrian system of military education, which he declared to be wooden, and to deprive the soldiers of all initiative and resource. That lecture was a veiled attack upon the Archduke Albert, the victor of Custozza; so the Archduke John Salvator was once more politely exiled—this time to a command at Linz.

Decidedly this Archduke was *frondeur*, with inclinations towards Liberalism; and there were precedents for those inclinations in his family. He was the grandson of that Grand Duke of Tuscany who put an end to the Inquisition in his dominions; and an ancestor of his had been the first legitimate potentate to recognise the French Republic after the Revolution. Nothing was more natural, therefore, than that he should have a good word to say for the Austrian rebels of 1848; though it was inevitable that his praise of them should shock conservative circles. So he sulked at Linz, while officialdom sulked at Vienna; and there was further commotion when he posed his candidature, without asking the Emperor's leave, for the vacant throne of Bulgaria. The Crown Prince was sent to him, to inform him that he had incurred Francis Joseph's displeasure; and he was stripped even of his rights over his own regiment of artillery.

If he and Rudolph *did*, as Countess Marie Larisch suggests, put their heads together and talk about a *coup d'état* and the usurpation of the throne of Hungary, that punishment may well have furnished the starting point of their treasonable confabulations. The two Archdukes were close friends and kindred spirits: among other enterprises, they had combined to expose the spiritualistic medium, Harry Bastian, to the horror and disgust of the superstitious sections of Viennese society. Moreover, the Archduke John Salvator may be supposed to have sympathised with Rudolph's love affairs, for he had, as we are about to see, a very similar love affair of his own. These facts no doubt furnish a prelude, more or less fitting, to his appearance in Countess Marie Larisch's narrative as the mysterious stranger to whom she handed Rudolph's steel casket of compromising documents; and if Countess Marie's recollection of what he said to her on that occasion is correct, he was himself the principal person whom those documents might have compromised:—

"Never mind," she reports him as saying. "Things have happened for the best; you could not save a coward like Rudolph, but you've saved my life."

And he added that he was going to "die without dying," because he was "tired of the hollow things of life"; and her comment is:—

"Has he died without dying? I think so. And I believe that the Archduke, despite all evidence to the contrary, will return in his own good time."

And Princess Louisa of Tuscany, it is to be noted, says pretty much the same. To her also, and to her brother Leopold, the Archduke John Salvator announced his intentions:—

"I am about to disappear, my dear children, and I shall do so in such a manner that no one will ever find me. When the Emperor is dead I will return, for then Austria will require my services."

And her comment is:—

"Papa was convinced to the day of his death that his brother was alive; and, as time proves all things, the Emperor's death will perhaps solve the mystery, for Austria may then require the services of John Orth in the international complications which will no doubt follow."

But all that is mere conjecture; and the conjectures belong to a later stage of the story. The solid fact to be set down here is that the Archduke John Salvator, having received the signification of Francis Joseph's displeasure, sought and obtained Francis Joseph's permission to quit the

Austrian army, and retired to live quietly at his Castle of Orth, on the shores of the Lake of Gmunden. But his position and aspirations had, meanwhile, been complicated by a love affair with a fascinating nymph of the ballet.

It was not his first love affair: the woman who first taught the Archduke John Salvator to love was English. He met her, when he was only a lieutenant of hussars, on an Austrian Lloyd steamer, in the course of a journey from Port Said to Trieste. One of his letters to her has got into the hands of those who collect such things; and it shows us the Archduke already cherishing the dream dreamt by so many Habsburgs of flying from pomp in order to indulge an honourable passion, and proving himself as capable as any meaner man of supporting a family by honest toil. It will be seen that he expresses his contempt for his illustrious title by a pretty play upon words. This is the communication:—

"Most darlingest of angel girls. I must lavish on you terms of endearment. You are my loveliest love, *mia cara carissima, ma petite chérie*, my own sweet rose of Kent. I thought myself often in love before I had the happiness to meet you, but was mistaken. You fill my soul as nobody else has ever done. I am in despair at being told I must not pay you further attention. My Imperial rank stands in the way, say you and your honoured mother, of courtship *pour le bon motif*. It should, did I not realise the utter vanity of being penned up with a tribe of seventy relatives on an isolated peak. I hate my position, and am determined to live as a man should, and not like a poor creature who must be spoon-fed from the cradle to the grave. It depends on you whether I shall go on as an 'arch-duckling' or not. You spoke of the sad life of Penny Smith. Yes, it was a sad one; but why? The Prince of Capua had not the manliness to go and work for a living for himself and his wife. My courage is equal to emigrating to Australia, where I am sure I should fall on my feet. I could be a manager of a theatre, a teacher of French, German, Italian, or the curator of a zoo or a botanical garden, or I could be a riding-master or a stock-rider. Without going so far as Australia, I might get married in Italy to the girl of my choice. I was born a Tuscan, and the statutes of the grand-ducal family are dead letters there. As you can never be an

Archduchess, I shall be only too happy to cease to be an Archduke, but hope ever to be counted your darling Archduckling.

"JOHANN.

"———or, since you like my soft Italian name, Giovanni—but not on any account (Don) Juan."

It is, in very truth, a remarkable document; but it is the sort of document which never surprises one when emanating from a Habsburg pen—and perhaps ought not to surprise one when emanating from any royal or imperial pen. In the House of Habsburg, as in many other royal and imperial houses—and notably those of the Wittelsbachs and the Neapolitan Bourbons—we find many men and women who have combined great ardour in love with a passionate desire for the domestic tranquillity of the common lot, and the lives of obscure citizens of the middle classes. Examples which occur on the spur of the moment are those of Queen Cristina of Spain, who married ex-Private Muñoz, the son of a Madrid tobacconist, and played parlour games in the Palace with that tobacconist and his family; of Queen Cristina's sister, the Duchesse de Berry, who married, *en secondes noces*, the impecunious young diplomat, Lucchesi-Palli, and bore him innumerable children; of that Archduke John, who was united so happily to the daughter of the village postmaster; of that Archduke Henry, whose wife, Leopoldine Hoffmann, the actress, was created Countess of Waldeck.

Such were the exemplars—though one could name many more—whose temperament and tastes the Archduke John Salvator shared; but his advances, as both the letter and the sequel show, did not this time inspire confidence. The lady, it seems, did not love him for himself alone—saw no beauty in the prospect of becoming the bride of a teacher of languages, or a riding-master, or the curator of the Zoological Gardens at Sydney or Melbourne; and perhaps she was, from the worldly point of view, wise. Habsburgs who are ready to turn their hands to anything have sometimes had to turn their hands to very menial occupations. Within the last few years an appeal was made to Francis Joseph to do something for a Habsburg—a descendant of the Archduke Ernest—who had fallen (or risen) to be head waiter in a *café* at Buda-Pesth. The lady whom the Archduke John Salvator had once proposed to support in modest comfort by means of honest toil may since perhaps have heard of that incident with curiously mixed emotions.

At all events, she did not marry the Archduke—her mother, as appears from the letter, intervening; and he, on his part, did not keep single for her sake—or, at all events, did not keep unattached. Princess Louisa tells us that he wanted to marry her, his niece, the future bride of Signor Toselli; but that is as it may be. His desire to do so was, at any rate, kept under control. One thinks of him rather as one of those Habsburgs whom the bare idea of consanguineous marriage revolts; and one knows that he met his fate, in a sentimental sense, while shooting with some of his brother officers in the Semmering district. One cannot do better than borrow the poetical picture of the scene presented to us by his biographer, Mme. de Faucigny-Lucinge:—

"It was one of those moments when the human soul feels the need of fusion and communion with the mysteries of nature. The Prince was walking in a favourite path of his—a discreet refuge in which his companions had always been accustomed to leave him alone. Of a sudden he found himself in the presence of a girl whose delicate features and pensive gaze attracted his attention. Her eyes were gentle, and her lips were lighted with a smile. As he overheard her talking with her parents, it seemed to the Archduke that he had long been familiar with that melodious voice, so fraught with enchantment to all who listened to it; for the things which most delight us always seem like reminiscences of some previous life."

Nothing happened, however, at the moment. The Archduke passed by without speaking—too shy to speak, perhaps, though that, in the light of the letter which we have just read, is not very easy to believe; but he did not forget. To quote the same narrator:—

"His thoughts came back, again and again, to the girl who had appeared to him in such poetical circumstances, in an Autumn twilight. He wanted to know who she was; and having learnt that her home was in Vienna, where she lived with her parents, and that her name was Milly Stübel, and that she was one of the artistes employed at the Opera, he sought and found an opportunity of meeting her again. Every time that he met her, it was a fresh pleasure to him to remark the originality and the attractive complexity of her gifted nature. Soon they were passing long hours in each other's society; and it was the unspeakable joy of musical harmony which attached him, for ever more, to Milly; for music is far more eloquent than words."

One has no difficulty in believing it; for that is what the Habsburgs are like. One after another, they find their way to the common lot by taking a perfectly sincere and simple interest in the ordinary occupations and amusements of ordinary people. Sometimes those interests are domestic, as in the case of the Archduke Charles Ferdinand, who is said to have proposed marriage in the kitchen; they sometimes are artistic, as in the case of Princess Louisa of Tuscany, who was at the piano when she first spoke of love to Signor Toselli. So that it was quite in conformity with the family traits that the Archduke John Salvator should forget his rank, in order to talk musical criticism with the ballet-girl; and it was equally in accordance with the family traits that the talk should soon become affectionately intimate.

They talked of marriage: to the Austrian ballet-girl, as to the English lady, the Archduke spoke of his ability to earn a competence by the sweat of his brow—not, this time, as a teacher of languages or a keeper of wild beasts, but as a skipper in the merchant service. In a sense it was idle talk, for he had money enough in the bank to keep both himself and a wife in comfort; but he wanted the common lot, and labour, as well as matrimony, was a part of it. Nor was he making an empty boast; for he had passed the tests, and held a master mariner's certificate. That was the condition of things with him when, not long after the Meyerling tragedy, he had his final quarrel with Francis Joseph.

The ultimate grounds and the immediate occasion of that quarrel remain uncertain. From Countess Marie Larisch's narrative one would gather that, whatever the proximate cause may have been, the final cause was the Hungarian plot. Princess Louisa, on the other hand, has a story that Francis Joseph ordered him to apologise for language which he had used to the Archduke Albert, and that he refused to do so. Both stories may be true; and the Archduke's determination to marry an opera nymph may also have been a contributory cause of disagreement. The actual scene is described by Princess Louisa, who may be supposed to have had her information from the Archduke himself:—

"Uncle John" (she tells us) "said in his bold way that he would leave the army and the Court rather than be dictated to, and he concluded by declaring that he did not care in the least whether he was a member of the Imperial House. A storm followed this rank apostasy, and my uncle, in a fit of ungovernable rage, tore off his Order of the Golden Fleece, and flung it at the Emperor."

The Emperor, as may be supposed, was not melted, but rather hardened, by that appeal to his feelings; so that, when the Archduke presently announced his desire to resign his rank and titles, take the name of "John Orth," and leave Austria, Francis Joseph replied that he might take any name he chose, and go where he liked, but that, if he ever attempted to return, he would find that the Austrian police had orders to arrest him as soon as he crossed the frontier. Those were the circumstances in which he departed; and Milly Stübel departed with him. He could not marry her in Austria, but he had promised to marry her in London.

CHAPTER XXIV

John Orth—Had he been plotting with Rudolph?—Indirect confirmation of story told by Countess Marie Larisch—Did John Orth really marry Milly Stübel—Failure to find the proofs of the marriage—John Orth's letters written on the eve of his departure for America—Disappearance of his ship off Cape Horn—Is John Orth really dead—Examination of the reasons for believing that he is still alive.

We will now definitely call John of Tuscany John Orth; but a cloud of uncertainty overhangs both his assumption of that name and his subsequent adventures. Ostensibly he assumed the name, and shook the dust of Austria off his feet, to please himself; but there are not wanting those who declare that, if he had not resigned his rank, he would have been deprived of it, and that he only banished himself because the Emperor had threatened to banish him.

The narrative of Princess Louisa does not help us much. Princess Louisa only knows what her uncle told her, and he evidently told her very little. It is reasonable to trust her for the passionate scene in Francis Joseph's cabinet; but that is all. She was only a girl of twenty when she heard of it, and there was no reason why the hidden causes of the scene should be confided to her. Nor does one get much light from Countess Marie Larisch's story of the plot to seize the throne of Hungary, if one accepts her version of that story; for, if all the evidence relating to that plot was contained in the mysterious steel casket, then Francis Joseph would have known nothing of it, and John Orth would have had nothing to fear when once the casket was in his hands.

But was all the evidence of that plot contained in that steel casket? Had not a portion of it found its way, by some means or other, into the hands of the Austrian secret police? That is our problem; and it will be useful to turn back to the half-forgotten gossip of the time, and see if we can find in it any indications that Countess Marie Larisch's "revelation" has, at least, "something in it."

We can. It was assumed by Countess Marie's reviewers,

when her book appeared, that her story connecting John Orth's departure with the Meyerling tragedy was, whether true or not, at all events quite new. But that assumption was erroneous. Countess Marie was only putting the dots on the i's—whether she put the right dots on the right i's or not—of a contemporaneous rumour. One may find the rumour in a work entitled *The Private Life of Two Emperors—William II. of Germany and Francis Joseph of Austria*—published in the United States, nine years ago, and written, as the publisher's note states, as far back at 1899. It possesses no sort of authority; one dares not go to it for "inside information"; but it does reflect—for what it is worth—the gossip of the hour. This is what the writer says:—

"There is, it may be added also, a story as to the Archduke's disappearance which I have never yet seen in print. It connects his exile and his disappearance from the ranks of the members of the Imperial family of Austria with the tragedy of Meyerling and the death of Crown Prince Rudolph. It is difficult to account for the origin thereof, except for the fact which I have just mentioned that the two Archdukes had already once quarrelled, and had been prevented from fighting a duel only by the intervention of the Emperor. There could, therefore, be no longer any love lost between them. Moreover, Archduke Rudolph died at Meyerling in the early part of 1889; Archduke John left Austria and relinquished his military and imperial dignities during that same year, after having been suspended from his divisional command just about the time of the tragedy at Meyerling."

What is important here is the rumour itself; the inferences drawn from it by the writer do not matter. The suggestion that John Orth was directly concerned with Rudolph's death is obviously no more than a conjectural explanation of the rumour. How, people were evidently asking themselves, could John Orth's departure be associated with Rudolph's death except on the assumption that he had done, or procured, a deed of violence? Countess Marie's story at least accounts for the association without invoking that hypothesis; and it also accounts for the quarrel between the two Archdukes. It was a quarrel, according to her, between conspirators—the one eager to press forward, and the other frightened into wishing to hang back; and though one gathers from one page of Countess Marie's book that the secret of the conspiracy was locked up in the steel casket, one reads on another page that the Ministers had an inkling of it. That fact transpires in her account of her interview with Count Julius Andrassy:

"Count Andrassy" (she writes) "said plainly that something beyond a love drama was responsible for the tragedy; the Archduke John corroborated this statement, and the affair of the steel box makes me absolutely certain of it."

Count Andrassy, that is to say, knew something, but did not choose to tell Countess Marie how much he knew. What was known to him was presumably known to the Emperor too; and their joint knowledge may have been enough to induce them to drive John Orth into exile with menaces. Still, though the conjecture is plausible, certainty is unattainable.

Nor is certainty attainable with regard to John Orth's alleged marriage to the ballet-girl, Milly Stübel. The stock statement is to the effect that he married her in London; but none of those who make the statement have seen the "marriage lines." They have been sought for; but the search has been unavailing.[5] One suspects that a ceremony of some sort was performed somewhere—*pour acquit de conscience*—but that it was a ceremony without legal value. One only gets back to certainty when one comes to speak of John Orth's voyage to the New World, whither he set sail, on his own ship, the *Sainte-Marguerite*, on March 26, 1890. But he had passed by way of Switzerland; and it was while he was in Switzerland that he and Francis Joseph exchanged their last communications. That story has been told, in the *Berliner Tagblatt*, by Marshal Czanadez, at that time attached to the Emperor's military cabinet:—

"John Orth" (Marshal Czanadez wrote) "had hardly left the Empire for Switzerland when the Emperor instructed me to follow him, to deliver a letter to him, and to induce him to

---

[5] Mr. Eveleigh Nash, the publisher, assures the author that he has himself engaged in the investigation very carefully, but with purely negative results.

return to Vienna. I fulfilled my mission; but I could not influence the Archduke. He told me that he wished to live on his private means in accordance with his tastes. He said that he had a capital sum of 70,000 florins, and proposed to lay it out to the best advantage. Seeing that he would not listen to my arguments, I took Francis Joseph's letter from my pocket and handed it to him. He ran his eyes over it and turned pale. Trembling with emotion, he handed the letter back to me and pointed to a passage in which the Emperor told him that his renunciation of the title of Archduke was accepted, but that he must never set foot in Austria-Hungary again. My mission was terminated. I returned to Vienna. I told the Emperor its result, and informed him of the details of my conversation with the Archduke. The Emperor made no remark."

It seems a little confused. The bearer of a letter forbidding John Orth to return to Austria can hardly have been instructed to try to persuade him to return there; so one scents inaccuracy. All that is established is that there were negotiations of some sort, even after John Orth had passed the frontier. We must make what we can of that imperfect information; and we must also make what we can—which is not much—of the letters in which John Orth himself bade his friends farewell. In a letter written to Herr Heinrich, on December 8, 1889, we find him protesting against constructions which have been placed upon his conduct:—

"I give you my word of honour" (he writes) "that my relations with our illustrious and benevolent sovereign have undergone no change. The impossibility of my return to the army must not, any more than my own resolution, be attributed to him....

"Francis Joseph's behaviour in the matter has been that of a magnanimous, just, and noble monarch. I have received from the hands of M. Csanadez of the Military Chancellery, the letter granting my request; but that letter forbade me to return to my own country without special permission. Hard as I find that condition, I recognise that it is not an act of excessive or exaggerated severity. No dynasty can allow one of its members to live the life of a *bourgeois* in his own country without his Emperor's leave.

"What really troubled me was the order intimated to me

by the order of the Minister of the Imperial Household to get myself naturalised in Switzerland. What a cruel dilemma was that! On the one hand I should have liked to demonstrate my gratitude and affection to the Emperor by acting in accordance with his wishes. On the other hand I was anxious to continue to be his subject, partly on account of my admiration for his august person, and partly on account of my passionate desire to continue to be a citizen of my beloved fatherland. I made an appeal, therefore, to the Emperor's gracious kindness; and I have been a whole month without a reply letting me know whether I am or am not to be permitted to be an Austrian."

The letter, which was published, was obviously written for publication. It was a manifesto rather than a confidence—designed to tell Austria, not the truth, but what John Orth wished to be accepted as the truth. We seem to see the writer laying his hand upon his heart and bowing, as he makes his exit speech. He goes on to speak of his intention to obtain a master mariner's certificate; and then he becomes poetically vague:—

"My longings and my dreams will doubtless disappear among the ocean waves: not so the ideal which I cherish in my heart. Shall I be happy? I do not know; but at least I am satisfied that I have no reason to blush for anything that I have done. What will become of me if I do adopt the Swiss nationality? That, too, I do not know. The time for idle and empty dreams is past....

"... Need I add that, even if I have to become Swiss, my heart and soul will continue to be entirely Austrian?

"Perhaps my words are the outcome of morbid excitement. However that may be, I hide my thoughts from no one, and cling to the hope that, some day, I shall be able to seal my fidelity to my country by my actions. In truth, my impatience to do so is great—especially great in view of the impossibility of bringing my plans to realisation."

There are also a few later letters. In one of them, written on the eve of departure, we read:—

"To-day I bid farewell to Europe—the quarter of the globe in which the first years of my life have been passed; and I am now beginning to realise, in the shadow of my old flag, my project of a voyage to the New World. The tug which awaits me will slowly and silently tow my ship out to sea, without any firing of salutes. And so we shall float down the Thames—the golden Thames; and, in a few hours' time, we shall be unfurling our sails in the midst of fog and rain."

The last letter is written after the arrival in South America:—

"Once away from Vienna, I find everything peaceful. My loyalty to my fatherland cannot be shaken. Across the wide waters I waft it a salute."

That is the final gesture; and one can get little out of it beyond the fact that John Orth was a true Habsburg, who must needs strike an attitude. His exit speeches to Herr Heinrich are, *mutatis mutandis*, in the same tone as his exit speeches to Countess Marie Larisch and Princess Louisa. We have already given a portion of his farewell speech to the latter; and the rest of it may be quoted here:—

"My uncle looked at us tenderly, for we were on the verge of tears at the idea of losing our kind and brilliant kinsman, and he then said, with calm gravity: 'I am about to disappear, my dear children, and I shall do so in such a manner that no one will ever find me. When the Emperor is dead, I will return, for then Austria will require my services.

"'I wish, Louisa and Leopold, that you could come with me, for we three should live the life best suited to us. It cannot be, however, and our ways must part here. You are both, like myself, individualities, and, like me, you will work out your destinies. But we shall become forces that will eventually be felt.'"

One suspects here, of course, that Princess Louisa's self-consciousness has impaired the exactitude of her recollections. She wants us to believe that the seal of mystery was imprinted, at an early age, on her own brow, and that the Man of Mystery among the Habsburgs recognised her, even in her childhood, as a kindred spirit. Perhaps he did, and perhaps he did not—it matters very little. What really matters is the impression which John Orth left behind him—the impression of a man with dark secrets and deep designs, which he hinted at but would not communicate; one who meant to evaporate like a subtle essence—to be materialised again when there once more was work for him to do in the flesh. That was how he impressed Countess Marie Larisch, when he kissed her hand and left her standing alone on that dark night in the Ring:—

"I watched John of Tuscany as he passed into the fog and disappeared in the gloom of the night. And, when I read later that he had been drowned at sea, I thought of that evening in Vienna when he bade me farewell. Has he died without dying? I think so. And I believe that the Archduke, despite all evidence to the contrary, will return in his own good time."

But what became of him?

The actual known facts are very few. The *Sainte-Marguerite*, navigated, not, as Princess Louisa says, by John Orth, but by Captain Sodich, set sail on March 26, 1890, and duly reached La Plata. There she took a fresh crew, and started, with John Orth himself in command and Milly Stübel on board, on a voyage to Valparaiso. Furious gales were raging round the Horn at the time of her passage; and she never reached her destination. The presumption that she had gone down, with her captain and all hands, was very strong; but still hope was not abandoned. There was just a chance that she might have been wrecked on one of the desolate islands off the coast of Chili—islands which have no harbours and no means of communication with the rest of the world. The thing had happened to other ships, and it was just possible that it might have happened to the *Sainte-Marguerite*. So Don Agostino Aroyo, Minister of the Argentine Republic at Vienna, argued; and Francis Joseph sent an Austrian cruiser to search the coast, in accordance with his suggestions. But without result. The cruiser searched diligently, and found nothing. The sea guarded its secret, and the mystery was as deep as ever.

And then legend got to work, and refused to be stifled, alleging that John Orth was still alive.

There were those who declared that the *Sainte-Marguerite* had not been lost at sea, but had been given another name, and had either been marooned or entered another port than that for which she was cleared; but that is quite incredible, if not materially impossible. The ship could hardly have been marooned anywhere where she would not, by this time, have been found; and one can imagine no means whereby the silence of the survivors could have been secured. Moreover, the police of the seas and the ports does its work very effectively; and every sailor man is a potential detective who boasts that he can recognise any ship known to him, without needing to read the name painted on her stern. This first theory, therefore, will not by any means hold water; and it was quickly supplanted by the second theory that, though the *Sainte-Marguerite* was lost, with all hands, John Orth was not on board of her. That is the theory to which Princess Louisa adheres:—

"The chief officer of this vessel" (she writes) "came to Salzburg expressly to see papa, and this man told me he was positive John Orth was alive, and had never gone to Valparaiso. He described how, as the old crew stood watching the *Margherita* disappear into the evening mists, the person who stood on the bridge, enveloped in a great-coat, and muffled to the eyes, was NOT John Orth, but some one impersonating him. The crew in question returned to Trieste, and one and all believed the evidence of their own eyes at La Plata, and refused to put any credence in the report that their captain had been drowned at sea."

That was the starting-point of the legend; and it was soon embroidered, as such legends always are. From this, that, and the other source came reports that this, that, and the other traveller had met John Orth and recognised him. One may as well make out a list of these stories:—

1. A visitor to a Spanish convent recognised John Orth there in the garb of a monk.

2. A French immigrant to the Argentine Republic, returning to France in 1893, declared that he had met John Orth at Buenos Ayres, and again at Rio Quarto.

3. A citizen of Trieste claimed to have met John Orth at Buenos Ayres in 1894.

4. An explorer of the Polar regions related that he had encountered John Orth in the midst of the eternal snow and ice, carrying a pocket-book on which the arms of the House of Habsburg were emblazoned in gold.

5. An explorer of the Chaco discovered John Orth, living in a lonely hut, sixteen miles from the nearest house, in the

disputed territory close to the Chilian frontier. The man, who spoke German, called himself Frederick Otten; but the traveller was not to be deceived by his false name.

THE ARCHDUKE JOHN OF TUSCANY
(John Orth.)

Some of these stories are more plausible than others; and the one of them which has stuck in the minds of men is that which identifies John Orth with Frederick Otten, or, as some versions of the story style him, Baron Ott. But another story, never before printed, may be added here. A gentleman who spoke English fluently with a German accent, was in England a little while ago, attended by a well-known London solicitor, and prepared to negotiate with publishers. The solicitor invited Mr. Eveleigh Nash to meet him; and he dropped the hint which gave the opening for overtures, by saying something about "my niece." "Then you," said Mr. Nash, "must be the Archduke John of Tuscany." "I am," replied the mysterious stranger; and then the conversation turned on literary matters. "I can't write my life under my own name," said the stranger, "but if you want reminiscences of the House of Habsburg, I can provide you with plenty of them."

There, for the moment, the matter was left; but presently there was a sequel. Information was received that the same traveller had also visited Paris, and, there also, had been invited to a little dinner in a restaurant; but, in Paris, the inquiry into his representations was pursued more carefully. Princess Louise of Saxe-Coburg, who was then in Paris, and who had known John of Tuscany well, consented to come to the restaurant, and look at the stranger, without making herself known to him. He did not recognise her, and she did not recognise him. "That man," she said, "is no more John of Tuscany than I am"; and when Mr. Nash subsequently tried to get into communication with his mysterious acquaintance at the address which had been given to him, his letter was returned to him.

So that that identification falls to the ground; and, indeed, the plausibility of the most plausible of the identifications weighs but little in the balance when set against the difficulty of vanishing, as John Orth is supposed to have vanished, from human ken. What Jabez Balfour failed to do, in the same part of the world, with considerably stronger motives for doing it, John Orth is not in the least likely to have done. Nor need his melodramatic exit speeches—if he really delivered them—influence our judgment in the matter; for there is nothing in a determination to "die without dying" which can avail to save a sailor from the perils of the sea.

Nor is anything proved by the fact that John Orth's mother, believing one or other of the stories, suddenly ceased to wear mourning for her son. Her case, in that respect, was only like that of the mother of Sir Roger Tichborne; and, like the mother of Sir Roger Tichborne, she gave large sums of money to an impostor who claimed to be her son. So we may take it as proved beyond all reasonable doubt that John Orth is really and truly dead; and the law courts recently took that view, and gave leave to presume his death, to the advantage of his heirs. His death is the second of the major tragedies of Francis Joseph's reign. The assassination of the Empress was to be the third.

CHAPTER XXV

The revolt of the Archdukes—Instructive analogies—Later years of the Empress Elizabeth—Her manner of life described by M. Paoli, the Corsican detective—Her fearlessness—Her superstitions—Various evil omens—The last excursion—Assassination of the Empress at Geneva—How Francis Joseph received the news.

Many Archdukes besides John Orth were destined to surprise and shock Francis Joseph by their aspirations after the common lot, and their repudiation of family pride in their conduct of the affairs of their hearts. We shall see them all in a moment—Archdukes and Archduchesses as well—placing love on the pedestal which the Head of their House assigned to rank, and rising, like a cloud of witnesses, to testify against the Habsburg principles and system.

The revolt is instinctive, though the vast number of the rebels sometimes gives it the appearance of being concerted. There are no precedents for it in history, and the most luminous analogies are religious ones. One may be reminded of the case of those Essayists and Reviewers who, in the 'sixties, split the tight vestments of the Church of England by the impatient movements of their broad shoulders, and were denounced as the Seven against Christ; or of the case of those Modernists of the Roman Catholic Church whom Pius X. from time to time rebukes for bringing scholarship and intelligence to bear upon theological propositions. In any case, the attack is, and has been, an attack from within,—the deadliest kind of attack; and the resulting spectacle is strange, and, to many, painful.

Here, it seems, is the House of Habsburg betrayed by the members of the household; here are the very pillars of the temple, getting up, one after the other, and walking—or even running—away, careless whether the roof falls in, so long as they are not involved in the ruin; while Francis Joseph is left to sit almost alone in the midst of the scene of desolation: a pathetic figure, like Marius alone among the ruins of Carthage—or perhaps an heroic figure, like that strong man of whom Horace wrote that even the collapse of the universe would find him undismayed. We are coming to that spectacle in a moment; but the time for ringing up the curtain on it is not quite yet. The *tableau* must be preceded by the scene of the assassination of the Empress.

We are told that the Empress wrote Reminiscences, which will some day be published. Until they appear—if they ever do appear—the full history of her inner life cannot be written; and it may be impossible to write it even then. The gift of self-revelation is as rare as genius, if it is not, indeed, a kind of genius; and the men and women who have the art of communicating the secrets of their souls are far fewer than those who have secrets to communicate. It often happens that the world, asking for bread, is given a stone; asking, that is to say, for a confession, is given dark hints, and trivial tittle-tattle. It may prove to be so in this case; but no one knows.

For Elizabeth guarded her secret to the end; and the world has no real knowledge of her, but only an impression, arising out of dark sayings, and a curious way of life. She was restless, and she sought solitude—one can say little more of her than that. What gadfly stung her, and drove her continually from place to place, one can but guess; and one is tempted, from time to time, to contradictory guesses. Perhaps the contradictions could be reconciled; perhaps more than one gadfly tortured her. She spoke of herself as a woman who dreaded death and yet saw nothing in life worth clinging to. She said that she had religious beliefs, and yet her favourite poet was Heine, who had none; and when Countess Starztay spoke to her of a peace beyond all understanding awaiting her when death had done its worst, she turned on her with the retort:

"What do you know about that? No traveller who has taken that journey has ever returned to tell us what he found at the end of it."

That is hardly the language of Pantheism; and yet there were pompous believers who pointed at Elizabeth reproachfully as a Pantheist. One may conjecture that she tried to be a Pantheist, and succeeded sometimes, for a little while, and relapsed, from time to time, into uneasiness, and the sense of her personality as an Old Man of the Sea always on her back, and by no means to be thrown off. It often happens so when personalities are very pronounced, and experiences have been vividly individual. Inherited superstitions naturally confirm the tendency; and Elizabeth—sceptic though she seemed in orthodox circles—must have inherited more superstitions than she abandoned.

She evidently felt herself to be—and, in a sense, doubtless was—a woman who had survived herself. Something, as she said, had died in her; and life, after that death, was no more than a mechanical physiological round. Ill health may have helped to fix a sensation which, in good health, would only have been transitory; she was an invalid—albeit rather a vigorous invalid—during her later years. Her knowledge that there was madness in her family—the consequent sense of doom impending—may have conjured up the picture of Nemesis in pursuit of her; and she was not without reasons for telling herself that her failure in life had been signal. Even if she did not know just what it was that she had wanted, she must have been quite sure that, whatever it had been, she had failed to get it. There had been no happiness for her in family life, and as little happiness in love. In the former she had had the sense of tragedy without the compensation of affection; and, if the obvious interpretation of Countess Marie Larisch's story be the true one, she had known what it was for a lover to ride away, leaving her to cynical reflections. So she went through life wearing a mask, and letting everyone see that she was wearing it.

So far as externals go, the picture can, of course, be given more detail. M. Xavier Paoli, of the Sûreté, whose function it was to shadow royalties in France, and protect them from assassins, has recorded many particulars of her eccentricities. She resented his attentions at first, and wanted to be left alone. "We shan't want anybody," were General Berzeviczy's words to M. Paoli when he first introduced himself, and offered his services; but M. Paoli was a discreet man who knew how to make himself acceptable, always there when wanted, and never in the way when not wanted; and he observed what he saw with the keen eye of a detective for whom nothing is too minute to be remarked. From him we learn that the Empress bathed daily in distilled water, and took only one biscuit with her tea at breakfast, and refreshed herself later in the morning with "meat juice extracted daily from several pounds of fillet of beef by means of a special apparatus which she always carried with her," and dined off iced milk, raw eggs, and a glass of Tokay.

M. Paoli also speaks of her long walks; for these, of course, were occasions on which the burden of his responsibilities weighed heavily upon him. Elizabeth often walked as much as fifteen or twenty miles in a day, with no one but her "Greek Reader"—some student, as a rule, of the University of Athens—in attendance. His function was not only to read Greek, but also to carry the Empress's spare skirt. She walked "clad in a black serge gown of so simple a character that no well-to-do trades-woman would have cared to be seen in it"; and she often changed her skirt in the midst of her perambulations, behind trees, or any other screen which the landscape afforded, while the reader dutifully looked the other way. Sometimes, too, she perambulated the streets of Paris with equal recklessness. Once, M. Paoli recalls, she went to see Notre Dame by moonlight, and insisted upon being taken afterwards to eat onion soup in a popular *café*.

Biarritz and the Riviera, however, were the places at which M. Paoli saw most of her. At both resorts she was known as "the lady in black" who went about with a full purse, dispensing charity when the fit came upon her. Whenever she visited Biarritz, she never failed to buy a cow, to be sent to her farm in Hungary. At Cap Martin, where the Empress Eugénie recommended her an hotel, Francis Joseph sometimes came to see her; but he does not seem to have seen very much of her when he did come. Elizabeth "sometimes," but by no means always, dined with him; and she invariably lunched alone. The visits, one cannot help feeling, were little more than tributes to those appearances which are so terribly important in imperial circles. It is added that the billiard-room was consecrated as a chapel; and perhaps in that act also a regard for appearances may be discerned.

A more important fact, from M. Paoli's point of view, was Elizabeth's reluctance to let him know where she was going, when she started for one of her walks. He generally managed to find out; but he nevertheless remonstrated, and received a characteristic reply:

"Set your mind at rest, my dear M. Paoli. Nothing will happen to me! what would you have them do to a poor woman? Besides, not one of us is more than the petal of a poppy or a ripple on the water."

He assured her that there really was danger—that he had heard rumours; but she still refused to let herself be scared:

"What!" she exclaimed. "Still more of your fears. I repeat, I am not afraid; and, mind, I make no promises."

But there were omens which others noticed even if Elizabeth herself was blind to them. It was observed that, while her reader was reading aloud from Marion Crawford's *Corleone*—a romance dealing with the crimes of the Mafia—a raven wheeled and circled round the Empress, returning as often as it was driven away; and she told her suite, one morning, that the moon, seen at midnight from her bedroom window, had looked like the face of a woman weeping. Moreover, the Parisian sorceress who prophesied under the name of the Angel Gabriel had made a significant prediction: that one of the sensational events of the year would be—*l'assassinat d'une souveraine au cœur malade*. No Queen or Empress of the time was known to be suffering from physical heart disease; but Elizabeth was living as a woman whose heart was bowed by grief and sickened by disappointments. It must be to her, the superstitious whispered to each other, that the warning of the Angel Gabriel pointed.

The fatal year was spent, as usual, in whirling about Europe: from Biarritz to San Remo; from San Remo to Caux; from Caux to Kissingen; from Kissingen to Bruckenau; from Bruckenau to Vienna—where Elizabeth shut herself up, and refused even to receive a newly-accredited ambassador; from Vienna to Lainz; from Lainz to Ischl; from Ischl to Nauheim; and from Nauheim back again to Switzerland, where she established herself in one of the hotels at Caux. At Caux she had, or thought she had, a vision which foreboded evil. A mysterious woman in white appeared in the hotel grounds, when the Empress was sitting on her balcony, and stared up at her with a fixed and menacing gaze. The sight made her nervous, and she told one of her retinue to send the woman away; but though every path in the hotel grounds was searched, and every bush was beaten, no woman in white could be discovered anywhere, and people remembered and recalled an old Austrian legend: that a woman in white always appeared on the eve of a Habsburg tragedy—had appeared at Schönnbrunn in 1867, and again in 1889, on the eve of the tragedies of Queretaro and Meyerling.

Whether the suite believed in that legend none can say; the normal attitude of unphilosophic mankind towards such a legend is to discredit it, and yet, at the same time, to wonder whether there may not be "something in it." The thing really to be dreaded was its possible effect on the Empress's mind, already impressed by the omen of the circling raven, and the resemblance of the midnight moon to the countenance of a weeping woman. It was thought unwise, in the circumstances, to let her pay a promised visit to Baroness Adolphe Rothschild, in her villa at Prégny, near Geneva. But, though she was nervous, she was also obstinate. She spoke, as it was her habit to speak, as a fatalist:

"I am always on the march," she said, "to meet my fate. Nothing can prevent me from meeting it on the day on which it is written that I must do so. Fate often closes its eyes; but, sooner or later, it always opens them again, and sees us. The steps which one ought to avoid in order that one may not encounter Fate are precisely those which one inevitably takes. I am well aware that I am taking such steps every day of my life."

So she insisted, and set out; and, this time, Fate was indeed waiting on the road which she chose to travel. She met Fate, just as one may meet any chance acquaintance when going on any journey. She was not the object of any individual hatred; she was merely the tallest poppy in the path of one of those anarchists who conceive it to be their function to lay the tallest poppies low. The assassin said as much to M. Paoli, who went to see him in prison:

"I struck" (he said) "at the first crowned head that came along. I don't care. I wanted to make a demonstration, and I succeeded."

His name was Luccheni; he made his demonstration

while Elizabeth was walking along the Quai du Mont Blanc towards the landing-stage of the steamer. His weapon was a shoemaker's awl, sharpened to a deadly point; he sprang like a panther, and drove it into her heart; then he ran for his life—soon to be overtaken, and caught, and held. It was all done so quickly that no one—not even the victim—realised what had happened. She could still speak, and supposed that she had been hustled by a pickpocket with a view to theft. "What is it?" she asked, with rather a dazed manner; and it was not until she had got on board the boat that she first sat down, and then fainted. There was only a single spot of blood—the weapon having closed the wound it made; but Elizabeth was now unconscious—dying of internal hæmorrhage. The steamer, which had started, was put back; a litter was improvised with the oars and sail of one of the boats; but it was all over by that time, and the doctors could do nothing. Luccheni, in custody, was already boasting cynically:

"I struck well. I feel sure I must have killed her. I hope I didn't bungle it. I hope she's really dead."

Such was her end: as sudden and tragic as her son's, though not, like his, enveloped in any shroud of mystery. It only remained to break the news to Francis Joseph; and Countess Starztay despatched two telegrams to Count Paar. The first ran thus:

"Her Majesty has sustained a serious injury. I hope you will announce the fact to the Emperor with all possible consideration for his feelings."

The second despatch added that the injuries had proved fatal; but the two arrived simultaneously. Count Paar had them both in his hands when he waited on the Emperor, who gathered from his face the nature of the news he bore. He read the messages, and sank into his chair like a man stunned. When he mastered himself, and looked up, he saw the Archduke Francis Ferdinand standing beside him. "What!" he cried to him bitterly. "Is there no calamity known to this world which is to be spared to me?"

None, it would seem; and the accumulation of tragedies on the bent white head may well have seemed the more rather than the less overwhelming, because of the dearth, in each case, of those endearing memories which can be relied upon to mellow grief after the first sharp shock of calamity has passed. The brother who had been shot for pretending to be Emperor of Mexico had been, in Austria, the leader of a hostile faction. The son who took his own life so ignobly at Meyerling had at least toyed with treason. The more distant relative who died at sea had defied him and insulted him. Between him and the memory of his early romantic love for his wife there loomed other interrupting memories. So that it was in a double sense that time had brought the fulfilment of the curse of the mother who prayed God to punish the Emperor for taking the life of her son by smiting him in the person of every member of his family.

His language, nevertheless, was that of a man who had really loved the wife whom he had lost. One of his intimates has reported it:

"No one" (he said) "can ever know how great is the loss which I have sustained. I can never tell you how much I owe to my well-beloved wife, the Empress, and how great a support she was to me during the years in which I endured so much. I never can thank God sufficiently for having given me such a companion in life. Repeat what I say to you; tell every one; I shall be grateful."

The speech may seem, indeed, an unnatural sequel to some of the facts related in these pages: an unnatural sequel, in particular, to the account given of the Empress's restless wanderings—her ceaseless search for something which she could neither discover nor define—and her long and frequent absences from the home of her adoption. But we need not, for all that, read it with any suspicion of insincerity. Francis Joseph, it is quite clear, set forth in it, not only what he wished to be believed, but also what he wished to believe. He had dreamed love's young dream in his youth, and had not merely pretended that he was dreaming it. It had seemed to him, in those years of illusion, that the dreaming of it was not incompatible with the Habsburg system of consanguineous marriages with the members of houses as tainted as their own.

Nor was it through any overt act of his that incompatibilities irreconcilable with that dream had come to light. The handsome young man, united to a beautiful young woman, had only by degrees discovered that his case was also that of a simple man of soldierly directness, united to a woman who was a mysterious enigma, living an inner life into which it was impossible for him to penetrate. He had done his best, and hoped against hope that the dream which he had dreamed would come true. There is no reason to suppose that he abandoned the hope because he found himself taking a keen pleasure in the society of Frau Schratt; and there is every reason to believe that he liked to recall the dream, and live in it again, and deceive himself.

But his marriage had, nevertheless, been a proof of the failure of the Habsburg matrimonial system; and further proofs of its failure, together with many instances of revolt against it, were to be pressed upon his notice in the years immediately in front of him. His future trouble with the Archdukes and the Archduchesses was to be trouble mainly of that kind.

CHAPTER XXVI

"Austria's idiot Archdukes"—A *catalogue raisonné*—The Emperor's brothers—The Archduke Rainer—The Archduke Henry and the actress—The Archduke Louis Salvator, the Hermit of the Balearic Islands—The Archduke Charles Salvator—The Archduke Joseph—The Archduke Eugéne and his vow to be "as chaste as possible"—The Archduke William and his courtship in the *café*—The Archduke Leopold—The awful Archduke Otto and his manifold vagaries.

"Austria's idiot Archdukes"—that is the scornful phrase in which Bismarck summed up the pillars of the House of Habsburg; but we must neither adopt it as a definition nor discard it as an insult.

Archdukes, it is true, have been bred to deviate from the normal human type; but they have not all deviated from it in the same direction. Brilliance, as well as beauty, may go with decadence. Genius and madness are allied, and eccentricity is the cousin of both of them; the diseased fruit of a diseased stock may sometimes seem to make up in splendour for what it lacks in strength. We shall see how the various cases of the Archdukes and Archduchesses confirm that truth—Francis Joseph alone among them combining a fair endowment of ability with a plausible resemblance to the average man.

Indeed, we have already seen him doing so. In his married life we have seen him as the average man puzzled by the exceptional woman—puzzled but pursuing to the last. In his political life we have seen him flexible rather than strong, wise in his selection of counsellors, but sometimes knowing better than they did, and always, in later years at least, cutting the right figure in the eyes of the world: an Emperor, indeed—"something like an Emperor," as people say— magnificent, authoritative, genial, and affable, though of an affability on which none must venture to presume. It may be, of course, that there is more here of appearance, carefully kept up, than of the reality which compels appearance to conform to it; but one's impression, in any case, is of an Emperor whom the discipline of a strict education and early responsibilities has, as it were, standardised.

But, if the Emperor has been standardised, the Archdukes have not. They have gone as they have pleased, differing from other people as Habsburgs must, but not differing from them in the pursuit of any uniform ideal— often, indeed, striking extraordinary attitudes in their strenuous endeavours to get back to the manners and methods of ordinary mankind. Already we have met a few of them: the Crown Prince Rudolph, a man of letters, a rake, and perhaps a potential rebel; "John Orth," a musician, a pamphleteer, and a hot-tempered visionary pelting the Emperor with the insignia of the Golden Fleece. It remains, leaving those stories behind us, to complete our picture of the Habsburg Court with a review of the proceedings of some of the others.

We may even go back a little way for the purpose; for, though the memory of the more distant events has been effaced by recent excitements, Francis Joseph has had trouble with his brothers as well as his son, his grandchildren, his nephews and nieces, and his cousins. Maximilian, as we have seen, wounded his feelings by more than one offensively pointed bid for popularity at his expense. Charles Louis is described by Countess Marie Larisch as "a fat old man with brutish instincts," and accused by her of ill-treating his wife, who, on her part, was understood to be in love with her Chamberlain. The proceedings of the third brother, Louis Victor, are still wrapped in a shroud of mystery which it might be indiscreet to try to tear; but his career as a butterfly of fashion was cut suddenly short by Francis Joseph's peremptory command to him to leave Vienna for Salzburg and stay there.

That is the end of the list of brothers, but only the beginning of the list of eccentric or otherwise unsatisfactory Archdukes. Whether any general impression of an abstract Archduke will result from an enumeration of the performances of several concrete Archdukes is dubious; but it will nevertheless be worth while to make out a list in the hope that the figures will somehow group themselves into a subject picture.

1. The Archduke Rainer, a second cousin, was long the most brilliant representative of Habsburg culture: a Doctor of

Philosophy of the University of Vienna, the Head, for fifty years, of the Imperial Academy of Sciences, the organiser of more than one International Exhibition, and a collector who ransacked the Coptic monasteries of the Lybian Desert for papyri, and brought two entire ship-loads of them home with him to Trieste—a collection which Orientalists have not yet finished sorting, though they have been at the task for half a century. His marriage caused no trouble, for he was united in time to an Archduchess who shared his simple tastes. He always, indeed, had his aspirations after the simple life and the common lot; but his manifestations of those longings did not cause much inconvenience. Just as the Empress Elizabeth once startled the company at a Court banquet by calling for a slice of sausage and a glass of beer, so the Archduke Rainer is said to have expressed a desire, on a similar occasion, for boiled mutton and caper sauce—a dish first served to him by the landlady of a Brighton lodging-house. But there certainly was no harm in that; nor was there any harm in the Archduke's passion for travelling in Switzerland under an assumed name, dining at *table d'hôte*, and so hearing at first hand the gossip current about his more lively relatives. The Archduke Rainer was an Archduke for whom his collection of papyri was Archdukedom large enough; and he was an ornament to the House of Habsburg, as he would have been an ornament of any house of which he was a member.

2. The Archduke Henry—Archduke Rainer's brother—was chiefly distinguished for his morganatic marriage with the actress, Leopoldine Hoffmann; and that story is chiefly interesting for the light which it throws upon the gradual evolution of Francis Joseph's attitude towards such marriages. He accepted such a union in the case of the brother of the Empress who married the actress Henrietta Mendel; but Bavarian *mésalliances* were, of course, outside his purview. Habsburgs, he considered, should maintain a higher standard of matrimonial exclusiveness than Wittelsbachs. He expressly forbade the Archduke Henry's marriage; and the priest who performed it is said only to have been entrapped into doing so by a trick played on him at a luncheon party. However that may have been, the Archduke fell into disgrace, and was absent from Vienna for fifteen years, spending most

of the time in Switzerland. Then he was recalled, and pardoned, and restored to the dignities of which he had been deprived. A title of nobility was, at the same time, bestowed upon his wife; and when both he and she died, as they did almost immediately afterwards, the Archduke Rainer, who had no children of his own, adopted their orphaned daughter. The promotion of the "unclassed" bride and her child—unclassed, of course, only from the haughty Habsburg viewpoint—may be said in some measure to have foreshadowed events which were to befall thereafter.

3. The Archduke Louis Salvator—John Orth's elder brother—has acquired for himself a kind of renown as the student hermit of the Balearic Islands. He lives the simple life there, attired, according to his niece, Princess Louisa, in "sandals and loose linen trousers," toiling like a labourer, with a sunburnt visage, in a vineyard of his own, with a yacht always at hand, ready to take him to sea whenever a fit of restlessness comes upon him. They speak of him as a pagan in his tastes, a worshipper of the sun, and of what else one knows not—perhaps of houris, for he is a bachelor, and perhaps not. He has erected statues in his mysterious grounds to a private secretary, to whom he was attached; he has been shipwrecked, and he has written books. The Empress Elizabeth was the only member of the House who showed much sympathy with him, sharing, as she did, his love of solitude, his aversion from splendour, and his detestation of the well-dressed crowd which has so little to do, except to be well-dressed. What the Russian novelists—or their French critics—call *impuissance de vivre* would seem to be the note of his passion for undisturbed seclusion; and he has written of his yacht as his sole place of refuge:

"It was the only place which I could call my home—the only place in which I really felt at home. In all my palaces and places of residence in Austria and Hungary, and even on my beloved Island of Majorca, I feel just as if I were in a hotel, and almost as if I were in a prison. There is no sense of home in such places—no sense of home whatsoever."

4. The Archduke Charles Salvator—another of John Orth's brothers—also fled from splendour, but fled in another direction. His manner of seeking the common lot was to

mingle with the common people; and he mingled with them in third-class railway carriages, and on the tops of omnibuses and tram-cars. He also taught himself a trade—Louis XVI.'s favourite trade of locksmith—and is said to have excelled at it. The police did not like him, for his habits gave them trouble; but the accidents which they feared never happened. A traitor to the Archducal ideal, perhaps, he was a traitor to nothing else; and he lived and died harmlessly.

5. The Archduke Joseph—one of the Emperor's cousins—was clever in more ways than one, being a man of learning and also a man of business. He counted among the authorities on the folk-lore of the Hungarian gypsies; and he was a valuable administrator of commercial and industrial concerns. His name figured on the official list of registered licensed victuallers; and he distilled an admirable brandy. Moreover, he was the titular head of a Casino on the Danube near Buda-Pesth: a versatile Archduke, in short, who made himself generally useful, and was appreciated.

6. The Archduke Eugène—the Archduke Joseph's brother—has specialised in religion, though he was educated as a soldier, and was, at one and the same time, a colonel of cavalry and a doctor of divinity. At one time he was anxious to resign his commission in the hussars in order to become an Archbishop, like Beethoven's patron, the Archduke Rudolph; but Francis Joseph would not permit the transformation. As a compromise, he undertook to make him Grand Master of the Teutonic Order, as soon as that office fell vacant: an office the taking up of which is preluded by the singular vow to be "as chaste as possible." It is said that the Archduke Eugène, who looks his part to the life, has taken the vow as well as the office seriously.

7. The Archduke William—the uncle of the Archduke Eugène—preceded him in the Grandmastership; but, in his case, the possibilities of chastity appear to have been limited. The stories of his assignations with ladies in the *cabinets particuliers* of restaurants are numerous, and some of them are diverting. The landlord, on one occasion, was so proud of his patronage that he could not keep the secret of it. Not realising what the consequences might be, he whispered to a friend that the Archduke William was, at that moment, doing

him the honour of pursuing a courtship in an upper chamber. The consequence was that, when the Archduke descended with the lady from the upper chamber, to take his carriage, he found a vast crowd of loyal supporters assembled on the pavement, to receive him with musical honours. His case must have been even more embarrassing than that of Francis Joseph, when the cook knelt at his feet and sang the national anthem, in the small hours of the morning, in Frau Schratt's villa.

8. The Archduke Leopold—brother of the Archduke Rainer—was, at one time, commander-in-chief of the corps of engineers; but he suddenly disappeared, and people wondered what had become of him. Epilepsy—that curse of the House of Habsburg—had struck him down. He was removed to the remote castle of Hornstein, where he had to be kept in the seclusion of a mental invalid until he died.

9. The Archduke Otto—brother of the present heir-apparent, and consequently Francis Joseph's nephew—was the most amazing of all the Archdukes, and the one whose case most fittingly illustrates the usual generalisations about Habsburg degeneracy. The common people rather liked him; for he had the negative merit of not being proud, and was, in the main, the sort of gay and festive buffoon to whom the hearts of the common people, when untrammelled by considerations of morality, go out. But people who were not so common took a different view of him; and Austria was filled with stories of his misdeeds and the discomfiture which they brought him.

Meeting a funeral procession, when he was out riding, he insisted that the coffin should be laid upon the ground in order that he might leap his horse over it. Getting drunk in a fashionable *café*, he more than once executed a dance, apparelled in nothing except a képi, a sword-belt, and a pair of gloves; and once, in order to express his contempt for things in general and Habsburgs in particular, he poured the contents of a dish of spinach over the Emperor's bust. A furious lady cyclist once assailed him with a whip for breaking up a cycle race on the high road on which he was driving; and the Austrian journalists who aspersed his private character were acquitted by the juries when he ventured to take proceedings against them.

The worst thing that he ever did was to invite his boon companions to pay a surprise visit to his wife's bedchamber, at two o'clock in the morning, at a time when she was just about to become a mother, and to strike the one boon companion who was sober enough to draw his sword and protect the Archduchess from the indignity. The matter was reported; and, as it was impossible for the offended officer to avenge his honour by challenging a member of the Imperial house, the Emperor took the matter under his own hands. He thanked the officer, it is said, in Otto's presence for the service which he had rendered; he smacked Otto's face in the officer's presence; and he put Otto under arrest.

And so on, and so forth; for the scandalous stories about Otto are endless. It need only be added that he died young, as the result of his dissipations—the structure of his once handsome nose having first collapsed.

There we may end our *catalogue raisonné* of those Archdukes whose connection with this biography is only incidental. Decidedly it is difficult to generalise about them, for they are, and have been, no more like each other than like other people. There have been good Archdukes as well as bad; clever Archdukes as well as stupid ones; and, at the end of the list, one finds oneself asking: Is there any single trait on which we can lay our fingers, declaring that it is common to them all?

At the first blush one would be disposed to say that there is none; that the recluses, and the rowdies, and the students, and the men of business of the House of Habsburg are like a fortuitous collection of incongruous atoms. But when one looks again, and looks more carefully, one becomes conscious of a common force which is at work among them all. One may describe it, in the language of the physicists, as a *centrifugal* force: Nature's reply, as it were, to that centripetal force which has been at work from a distant past through the media of the doctrine of divine right, and the systems of specialised princely education, and consanguineous marriages. There is, to sum the matter up, a Habsburg ideal, forming the centre of the circle—an ideal to which Francis Joseph himself has remained as faithful as possible for as long a time as possible; but there is also that centrifugal force whirling all the individual Habsburgs away from that centre in all imaginable directions.

Most of them, as we know, have been whirled into marriages incompatible with the ideal; but there have been exceptions to that rule, as to any rule which one might endeavour to lay down. The only feature really common to their very various adventures and ways of life is that the force has affected, and the whirl has caught, each one of them. Otto stripping himself in public; Charles Salvator boarding the tram; Louis Salvator hiding his face in the Balearic Islands; Eugène clamouring for an archbishopric; and Rainer sighing for boiled mutton and caper sauce—all these are multifarious manifestations of an identical phenomenon; that phenomenon being Nature's centrifugal force which is making, and will continue to make, havoc of the imposing Habsburg system.

It is in the matter of matrimony, however, that the manifestations of that force have excited most attention, and promise to be most fruitful of consequences; and it is of those matrimonial divagations from the central ideal that we shall next have to speak in detail.

Chapter XXVII

The centrifugal marriages of the Habsburgs—Francis Joseph's attitude towards them—His attitude towards Baron Walburg, the Habsburg who had come down in the world—Where he draws the line—His refusal to sanction the marriage of the Archduke Ferdinand Charles to the daughter of a high-school teacher—The Archduke resigns his rank and becomes Charles Burg—Marriage of the daughter of Archduchess Gisela to Baron Otto von Seefried zu Buttenheim.

In one's survey of the centrifugal marriages of the Habsburgs it matters little with which marriage one begins. There can be no orderly scheme of progression in the narrative; and though one sometimes finds the Emperor, in his later years, unbending, resigning himself to the inevitable, and even going half-way to meet it, his condescension has been neither continuous nor graduated, but has proceeded by fits and starts and spasms. At one moment we seem to see good nature triumphing over pride; at another, the supple back once more stiffens itself to the rigidity of the days of old. Conflicting considerations have done battle in his mind. Did he dare resist? Could he afford to yield? Had he any tender feelings towards the individuals who pleaded for the concession? Only by considering how these several questions presented themselves to him can one discover unity of principle in his contradictory responses to the innumerable appeals.

The rule, theoretically absolute, is modifiable by the Emperor's caprice. Francis Joseph is the Head of the House as well as the Sovereign Ruler of the Empire; his judgment seat is, in all family matters, the ultimate tribunal. He can grant dispensations, like the Pope; and he sits without assessors—to decide whether hallowed principles or personal inclinations constitute the Higher Law. There are times when he feels that he would like to yield but must not; times when he yields, against his will, to a pressure which wears down his resistance; times when, though there is no particular reason why he should not yield, he simply does not choose to. One can easily adduce both earlier and later examples of each of the three attitudes; but one can trace through them all a gradual weakening, due, in part, no doubt, to advancing age, but in part also to a dawning perception of the deleterious effect of the Habsburg system upon human happiness.

Marriage after marriage, arranged in accordance with the prescriptions of the system, has resulted in misery— sometimes to the point of making the welkin ring with scandal. The failure of Rudolph's marriage was notorious; the failure of Otto's marriage was hardly repaired by his wife's dutiful attention to him when he came back to her, a mental and moral, as well as a physical, wreck. There were rumours that the Archduchess Augustine—Francis Joseph's granddaughter, the daughter of the Archduchess Gisela— suffered violence at her husband's hands; and the union of the Archduchess Maria Dorothea to the Duc d'Orléans was equally unsatisfactory. That son of St. Louis had in his youth been tracked to a hotel in Paris by the outraged husband of a Queen of Song, attended by a French commissary of police; and he and the Duchesse d'Orléans have sometimes lived separately and talked about divorce. Yet another Archduchess—the consort of Leopold II., King of the Belgians—had reason to complain that she was forsaken for the French dancer, Cléo de Mérode, and many other ladies mostly of low degree and light repute.

Assuredly there is food for reflection on the Habsburg system in this array of connubial facts; and one cannot doubt that it has produced a cumulative effect upon Francis Joseph's mind and conscience. None the less, it has found other preconceptions and prejudices firmly entrenched in that mind and conscience; and the campaign between the two sets of ideas and points of view has been long and violent—the victory inclining sometimes to the one side and sometimes to the other. Quite recently, for instance—at a date subsequent to several remarkable concessions of which we shall be speaking in a moment—Europe heard of the morganatic principle being discountenanced with such severe success that seven Habsburgs (though they were no longer entitled to call themselves Habsburgs) came, as we say in England, "on the rates." This is how a Viennese correspondent chronicles the incident:

"Great sympathy has been aroused here by the sad condition of Baron Ernest Walburg, son of the late Archduke Ernest, the Emperor's uncle, by a morganatic marriage with a tradesman's daughter. His father gave him £2,000 a year while he lived, but these payments ceased on his death. Baron Walburg was an officer in the Austrian army, but he resigned his commission when he married a poor work-girl. He applied for an audience of the Emperor, who declined to see him. He then stopped the Emperor in the street at Buda-Pesth, and described his sad situation. His creditors had distrained on all his belongings, leaving the Baron, his wife, and six children absolutely destitute. The whole family of eight persons, seven of them having Habsburg blood in their veins, are now dependent on the public poor rate."

One of them, it was added, in a subsequent communication, obtained a situation as head-waiter in a café at Buda-Pesth.

The story,[6] it must be admitted, does not display Francis Joseph in a sympathetic light; and there are several other stories of the same sort concerning which the same thing may be said. One observes him, as it were, drawn this way and that by his feeling that an Emperor—especially if he be a Habsburg—must draw the line somewhere, and his doubts as to the precise point at which he ought to draw it. Presumably, too, he draws it in different places on different occasions, relating the drawing of it, whether wittingly or unwittingly, to the state of his temper and affections. The Archduchess Maria Henrietta was, of course, well on the right side of it when she married Prince Gottfried zu Hohenlohe Schillingfurst; and so, though by no means so much as a matter of course, was the Archduchess Eleanor when she married Naval Lieutenant Alfons von Kloss. On the other hand, the Archduke Ferdinand Charles—nephew of the Emperor and brother to the Archdukes Otto and Francis Ferdinand—found himself decidedly on the wrong side of it when he announced his desire to marry Fräulein Czuber,

---

[6] The responsibility for the story rests with the Vienna correspondent of the *Daily Mail*. It was not contradicted.

daughter of a teacher of mathematics in the Technical High School of Vienna.

His case is perhaps of all our cases the most provocative of sympathy; even respectable people of the upper middle classes may properly permit themselves to be moved by it. It was no case, this time, of a precociously dissipated youth haunting the stage doors of the theatres given over to musical comedy, and suffering his inexperience to be beguiled by the meretricious attractions of a minx. The daughter of a high-school teacher is—the daughter of a high-school teacher; one need add nothing, for the rest is understood. The description implies culture conjoined with decorum, and set in a frame of homeliness—a high moral tone, and an atmosphere of useful respectability. Whatever one may think of the theatrical ladies whose fascinations have been so fatal to the Habsburg system, one cannot but admire and respect a lady who induces an Archduke to prefer an educational environment to the purposeless frivolities of the gayest Court in Europe.

And that was what Fräulein Czuber achieved. For some time Viennese Society had been diverted by the rumours which reached it of Archduke Ferdinand Charles's homely tastes and habits. He liked, it was said, to mix with the middle classes—not condescendingly, but as if he were one of them; he liked to retire to a middle-class kitchen, and help a homely girl to shell the peas or make the jam; he did not mind being seen looking out of the window of a middle-class flat, with his arm round a homely girl's waist. So gossip whispered; and presently gossip was reinforced by the solid fact that the Archduke, taking his middle-class friends as seriously as he took himself and the Imperial family, had sworn King Cophetua's royal oath that the homely girl should be his bride, and had asked her father's permission, just like any middle-class suitor, to pay his addresses to her.

Nothing, surely, could be more admirable; and yet Francis Joseph did not admire. He had not always drawn the line at actresses, though he knew that he ought to have done so. He had been on terms of personal friendship with more than one actress; and it is not unlikely that his particular friend Frau Schratt found occasional opportunities of putting in a good word for the ornaments of an unjustly aspersed profession. But the daughter of a high school teacher—a lady who was not even notorious—in whose favour there was nothing to be said except that she was well bred, well brought up, well educated, modest, domesticated, and respectable—that was another matter altogether. There are men, as we all know, to whom the open scandal of marriage with a woman of the town seems less discreditable than the commonplace ignominy of union to a well-conducted social inferior; and Francis Joseph seems to have analogous habits of thought.

At all events, in this particular case, he put his foot down. One must draw the line somewhere—that was generally admitted; and he proposed to draw it at the daughters of high-school teachers. They might come of healthier stock than Archdukes and Archduchesses; their blood might be freer from the taint of insanity; and they might be less likely to leap their horses over poor people's coffins when they were sober and undress to dance in cafés when they were drunk. Nevertheless they were unfit—grossly and impossibly unfit—to be married by Archdukes; and if the Archduke Francis Charles did not take that view of the matter, then he should be an Archduke no longer, but should depart—an imperial castaway—and hide his shame in a foreign land.

But the Archduke Ferdinand Charles had not Francis Joseph's reverence for caste, and was not to be browbeaten. His rights as a man and a lover were more to him than his rights as an Archduke and a possible heir to the throne; and his instinct told him that he was choosing the better part. Fräulein Czuber had never hoped to be an Archduchess; and he would be delighted to relieve her of awkward embarrassment by ceasing to be an Archduke. If he needed a new name, he had a little property at Burg which would supply one. Fräulein Czuber would love him as Charles Burg just as much as she had loved him as Archduke Ferdinand Charles—better, perhaps, seeing that he would have made a sacrifice for her sake. As Herr and Frau Burg, therefore, he and she would face the world together.

So he spoke; and the thing which he said that he would do he did—renouncing, and then disappearing. He passes out of our narrative as an ordinary passenger, driving in an ordinary cab to catch an ordinary train, bound for the

Riviera—starting without even a crowd to note whether rice fell when he shook himself or luck-bearing slippers pursued him. May all good things attend him in the middle-class retreat which he has found! His demonstration against the Habsburg system has been a fine one, and has been made in time: a safe escape from decadence before the doom was yet in sight; a sane escape, and not one of those—too frequent among the Habsburgs—of which the true nature and underlying motive have been obscured by bizarre eccentricities and crying scandals. Whether Francis Joseph classes the case among those in which Nemesis has smitten him through the members of his family is more than one can presume to say. We will pass from it to some of those cases in which Francis Joseph has given his consent—sometimes with his blessing, and sometimes without it.

The first case was that of Princess Elizabeth, his granddaughter—the eldest daughter of the Archduchess Gisela, and the sister of that Princess Augustine, already mentioned as the wife of the Archduke Joseph. She sought a private interview with her grandfather, in order to tell him a secret which she had not ventured to tell her mother; and the secret was that she had given her heart to Baron Otto von Seefried zu Buttenheim, a dashing young lieutenant of cavalry in the Bavarian army. It was very objectionable—the more so because love, in this instance, was laughing not only at rank, but also at religion. Otto von Seefried zu Buttenheim was a Protestant; and the Houses of Wittelsbach and Habsburg resemble each other, not only in their liability to mental derangement, but also in the soundness of their Catholic principles.

Still the case was one in which excuses and allowances could be made. Princess Elizabeth, though a granddaughter, was not an Archduchess; the disgrace, if disgrace there was, would fall not on Austria, but on Bavaria. Moreover, Otto von Seefried zu Buttenheim, though a subaltern, was a baron; and we have several times noted the ancient maxim of the Austrian aristocracy that "mankind begins with the baron." Creed may count for more than lineage in church, and before the throne of grace; but lineage counts for more than creed at Court and in Society. If principles might be tampered with at all, this was a proper time for tampering with them—especially as Princess Elizabeth pleaded very pitifully and prettily. So Francis Joseph tampered—showing, as it were, that the Habsburgs could afford to be more tolerant than the Wittelsbachs because they were greater and grander. He not only consented to the marriage, but gave the young Bavarian bridegroom a refuge in his dominions and a commission in his army. Nor has he had any reason to regret his indulgence; for this is one of the happy marriages which have no history.

And what one says of that marriage—the one which made the first effective breach in the wall of Habsburg pride and prejudices—one may say of the marriages of various other bridal couples who presently insisted on following through the breach which had been made: the marriage of Archduchess Stéphanie to Count Lonyay; of Stéphanie's daughter, the Archduchess Elizabeth, to Otto von Windischgraetz; and of the Archduke Francis Ferdinand to Countess Sophie Chotek.

Even against those marriages—or against some of them—the breach which Princess Elizabeth and Otto von Seefried zu Buttenheim had made was to be defended; but the stories are of sufficient interest and importance to be related separately.

CHAPTER XXVIII

The marriage of Archduchess Stéphanie to Count Lonyay—Attitude of the King of the Belgians towards that marriage—Attitude of Francis Joseph—He sanctions the union, but snubs the bridegroom—Marriage of the Archduchess Elizabeth to Otto von Windischgraetz—Francis Joseph's approval—The Windischgraetzes raised to the rank of Serene Highnesses.

Through the breach which Princess Elizabeth had made the Archduchess Stéphanie presently insisted upon marching; and it would indeed have been cruel to have hindered her from doing so. Her life had been an unhappy and a lonely one; she had been made to feel that, wherever she might be, she was not really wanted. She wished, after Rudolph's death, to return to Brussels; but the King of the Belgians would not have her there—his treatment of her being only less shameful than his treatment of her sister, Princess Louise of Saxe-Coburg. Remaining in Austria, she realised that neither the Emperor nor the Empress liked her, though they had no grievance against her beyond the fact that she had not attracted Rudolph sufficiently to save him from himself. Her estrangement from Rudolph was perpetuated after his death by the discovery that his will deprived her of the guardianship of her only child.

Of course there was talk to the effect that she was consoling herself—there always is such talk in such cases, and there is no need to attach importance to it. Presently all the other rumours were silenced by the announcement that she loved, and was resolved to marry, Count Lonyay, a gentleman of her household. His quarterings were few; but experience had not taught Stéphanie to associate blue blood with devotion and fidelity. Nothing was more natural than her desire to make a dash for happiness without reference to equality of rank; and as her imperial relatives were treating her as a person of no importance, there was no particular reason why they should object. As a matter of fact Francis Joseph did object, and did defend the breach; but his resistance was weakened, and his surrender precipitated, by the uninvited appearance of Stéphanie's father as his ally.

For who, after all, was this King of the Belgians that he should make himself the champion of royal and imperial exclusiveness? He was a mere *parvenu* among Kings: one whose territory had, within quite recent times, formed a portion of the Austrian dominions, and whose subjects were such aggressive democrats that they did not even allow him to possess a crown; a scandalous King, too, whose ostentatious intrigues with dancing girls were derided in all the comic papers of Europe, and who punished no one for *lèse-majesté* when his portrait and theirs were offered for sale side by side in the kiosks at Ostend. How could the Head of the House of Habsburg stand shoulder to shoulder in support of his caste with such a man as that? The cause was obviously compromised by the alliance, and the dignified course for Francis Joseph was to show that he could afford to be magnanimous, even if Leopold II. could not.

He took that dignified course, and made that magnanimous gesture. "In the name of tradition," Leopold II. stopped his daughter's allowance—it was only £2,000 a year—and deprived her of her title of Royal Highness. Francis Joseph retorted by giving his daughter-in-law a considerable sum of money, and announcing that she might retain her imperial dignities. He cut the nobler figure of the two; and praise of his magnanimity rewarded him. But his pride nevertheless had to find utterance; he had to make it clear that, though he consented, he did not approve, but regarded Count Lonyay as an intruder in a family infinitely above him. When Stéphanie came to Court, she had to come without her husband; and when Stéphanie's daughter was married, Count Lonyay, though suffered to be present in the crowd at the religious ceremony, received no invitation to the subsequent luncheon.

It sounds petty; and one need not suppose that Stéphanie did not care. But if Francis Joseph could make her unhappy for a day, he could not make her unhappy on the whole. One cannot leave the subject of her marriage without quoting once again her own joyous anticipation of it:—

"Is it possible? A long, long terrible night has gone by for me, and I see a rosy dawn of hope on the clouded sky, a ray of light which tells of the rising sun of joy. Will the sun rise in full glory? Will he warm me with his rays, and dry the tears from my cheeks? Come, my sun, come! You find a poor faded flower whose freshness has been destroyed by the hard frost of fate."

With that we may leave Stéphanie, and pass to the story of her daughter's marriage—the marriage to which Count Lonyay received no invitation.

Of all his relatives the Archduchess Elizabeth was probably the one whom the Emperor loved the best. She saw but little of her mother, who travelled a great deal, both before her marriage to Count Lonyay and afterwards. Her principal companions were the daughters of the Archduchess Isabella; and her tastes are said to have been simple. She was fond of gardening—selling vegetables, to give the proceeds to the poor; and a pleasant story is told of her devotion to her foxterrier. The place was the Schönnbrunn Park, and the time was winter; her only attendant was a footman:—

"The lively little dog jumped on the fresh ice of a fountain, which broke under him. The little animal struggled in the water, and Princess Elizabeth called to the footman to save it. The man found an excuse and did not move a hand. Then the Princess screamed at the top of her voice: 'You nasty coward! I'm not half so big as you, but I'll go in, even if I get drowned.' The man held her fast, although she shrieked and struggled, and, a gardener coming to the rescue, the little dog was saved. But Princess Elizabeth dislikes all footmen and flunkeys since that day."

It seemed as if a destiny of great distinction was in store for her. There was even talk of marrying her to the German Emperor's son, Prince Eitel Fritz, and raising her to the Austrian throne. Whether that plan would have proved agreeable to public opinion is doubtful; but a circumstance soon occurred which removed it from the sphere of practical matrimonial projects. At her very first ball Elizabeth met young Otto von Windischgraetz, a lieutenant in the lancers. She met him again at tennis-parties at Laxenburg; and presently she announced to one of her aunts that she meant to marry Otto von Windischgraetz, and that, if she were not allowed to marry him, she should spend the rest of her days in a convent. "Tell your grandfather about it," said her aunt; and she went into the next room and told him.

Otto von Windischgraetz was one of *the* Windischgraetzes, and Francis Joseph owed a great deal to them. To Alfred von Windischgraetz, indeed, as was shown in an earlier chapter, he may almost be said to have owed his throne. But no one expected that fact to count with Francis Joseph—especially as Otto only belonged to a junior branch of the family; and it is quite likely that it did not count with him. What did count was his affection for his granddaughter. As a rule he inspired his relatives with awe rather than affection; but Elizabeth was really fond of him, and he was fond of her, and could not bear to see her cry. So he listened patiently, and promised to see what could be done. For the sequel we may quote Sir Horace Rumbold's "Austrian Court in the Nineteenth Century":—

"A few days later he sent for the father, Prince Ernest Windischgraetz, and talked the matter over with him, ending what must have been a somewhat trying conversation for the parent of the aspiring young man, by telling him that he trusted his granddaughter would receive as kindly a welcome '*im Windischgraetzchen Hause*' as Prince Otto might be assured of from him and the Imperial family. On the occasion of the marriage, the entire junior branch of this old Bohemian house to which the bridegroom belonged was given the rank of '*Durchlaucht*,' or Serene Highness."

So love triumphed again, and triumphed, this time, not only without opposition, but also without the accompaniment of petty annoyances. One would be glad if it were possible to leave this matrimonial branch of the subject on that note; but it is not. We have already seen that the measure meted out to the Archduchess who loved the lancer was by no means meted out to the Archduke who loved the daughter of the professor of mathematics. The story of Francis Joseph's severe attitude towards the romances of "Herr Wulfling" and Princess Louisa of Tuscany has still to come; and before we reach those stories we have to hark back, and consider the case of the Archduke Francis Ferdinand and Countess Sophie

Chotek. That, of all the matrimonial encounters, has been the most interesting and the most important. It was not a single battle, but a prolonged campaign, in which we see Francis Joseph giving ground step by step. The final result of the conflict is still uncertain; and the full consequences of the victory gained by human affection over the Habsburg system cannot be measured and known until after Francis Joseph's death.

CHAPTER XXIX

The Archduke Francis Ferdinand—An invalid who delayed to marry—Report of his betrothal to the Archduchess Gabrielle—Announcement of his betrothal to Countess Sophie Chotek—Anecdotes of the courtship—Indignation of the Archduchess Gabrielle's mother—Attitude of Francis Joseph—-He permits the marriage on condition that it shall be morganatic—Francis Ferdinand compelled to swear a solemn oath that he is marrying beneath him, and that his children will be unworthy to succeed him—Reasons for doubting whether he will eventually be bound by his oath.

Francis Ferdinand is the son of Francis Joseph's brother, Charles Louis, and himself the brother of the Archduke Otto whose outrageous eccentricities we have reviewed, and of the Archduke Frederick Charles who wooed and won the homely daughter of the mathematical master, after helping her to shell the peas. He was not classed in his youth with the Archdukes who matter, for he was a delicate boy, and it seemed unlikely that he would live to grow up. Though he grew up, he remained delicate, and it was still assumed that he would die young. Hence the talk, which came to nothing, of marrying the Archduchess Elizabeth to Prince Eitel Fritz, and securing the succession to the throne to her by a fresh Pragmatic Sanction.

Whether we regard him as having been well or badly brought up depends upon our educational ideals. If it be good to be a Catholic, and better still to be a bigoted Catholic, then his upbringing was admirable. From his earliest years he was taught to walk, if not with God, at least with the Jesuits: the worthy son of a father of limited intelligence, who combined (if his portraits are to be trusted) the smug appearance of a sinister family solicitor with the fanaticism of an Ultramontane reactionary. There are those, to this day, who sum him up with the statement that he is "in the hands of the Jesuits"; but that is a phrase which may, in practice, mean anything or nothing. When princes and priests form a Holy Alliance, the wisdom of the serpent is quite as likely to be found in one partner of the combination as in the other. Their interests are seldom identical, and exploitation is a game at which two can play.

THE ARCHDUKE FRANCIS FERDINAND.

It mattered little as long as Francis Ferdinand was expected to die, at any instant, of consumption; but he did not die of that disease, and perhaps he never really had it. He wintered in warm climates; he took cod liver oil; he travelled. Treatment and medicine produced the desired effect. Francis Ferdinand became as well able as any of his relatives to take his place in public life, and had to be reckoned with. The question of finding a wife for him became urgent. There were plenty of Archduchesses available; why did he not choose one of them and beget an heir? That was what Francis Joseph wanted to know when he saw his nephew thirty-five or more, and still a bachelor. The resulting dialogues are said to have been rather heated.

Presently rumour began to whisper that Francis Joseph had got his way. It was observed that Francis Ferdinand paid frequent visits to the house of the Archduke Frederick and the Archduchess Isabella at Presburg. They had charming daughters—the Archduchess Gabrielle was particularly charming. Here, it was felt, well within the Habsburg ring-fence, was the opportunity of an ideal betrothal; and here, at any rate, was the journalist's opportunity for the intelligent anticipation of events before they occurred. Various newspapers, though not the official ones, grasped that opportunity and announced the betrothal. Official confirmation, they did not doubt, would come later, enabling them to boast: "I told you so." But those readers of the newspapers who had been admitted to the Archduchess Isabella's family circle shook their heads. They had seen what they had seen, and they anticipated quite other eventualities.

The Archduchess Isabella had a lady-in-waiting—Countess Sophie Chotek: a member of a Bohemian family, which, though old, was poor, and not of the highest order of nobility. Her father had held a governorship in Bohemia; her brother was a provincial official of moderate, but not excessive, dignity. But Francis Ferdinand, while charmingly polite to the Archduchess Gabrielle, was more often to be seen sitting in cosy corners with Countess Sophie Chotek. Often and often he sat a whole evening with her in a cosy corner, talking gloomily about his health, and complaining of the rigorous prescriptions of the doctors. Cod-liver oil, he said, was horrid stuff. It did him no good; he should stop taking it.

And Countess Sophie Chotek reasoned and pleaded with

him, as womanly women do. Of course, cod-liver oil was good for him—he mustn't be silly, and pretend that he knew better than the doctors; a peppermint lozenge would take away the taste. Anyhow, take it he really must, not only for his own sake, but for the sake of those to whom his life was precious.

"For my sake—to please me," she concluded coaxingly; and Francis Ferdinand promised, and found that the medicine did work the promised miracle. He got better and better, until he was quite well; and there was joy in the House of Habsburg, and all the Archdukes and Archduchesses were grateful to Countess Sophie Chotek. It delighted the Archduchess Isabella in particular to see that her lady-in-waiting had such a good influence over the heir-apparent, and had succeeded, after everyone else had failed, in modifying his attitude towards his medicine. It did not occur to her that cod-liver oil was a potion which could operate as a love philtre, or that the conversations conducted in the cosy corners might have run on from cod-liver oil to other and more intimate themes.

But so it was; and while the Archduchess Isabella was giving Countess Sophie Chotek great credit for her tact, Countess Sophie Chotek was, in truth, displaying even more tact than the Archduchess was giving her credit for. For it came to this: that while the Archduke Francis Ferdinand was supposed to be nursing himself with a view to proposing marriage to the Archduchess's daughter, he was, in fact, offering the devotion of a lifetime to the Archduchess's lady-in-waiting. He was not only taking his oil three times a day for her sake; he was also declaring that, if it cured him, he should feel that he owed his life to her, and should show his gratitude by begging her to unite her life to his. It was understood between them that, when he did ask her to do this, she would not refuse; but meanwhile they kept their counsel until an accident disclosed their secret.

That secret came to light because Francis Ferdinand—or perhaps his valet—was a careless packer. He had been at Halbthurn on a visit to the Archduke Frederick; and when he had taken his departure, a servant came to the Archduchess Isabella and told her that he had left a quantity of jewellery behind him on the dressing-table. It had, of course, to be sent after him; and the Archduchess thought it better to see to the matter herself. She went to the bedroom, therefore, to collect and review the jewellery, and the inspection gave her a shock. She spoke to a servant:

"Tell Countess Chotek I desire to see her immediately."

Countess Sophie Chotek obeyed her summons, and was greeted with:

"This calls for an explanation, miss. Pray, what have you to say for yourself?"

"This" being a medallion portrait of the Countess discovered among Francis Ferdinand's personal effects.

One can imagine that the blow was a severe one to an Imperial mother who had cherished the hope of marrying her Imperial daughter to the heir-apparent. One can further easily believe that the explanation, if any, which was offered was unacceptable. One can almost fancy that one hears the climax of the dialogue:

"That will do. You need say nothing more; but you will leave my house at once. I give you half an hour in which to pack."

Of course, Countess Sophie could not pack in half an hour, but had to go without her luggage; of course, too, the discovery of a portion of her secret entailed the revelation of the whole of it, though so far as the public were concerned it was only made known by degrees. First came the report that Francis Joseph and Francis Ferdinand were, for some unknown reason, not on speaking terms, and that the Court officials were snubbing Francis Ferdinand with educated insolence. Then came the rumour that Francis Ferdinand was going to renounce his archducal rights, marry Countess Sophie Chotek, leave Austria, and take up his residence with her at the Villa d'Este, at Rome. Finally came the official notification that the marriage would take place—that the Emperor had sanctioned it—but on terms.

And the nature of those terms?

This is not a Court history, and there is no need to gloss them over,—they shall be described with absolute frankness, and in plain language. The stipulation which the prestige of the House of Habsburg was held to require was this: that affronts should be publicly put on the bride before, during, and after the ceremony. The view officially taken of her may be said to be summed up in the carefully worded speech which the Emperor, gorgeously attired in his Field-Marshal's uniform, read at a special meeting of his Privy Council. Every phrase in it should be noted with care:—

"I have invited the members of my House, my Privy Councillors, and my Ministers to attend to-day's ceremony because the declaration which will be made is of the highest importance to the monarchy. Inspired by the wish always to provide as best I can for the members of my high House, and to give my nephew a new proof of special love, I have consented to his marriage with Countess Sophie Chotek. The Countess descends, it is true, from noble lineage; but her family is not one of those which, according to the customs of our House, we regard as our equals. Now, as only women from equal Houses can be regarded as equal in birth, this marriage must be regarded in the light of a morganatic marriage, and the children which, with God's blessing, will spring from it cannot be given the rights of members of the Imperial House. The Archduke will, therefore, to make this certain for all time, to-day take an oath to the effect that he recognises all this, that he recognises his marriage with Countess Chotek to be a morganatic one, that the consequences are that the marriage cannot be regarded as one between equals, and that the children springing from it can never be regarded as rightful children, entitled to the rights of members of our House. I beg the Minister of my Imperial House to read the oath which the Archduke will swear."

The Emperor's voice is said to have been "full of emotion" while he recited this solemn manifesto. One would like to attribute at least a little of the emotion to regret that his family pride required him to insult a woman who, far from doing him any harm, had saved his nephew's life by coaxing him to obey his physicians; but it is difficult to picture Francis Joseph as melted to tenderness by the idyll of the cod-liver oil. In any case, his emotion, whatever it may have been, was not allowed to interfere with the ceremony, which was continued with an ecclesiastical pomp indicating that Francis Joseph does, indeed, at times, mistake himself for God and the Archdukes for archangels, who are failing to behave as such.

It was Francis Ferdinand's turn. Bowing to the Emperor, he advanced to the table, on which stood a crucifix, laid his first and middle fingers on the Testament which was held up to him by the Archbishop of Vienna, and read the oath from a paper which he held in his left hand. This is the remarkable text of it:—

"I, Francis Ferdinand, by the grace of God, Archduke of Austria, swear to God the Almighty that I recognise the House Laws always, and, in the case of my marriage with Sophie, Countess Chotek, specially; that I accept the oath read to me, with all its clauses, and therefore recognise that my marriage with Sophie Chotek is a morganatic one; that the children which, with God's blessing, may spring from this marriage, will not be equal in birth, and, according to the Pragmatic sanction, will not be entitled to succeed to the throne, either in Austria or in Hungary."

The two speeches sound like the last lingering echoes of mediævalism; and Francis Joseph, in spite of the successive shocks which experience has given him, probably retains more mediæval ideas than any other contemporary ruler. The superiority of the Habsburgs to the rest of mankind—at all events, of Austrian mankind—is not, for him, a proposition which needs to be demonstrated; it is a law of thought. He does not argue about it, or expect others to argue about it, but finds it in his consciousness together with his conceptions of space and time. What others may do counts for nothing in comparison with what the Habsburgs *are*; and that though a simple-minded seeker after truth who should ask *what* they are, could be told little in reply except that they are the Habsburgs. Gold similarly is esteemed a nobler metal than iron, though it cannot be fashioned into such effective swords or ploughshares.

On that principle, therefore—the principle that to be is more than to do, and that the function of those who can do is to serve those who are—Francis Joseph took his stand: thoroughly believing in it—himself at once the worshipper and the worshipped; no more regarding his declaration of his own immeasurable superiority to other men as an insult to those to whom he declared himself superior than the judge so regards his admonition of the convicted prisoner in the dock. One can only insult one's equals. Any day on which the Head of the House of Habsburg decides a point of precedence takes rank as a Judgment Day—a day on which there can be only one answer to the question: Shall not the Judge of All the Earth do right? It was a matter of course that the prelates of the State Church lent themselves to the doctrine; for that is what the prelates of a State Church are for.

So that it was a matter of course that Francis Ferdinand should be required to proclaim *urbi et orbi* that he was marrying beneath him; that the marriage should be condemned to be a hole-and-corner affair which even the bridegroom's brothers did not attend; that the bride's status should be left so undignified that it was not permissible to her to attend the opera with her husband, or to sit in the Imperial stand with him at the races. But though that was Francis Joseph's official attitude as an Emperor and a Habsburg, he was also a man and a brother, capable of tolerance and condescension—increasingly capable of it as the years went by. Flexibility, good nature, weariness of the long struggle with the Zeit Geist—one does not know to which of these things to attribute the modification of his tone; but he has modified it. Francis Ferdinand has been taken back into favour and allowed to hold the highest offices suitable for him; and Countess Sophie Chotek has been promoted to be Duchess of Hohenberg. She does not yet rank with the Archduchesses, but she does take her place in the hierarchy immediately after them.

How will she rank eventually, after the inevitable day on which Francis Joseph is gathered to his fathers? That is a question which must soon, in the course of nature, present itself; and it would be a great mistake to suppose that it was settled, once and for all, when Francis Ferdinand stood before the crucifix and swore that his wife was, and that his children would be, inferior persons, unworthy to be related to him. It is not merely that "Jove laughs at lovers' perjuries," or that Francis Ferdinand's heart rejects the Habsburg superstition to which we have seen him rendering lip service. One must also remember that knots of this kind can never be tied so tightly that no way of untying them can be found by adroit and willing hands.

No doubt the Archduke is a religious man who understands the nature of an oath; but he was "brought up by the Jesuits," and one suspects that he has not been brought up by them for nothing. All Catholics are addicted to casuistry, and the Jesuits specialise in it; nor does one need any extraordinary shrewdness to divine the insidious questions which may be invoked as solvents of a situation which Francis Joseph believed himself to have made hard and fast. Let us set them forth in order:—

1. Granted that Francis Ferdinand had the right to swear away his own rights, had he any right to swear away the potential rights of persons still unborn?

2. Granted that Francis Ferdinand is personally bound by his oath, on what grounds can that oath fetter the freedom of action of the Hungarian and Austrian Parliaments?

3. Cannot the Pope, to whom God has given the power to loose and bind, free any man from any obligation, even though he has sworn by bell, book, and candle to bow to it?

4. Would it not be right and reasonable for the Pope to accord that dispensation to such a religious man as Francis Ferdinand? Would it not be to the interest of the Church that he should do so?

5. Is there any particular reason why the Austrian and Hungarian Parliaments should not petition him to take that course?

Upon the answers given to those questions, and not upon the text of the oath which Francis Ferdinand swore, the ultimate inheritance of the Empire will depend. They are questions to which, so far as logic goes, one answer is as good as another; which means that the answer actually given to them will be dictated by expediency and the wishes of the influential. Those who picture Francis Ferdinand dutifully abiding by his pledges because he is a religious man not only misjudge him, but misjudge religious people generally. There is always a Higher Law—the universe is full of Higher Laws. One can always appeal to them; and, if one is an Emperor, one may have the advantage of being judge in one's own case. Francis Ferdinand will enjoy that advantage presently; and it remains to be seen what use he will make of it. The issue is not yet, though it cannot be long delayed.

THE DUCHESS OF HOHENBERG
(Wife of the Archduke Francis Ferdinand).

Meanwhile, one may salute Francis Ferdinand respectfully as one who has fought a good fight, and has not been content with half successes. His wife is a clever woman who knows how to bide her time, and does not go out of her way to make unnecessary enemies. He himself has his party, which looks likely to be the party of the future. The blow which he has struck at the Habsburg system is the hardest blow which that system has yet sustained, because he has struck it with dignity and self-restraint, gratifying the instinctive Habsburg craving for the infusion of fresh blood without provoking any of those scandals which give the enemy occasion to blaspheme. If the Papacy was in earnest when it admonished the Habsburgs for their consanguineous unions, then he may fairly claim that the Pope is his ally in the battle.

One cannot say the same of the acts of rebellion which have to be reviewed next, though they too have served their purpose as object-lessons: crowning proofs to be cited in support of the thesis that the Habsburg system of in-breeding in order to develop an unique type of man and woman is a failure, and that nature, expelled with a pitchfork, is apt to return—an old friend with a new face, exaggerating even to the point of grotesqueness the normal man and woman's passion for romance.

CHAPTER XXX

The "terrible year" of the Habsburg annals—Proceedings of Princess Louisa of Tuscany—The taint inherited from the Bourbons of Parma—Princess Louisa's suitors—Her Marriage to Prince Frederick August of Saxony—She bicycles with the dentist—She runs away to Switzerland with her brother, the Archduke Leopold, and her children's tutor—Attitude of the Courts towards her escapade—Official notice on the subject in the *Wiener Zeitung*.

The "terrible year" in the family annals of the House of Habsburg began towards the end of 1902. Before then, though many Archdukes and Archduchesses had caused trouble, they had raised the flag of rebellion independently— one at a time. Now we see a brother and a sister making a simultaneous and concerted demonstration; Princess Louisa of Tuscany embarking on the adventure which united her, for a season (and still legally unites her) to Signor Toselli, and the Archduke Leopold Ferdinand adopting the style of "Herr Wulfling" in order to be free to follow the promptings of an impulsive heart.

Princess Louisa has told her own story. It is the story, of course, of a woman placed on her defence, replying to charges, making out a case for herself, and it therefore requires to be read critically; but the holes which criticism can pick in it do not affect the general verisimilitude of the picture. Most of the facts, after all, were too notorious to be disputed. All that was possible was a manifesto of motives; and Princess Louisa's exposition of these was entitled to an attentive and respectful hearing. She, at least, might be supposed to know why she did the things which the whole world knew her to have done. It may be, indeed, that she wrote some of her pages as one who desired to deceive; but that desire only related, at the most, to a few points of detail. The net impression of the narrative is one of winning candour. Princess Louisa could not, of course, criticise herself from a detached stand-point; but she explained herself.

There seems, at the first blush, to be a certain confusion of thought in her explanations. One cannot always make out whether she is excusing her conduct on the ground that she is a Habsburg and therefore mad, or patting herself on the back for having followed the sane and sensible, as well as the romantic course; but it is also a little difficult to make out which of the two lines would have been the proper one for her to take. There is a point of view—it has already been expounded in these pages—from which her precipitate descent from dizzy heights of grandeur presents some of the aspects of Christian's flight from the City of Destruction; but it must in justice be added that Princess Louisa, having been born in the City of Destruction, and having spent her impressionable years in it, had herself acquired some of the characteristics of the inhabitants. The true picture, perhaps, is that of an abnormal character stimulated by a sane instinct to sudden, unexpected, and eccentric action.

It was not on her father's side only that there was insanity in her house. Her mother was a Bourbon Parma; and about the Bourbons of Parma, Princess Louisa neither has, nor affects to have, any illusions. They are madder than the Habsburgs, and have none of their redeeming qualities. The character sketches which Princess Louisa gives us of her maternal great-grandfather, Duke Charles of Parma, and Lucca, and of her uncle, Duke Robert of Parma, are sketches of lunatics; though the instinctive perception that the royal family party was a City of Destruction from which it was imperative to escape for self-realisation in the atmosphere of romance appears in her account of his relations with his Duchess, who "bored him to tears":—

"She was *dévote* and excessively plain, and whenever he returned from a visit to Parma, he was wont to exclaim: '*Il faut absolument que j'aille me retremper auprès d'une jolie femme après ce tombeau de mon illustre compagne.*'"

Nor is that all; for Princess Louisa does not exhaust the subject. She might also have spoken of certain Parma cousins—nineteen children of a single father. Some sixteen of them are said to be, or to have been, of feeble intellect. One hears of one of them wandering about in the pathetic belief that she is Marie-Antoinette, carrying an orange with her, and insisting that it is her head which has recently been cut off. It is not difficult to picture Princess Louisa thinking her way to the conclusion that to be of royal birth was to come of tainted stock. She would be more likely to come to that conclusion if one may assume that the seeds of morbidity were latent in her even when her youthful high spirits concealed them.

It would not have mattered—or, at any rate, it would have mattered less—if the truths of eugenics had been revealed to her in time, and she had fought, while still a girl, for the right to dispose of her heart as she chose. That is to say that a genuine romance, at that age, might have saved her from a great deal. But love did not come; and she was only a girl, and a sufficiently "good girl" to do as she was told, though not without a high-spirited girl's disposition to laugh at uncongenial suitors. She laughed at Ferdinand of Saxe-Coburg, now King of Bulgaria, though she would probably have married him if there had not been a division of opinion in her family as to the desirability of the alliance; and she sums up the matter in retrospect thus:—

"I do not wish to imply that a princess is forced to accept the first suitor who presents himself. She can choose her future husband within certain limits, but as most princes and kings are very much alike, choice is not a difficult matter after all. Part of our education is to accept without question whatever lies upon the knees of the gods, and although every princess doubtless at some time dreams of an ideal Prince Charming, she rarely meets him, and she usually marries someone quite different from the hero of her girlhood's dreams."

There was some talk of marrying Princess Louisa to Dom Pedro—a sort of a cousin, the nephew of the Empress of Brazil; and she tells us what became of that suitor:—

"Poor Dom Pedro! Three years after our meeting he went mad, and he is now under restraint in a castle somewhere in Austria."

Then Frederick August of Saxony—the present King of Saxony—was presented. Princess Louisa rather liked him, and she married him; and it is noteworthy that, though she ran away from him—impelled by something not herself which made for liberty—she speaks of him in her book without any trace of bitterness. He meant well, one gathers, but was not intelligent enough to understand his wife, who certainly appears to have had many perplexing characteristics, and allowed the well of his natural affection to be poisoned by evil counsellors. The details are set forth in "My Own Story"; but it is, of course, necessary to remember, when reviewing them, that, though Princess Louisa has told her story, the King of Saxony has not yet told his.

One's first impression is of a conflict between natural instincts and artificial conventions. What with their devotion to religion and etiquette—and their inability to distinguish the one thing from the other—the Heads of the Saxon House were doubtless difficult companions for an impulsive child of nature. They were stiff and pompous out of all proportion to their importance—as if they had all swallowed pokers in the cradle; and Princess Louisa came among them like a Daughter of Heth, and behaved accordingly—but more so. It would be hopeless to attempt to make separate catalogues of the things which she did and the things which she is only said to have done; but it is clear that she was a romp deficient in veneration for the common objects of worship in royal and Catholic circles.

She had a gallery to play to. The common people admired and applauded; and there have, from time to time, been many indications that Princess Louisa's passion for publicity is not less strong and instinctive than her passion for romance. In a Protestant country ruled over by Catholic sovereigns, her obstinate refusal to confess to a Jesuit was naturally a popular demonstration. Protestants everywhere regard Jesuits as the most odious of all ecclesiastics, and confession as the most ridiculous of all modes of religious activity. In advanced democratic circles, too, enthusiasm was naturally aroused by the report that she had chosen a dentist for the companion of her bicycle rides in the Dresden Park. It was high time, in view of the democrats, that the royal family accepted the dentist as a man and a brother; for whereas several civilised countries had contrived to get on without Kings, a country without dentists would be intolerable.

The royal family, however, blinded by superstitious

prejudices, declined to take that view of the matter. Whether friendship for dentists or dislike of Jesuits was the more reprehensible trait in Princess Louisa's character, they either did not know or did not think it worth while to say. They summed the matter up by declaring that that was what came of reading Nietzsche; and one hears of an attempt to stem the tide of evil influence by tearing up Princess Louisa's copy of "Thus Spake Zarathustra." It was about as effective as the famous attempt to stop an earthquake by taking a pill; and the drama was quickly advanced another stage. The members of the royal family, putting their heads together, came to the conclusion that a woman who preferred bicycling with dentists to confessing her sins to Jesuits must be mad, and must, without delay, be locked up in a lunatic asylum. Whereupon Princess Louisa, having got an inkling of what was about to happen, took to flight.

No one will blame her; for no one will believe that her fears were illusory. If there is one circumstance which suggests scepticism of the fact that the percentage of insanity is higher in royal than in other families, it is the fact that members of royal families are unscrupulously ready to accuse each other of insanity, and place each other under restraint. The case of Princess Louise of Saxe-Coburg, whom Count Mattatich rescued from her prison like a gallant knight of old, is only one of many cases of which Princess Louisa of Tuscany may have bethought herself. Bethinking herself of it, she fled to her father's house at Salzburg; and when her father refused to help her—being one of those stupid old men to whom it is too much trouble to do anything definite—she fled, yet again, to Switzerland. But not alone, and not, it must be added, with the dentist. With her went her brother, the Archduke Leopold; after her came her son's tutor, M. Giron. We will say what needs to be said about M. Giron in a moment; but a word about the Archduke Leopold must come first.

Leopold, like Louisa, was, at that hour the hero of a romance; though it was not his first romance, and was not to be his last. His first love had been Elvira, the daughter of the Spanish Pretender, Don Carlos. The proposed marriage had, for some reason, fallen through; and Elvira had consoled herself for her disappointment by eloping with a married man. Now, Leopold was determined to marry Wilhelmina Adamovics, the daughter of a post office official at Iglau: a minor lady of the theatre, with two sisters, one of them on the stage, and the other married to an unimportant *employé* in one of the State tobacco factories. He had been sent to Egypt, to be out of the way of temptation; but he had returned to the temptation as soon as he got back to Austria. For the sake of Wilhelmina Adamovics he was prepared, not only to take the humble name of Herr Wulfling, but also to sacrifice his allowance of forty thousand crowns a year and his pay as a colonel in the Austrian army. He and she, and Princess Louisa, and M. Giron—a most respectable young man, and the nephew of the Professor of Public and Administrative Law at Brussels—were to face the cold world together as a Romantic Quadruple Alliance. And, meanwhile, Princess Louisa was being pursued with Olympian thunders from the various homes which she had left: thunders which took the various forms of denunciation, punishment, and prayer.

First of all, there was the official notification of her departure. It said nothing about the peril of the lunatic asylum from which she had escaped, but simply charged her with having "ignored all her family ties and proceeded abroad." Then came the Court Chaplain, who, similarly avoiding all reference to the essential fact, invited the prayers of the congregation for the Princess's return to "virtuous courses." He must have known that she could only return to those courses at the peril of her liberty; but he may be assumed to have taken the view that it is the function of a Court Chaplain to pray as he is told. Next followed the intimation that the Crown Prince of Saxony was considering by what means he could obtain the divorce to which, according to the law of his Church, he clearly was not entitled; and there also came a telegram from Grand Duke Ferdinand—"Nous avons d'autres enfants, nous ne pouvons nous occuper de toi"—and finally Francis Joseph himself took the steps which he considered incumbent on him. The following notice appeared in the *Wiener Zeitung* on January 28, 1903:—

"We learn that the Emperor, in virtue of the powers

vested in him as Head of the Reigning House, has considered it incumbent on him to direct that all the rights, honours, and privileges hitherto appertaining to the Consort of the Crown Prince of Saxony as an Archduchess of Austria by birth shall be suspended, and that this suspension shall also be maintained in the event of the impending divorce proceedings leading to the results provided for in paragraph 1577 of the Civil Code for the Empire; that the Princess shall again receive her original family names, and that she shall accordingly be prohibited henceforth from making use of the title of Imperial Princess, Archduchess, or Royal Princess of Hungary, etc., and from using her ancestral archducal arms with the archducal emblems. Furthermore, she shall no longer have any claim to the title of Imperial and Royal Highness, and all rights connected with such title shall in future be relinquished by her."

What does it all amount to?

On cold analysis it amounts to this: that, if Princess Louisa could have been caught, she would have been placed in an asylum on the assumption that she was mad, and that, as she could not be caught, she was to be punished, *in contumaciam*, on the assumption that she was sane. Whether she was actually sane or mad may be a point which it is beyond the province of Francis Joseph's biographer to settle; but he may, at least, permit himself to point out that she cannot have been, at one and the same time, both responsible and irresponsible for her actions, and that the readiness of the heads of both her own and her adopted family to pass from the one assumption to the other, to suit their convenience, betokens a shiftiness incompatible with the doctrine that Kings, Princes, and Emperors are necessarily upright, honest, or honourable men.

We will let that point go, however, and turn back to follow the fortunes of the members of the Romantic Quadruple Alliance in Switzerland, where their war against the House of Habsburg was witnessed by innumerable war correspondents from two hemispheres.

CHAPTER XXXI

The romantic Quadruple Alliance—The jarring notes—Princess Louisa's objections to her brother's companion Fräulein Adamovics—The sentimental life of the Archduke Leopold—He becomes "Herr Wulfling," and marries Fräulein Adamovics—Herr and Frau Wulfling run wild in woods—Herr Wulfling divorces his wife and marries again—His confidences to Signor Toselli—Princess Louisa's conception of the Simple Life—Her manners shock the Swiss—She dismisses M. Giron—Her marriage to Signor Toselli.

There were wheels within wheels; and the members of the Romantic Quadruple Alliance were not absolutely united. They could hold together in the presence of alarums and excursions; but intimacy and reflection discovered weak points in the combination. The dissidence was not quite so sudden or pronounced as in the case of those Balkan States which temporarily made common cause against Turkey; but lines of cleavage were nevertheless soon revealed, impairing the solidity of the *entente*, and introducing an appearance of comedy, not to say farce, into what should have been a drama of sustained and purely serious interest.

The first jarring note was struck when Princess Louisa made the acquaintance of Wilhelmina Adamovics. The ex-actress ran into the bedroom of the ex-Archduchess at Zurich, bursting with affection, and eager to take a new sister to her arms; but the ex-Archduchess was not so democratic as all that. Though she had bicycled with the dentist and made assignations with the tutor, she could not forget that she was a Habsburg, but retained enough family pride to feel that it should have been left to her to take the initiative in emotional demonstration. "The newcomer," she tells us, "was obviously not of my world"; and she continues:—

"I was taken aback. I had not expected this, and I did not want it. I knew, indeed, that Leopold had fallen in love with a beautiful girl of the people, but it never crossed my mind that he intended to marry her, and I felt instinctively that her arrival in our midst would upset all our plans.

"I tried, however, to disguise my annoyance, and to put some warmth into my greeting, but she was quite impossible, and I subsequently discovered that she had not even been trained in the rudiments of the art of behaving at table."

It was a bad beginning; and it was not made any better by the representations of the Vienna newspapers that "the flight of the Crown Princess was exclusively due to her brother Leopold's influence." Their cue seems to have been to depreciate Leopold; and this is the place in which to reproduce the character sketch of him printed in the *Neue Freie Presse*:—

"Archduke Leopold Ferdinand" (we there read) "is a very intelligent man, but somewhat eccentric, whimsical in a high degree, and difficult to manage. A prominent feature of his character is irony and sarcasm. He has in this way given much displeasure to officers of high rank, and this is the only reason why, in spite of his jovial and agreeable manner, he has made no friends in the army. While at Iglau he was constantly in conflict with the commander of the regiment. Thus, one day he went out riding disguised as a lady, in company with another officer, and was seen and recognised by his commanding officer, who, of course, took him to task. He hates etiquette, loves free and easy manners, and has always had little intercourse with the aristocracy, preferring lively young people of the middle class."

The free-and-easiness of the Archduke's manners had, indeed, manifested itself in the presence of Francis Joseph himself, on the day on which he was summoned to the Emperor's presence to be told that his way of life was dissolute and indecorous. He did not, like John Orth, pelt the Emperor with the insignia of his Orders; but he found another means, not less effective, of carrying the war into the enemy's camp, bowing politely and responding:

"I hear what you say, sir, but I fail to see why I should pay any attention to it. If there is a mote in my eye, there is a beam in yours. When you speak of such matters as these, I do not regard you as the Emperor of Austria—I merely regard you as Herr Schratt."

And so saying, he ceremoniously bowed himself out before Francis Joseph could lay his finger on the electric button which would have summoned the secret police.

Thus, by that *tu quoque*, he justified his own preference for "lively young people of the middle-class"; but it nevertheless seems that, in Switzerland, the particular liveliness of Fräulein Adamovics, after jarring from the first upon his sister's taste, came eventually to jar upon his own. It transpired in the course of time—in the course of a very short time, in fact—that the tastes, manners, and customs of Fräulein Adamovics deviated from the healthy norm no less than those of the more eccentric of the Habsburgs, albeit in a different direction. Her passion for the simple life and the return to nature lured her on to proceedings hardly compatible with sanity. The goal of self-realisation, it seemed to her, could only be attained if men and women divested themselves of their clothing, and climbed trees in order to crack nuts.

A strange doctrine truly, and one to be condemned by those pragmatists who bid us test every doctrine by the touchstone question: "Will it work?" It found its condemnation in this case, when "Herr Wulfling" began to translate theory into practice. After running wild in woods for a season, he was persuaded by the jeers of a passer-by to visit a barber's shop; and the sudden sight which he got of himself in the barber's mirror—the spectacle of a hirsute savage suggesting a Wild Man from Borneo—decided him to return to civilisation by the shortest cut available. He ran to the nearest slop-shop, put himself into a reach-me-down check-suit, engaged rooms in a *pension*, and shortly afterwards divorced the wife who had lured him into his amazing courses, and sought another wife of a more commonplace kind.

His second wife was a Swiss lady—Fräulein Ritter—and his union to her appears to have been more fortunate. He acquired the rights of citizenship in the Canton of Zug; and he presently obtained damages in a Swiss Court of Law against a journalist, who circulated the report that he had always lived, and was still living, a disorderly life, and had refused to pay his rates. The dispute about the rates was only a dispute about an assessment; and the tribunal endorsed counsel's favourable estimate of Herr Wulfling's personal worth. It is interesting to compare that estimate with the depreciatory paragraph quoted from the *Neue Freie Presse*; and we may borrow the report of the *Indépendance Belge*:—

"In Austria" (we there read) "M. Leopold Wulfling was indifferent to the attractions of fashionable life, but enjoyed himself in middle-class society. He was understood to be one of the most cultivated members of the archducal house. He speaks and writes ten or a dozen languages correctly, and has a knowledge of mathematics and astronomy which would qualify him to occupy a professorial chair in any University in the world. He is also an experienced navigator of the seas. At Salzburg, where he lived for a long time, he became very popular. His superiors considered him too considerate to the soldiers serving under his orders. His relations with his father continued to be extremely cordial even after he had retired from the army. It is absolutely untrue to say that he has been compelled to abandon the profession of arms; but the resignation of his titles involved the resignation of his commission. Note that of all his Orders he has kept only the modest Cross of Merit bestowed upon the young Archduke by the Emperor himself for saving two men from drowning."

Decidedly the Archduke Leopold had the *beau rôle* on that occasion. Not only did he leave the Swiss Court without a stain on his character, but his calumniator narrowly escaped imprisonment for defamation, and had to pay a heavy fine. It was at about this date that Signor Toselli made his acquaintance, and was inspired to the following pen portrait of the Archduke:—

"He was a tall, fine man, fair, stout, loud-voiced, and genial. He lived in an English boarding-house, where he did exactly as he liked. He trailed about most of the day in carpet slippers."

Some may think that that was carrying liberty to the verge of licence; but it is perhaps not less natural for an Archduke unwittingly to infringe the etiquette of boarding-houses than for a *parvenu* to infringe the etiquette of Courts. In Austria, it has been said, the aristocracy dare not ask the professors to dinner for fear lest, if they were worldly enough to dress for the banquet, they should wear green ties with their dress clothes. Herr Wulfling, at any rate, spoke his mind about Courts and Kings—and also about his sister:—

"Court life is stupid, dull, and wretched. Everything about it is insufferable. I cannot breathe at Court. A free man has the world at his feet, but a Prince or King is the puppet of his surroundings."

And also, on another occasion:—

"Kings are just like other men. Not one in a hundred is worth a cent; perhaps even that is an exaggerated estimate. As for my sister, she is a crazy creature. At her age she might surely keep out of mischief."

That was rather an unkind criticism, especially so soon after he and Princess Louisa had made the plunge into the simple life together; but it appears that, though Princess Louisa had, like her brother, the courage of her convictions, she was more a creature of impulse, more inclined to pose, and less consistent in her view of the obligations of simplicity. Half the journalists of Europe had assembled at Geneva, as we have seen, to give her a gallery to play to; and she played to that gallery like an operatic star, taking the air with M. Giron daily, amid the applause of the collected populace, and thereby somewhat shocking the opinion of the rigid City of Calvin. This is how, speaking to the wife of an artist who called on her, she manifested her joy in her emancipation:—

"What a happy woman you must be to be married to an artist who has a high standard, and tries to make his life square with it! Then you are free to do as you please, to dress as you like, to wear out your clothes. I have often to dress six times a day."

Perhaps. But Princess Louisa had engaged the whole of the first floor of the Hotel d'Angleterre for herself and her suite; and it was remarked that this proceeding seemed to reflect an Archduchess's rather than an ascetic's conception of simplicity. It was remarked, too, that her literary tastes, in so far as these could be inferred from the books which she borrowed from the Geneva libraries, appeared to be of a decadent modernity. Her favourite authors were discovered to be Gérard de Nerval and Baudelaire: excellent authors, indeed, but not authors whose message is for the simple and unsophisticated.

But let that pass: this work is not the life of Princess Louisa of Tuscany. Nor need we dwell upon the withdrawal of M. Giron from the Princess's *entourage*, or upon her own nervous breakdown and consequent retreat into a *maison de santé*. Very possibly the two events had some connection with each other; but it does not matter. Nor does the behaviour of M. Giron himself matter, though it is impossible not to commend him, before one dismisses him, for the chivalry with which he has kept silence. At the height of the romantic battle, indeed, he was no more discreet than the rest, and could hardly be expected to be so. He was very young; and he evidently believed that great things had happened, and that still greater things were about to happen. If he and Princess Louisa were going to defy the Habsburg system by living happily together ever afterwards, there was no reason why their gestures should not be as defiant as their actions; but that, as it turned out, was not to be.

Once more there were wheels within wheels; once more there was an interposition of some sort which threw the machinery out of gear. There is some reason to believe that the interposition was of a pecuniary character, though none for believing that M. Giron himself was "bought off." But the day nevertheless came when M. Giron discovered that his mission was terminated. As Princess Louisa puts it:—

"M. Giron did not remain long in Switzerland. My reputation being thoroughly compromised by his presence, my object was achieved, and he therefore returned to Brussels."

It is rather a cold-blooded way of putting it. M. Giron may well have felt that Princess Louisa was resuming as a woman all the rights which she had forfeited as an Archduchess. But he raised no public protest at the time, and he has raised none since, though the wealthy proprietors of sensational newspapers have often tempted him to do so. One need seek no other explanation than the fact that he was a gentleman, too chivalrous to bear malice if there was any to be borne, conscious that his chivalry had led him into mistaken courses, and only anxious that the world should forget his error. After all, how many private tutors of his tender age, however respectably connected, can lay their hands upon their hearts and vow that they, in his place, would have been irresponsive to the appeal of a fascinating Crown Princess?

But let that pass too; for our business is only with Princess Louisa, and with her only in so far as her case illustrates the failure of the Habsburg system, and the impulse of the family to revolt, as it were, against itself. No theory of her possessing a double dose of original sin can justly be invoked to account for her proceedings. The impulse to revolt was as physiologically sound in her case as in any of the others; but it was stirred in her too late. She was too radically affected to be saved by it. There is something pathetic in the picture of her efforts to recover her balance—so desperate, yet so unavailing.

In her restlessness, if in nothing else, she reminds one a little of the Empress Elizabeth. One sees her, as one sees the Empress, driven continually from place to place, seeking she knows not exactly what, but always failing to find it; but one does not see her, as one sees the Empress, guarding her secret like a delicate flame which must at all costs be sheltered from the wind. Her disposition is, rather, to expose the flame to all the winds which blow, in the hope that one or other of them may fan it to a blaze. For she is, after all, a Habsburg; and that is how the Habsburgs differ from the Wittelsbachs. The contrast has been pointed out already; but the point may be made again—in French, because there is no exact equivalent in English for the French phrases. The typical Wittelsbach, sane or insane, is *tout en dedans*; the typical Habsburg, conventional or unconventional, is *tout en dehors*.

Princess Louisa's career exemplified the distinction when she bicycled in the Park with the dentist, and when she summoned M. Giron to Switzerland to compromise her. A further illustration of it was furnished when she affianced herself to that promising young pianist, Signor Toselli. The contrast leaps to the eyes in Signor Toselli's report of the first compliments which she paid him:—

"I love the society of artists. Their views are so noble and so generous. They are far above the petty prejudices of other men. Their conversation is stimulating and inspiring. You cannot imagine how badly they are treated at the Court of

Dresden. They are simply paid their fee and dismissed."

Even M. Paderewski, the Princess added, would have been simply paid his fee and dismissed, if she had not herself run forward, with tears in her eyes, and clasped him by the hand.

The Wittelsbachs do not talk like that, but, entertaining similar sentiments, act on them more quietly, and more as a matter of course. Nor does one hear of the Wittelsbachs making their declarations of love with that dramatic directness with which, if one may trust Signor Toselli, who has not M. Giron's instinct for reticence, Princess Louisa made hers. One does not picture a Wittelsbach putting to a comparative stranger the straight questions: "Have you ever loved?... Tell me, do you feel capable of love?" Nor could one readily credit a Wittelsbach with the naïve vanity of the following announcement of artistic aims and gifts:—

"I shall write the words to your music. I feel a hitherto unused talent stirring within me. I can also do sculpture."

What wonder if Signor Toselli, being only twenty-four, was persuaded by such exclamations that all the fairy-tales were coming true? And that though he was warned.

"Do you really know the Crown Princess of Saxony, sir?" said Countess Fugger to him. "Do you realise her character and the life she has led? Rather than commit such folly I would advise you to go into the garden, this very instant, and put a bullet through your brain."

But the warning fell upon deaf ears; and it is impossible to feel surprise at its having done so—not only because a child was about to be born, but also for a good many other reasons. Rank does not cease to dazzle because the high-born condescend, but often dazzles all the more effectively, by causing the lowly-born to feel at ease in their preferment, as well as proud of it. The chances of really romantic adventure, too, are rare in modern life; and a young musician is even less likely than most other young men to turn his back on them in a calculating spirit of sober self-restraint. The blaze of publicity is not a thing from which the conditions of his calling have taught him to shrink.

Signor Toselli did not shrink from it, and doubtless he enjoyed his hour of rapture. He and his bride changed their names with the rapidity of genius. At the office of the London Registrar, they were, of course, Signor Toselli and Princess Louisa of Tuscany; but at the Hotel Cecil they were Signor and Signora San Marcellino, and at the Norfolk Hotel they were M. and Mme. Dubois. When they started for their honeymoon, their railway carriage was besieged by reporters; and they may well have believed that the acclamations of the world's Press saluted their definite entrance into the joys of an earthly Paradise.

But, if that was their belief, then they were mistaken in it. In Princess Louisa's case, as we have said, the hour of revolt had struck too late. Her spiritual revolution was, in some respects, rather like the great French Revolution, which continued to proceed from excess to excess, and from extravagance to extravagance, long after its ostensible purpose had been achieved. She might be able to "do sculpture"; but there were certain other things, more important than sculpture, which she found it impossible to do. Above all, she could not settle down and keep her allegiance fixed. She had no sooner settled down in one place than she wanted to move on and settle down somewhere else. Like Little Joe, she was "allus a-moving on"; and the meaningless migrations were a weariness of the flesh to her husband, and a hindrance to his professional prospects. "You are killing the artist in me," he said to the woman who had once assured him that artists were, of all men, the noblest and the worthiest to be loved.

After that there was estrangement, culminating in separation, but mitigated by collaboration in a comic opera— the plot of it based upon Princess Louisa's recollection of certain incidents in her career as Crown Princess of Saxony. The proof is clear that, in her case—if not also in his—the passion for publicity has survived the passion for romance; but the end is not yet, and is not likely to prove of a significance which would warrant the suspension of the publication of this work until it occurs. Princess Louisa's story has been an excursus, albeit a necessary one, seeing that it illustrates, even to the point of absurdity, the Habsburg habit of doing melodramatic things melodramatically, as if they felt conscious that, whether they sat on thrones or slid off them, they owed at once an entertainment and an object lesson to the admiring curiosity of the world.

PRINCESS LOUISA OF TUSCANY
(Ex-Crown Princess of Saxony).

And that, of course, is the reason why the Habsburgs have been at once so interesting and so troublesome to the Head of their House. When they have sinned, as he would account it—offended, at all events, against the ancient traditions of the House—they have not been contented to go out and sin quietly. They have, on the contrary, sinned, if not strongly, at least demonstratively, as if their business was everybody's business, and it behoved both the Courts and the peoples to take note. And Francis Joseph, on his part, has not failed to take note, protesting, as it were, against Habsburg side-shows, and re-asserting those Habsburg principles which the rebels have rejected, with a vigour which sometimes reminds one of the last roar of a dying lion.

We must return to him, though, in truth, there remains but little to be said.

CHAPTER XXXII

The summing up—The probable future of Austria—The probable future of the House of Habsburg—Questions both personal and political which will be raised when Francis Joseph dies—The extent to which he has been "in the movement"—The faithful companion of his old age.

Francis Joseph, at the moment of writing, has passed not only his eighty-third birthday, but the sixty-fifth anniversary of his accession. Since the death of the late Regent of Bavaria, he has been the *doyen* of European rulers; and his reign has been longer than that of any modern monarch except Louis XIV., who came to the throne as a small child. His health is naturally the subject of constant preoccupation and infinite precaution on the part of his *entourage*; and last year he was kept indoors at Schönnbrunn from the middle of October until the middle of April. To what extent he is now able to govern, as well as to reign, only his Ministers know; but it is understood that, while they mobilise the army, he prays that there may be peace in his time.

Most likely he will get his way. There prevails throughout Europe, as well as throughout Austria, a sentimental feeling that he has suffered enough, and that it would be cruel to disturb his last days with war or civil commotion. That sentiment may be expected to count for more than the impatience of those Ruthenian deputies who have taken to silencing their German rivals in the Reichsrath by banging gongs and sounding motor-horns. It might not be so if the problems to the discussion of which the sounding of those motor-horns is an emotional contribution were quite ripe for settlement; but the day of reckoning must still be deferred a little. It is not before the blowing of motor-horns that the walls of Jericho will fall down flat; and it is improbable that Francis Joseph will live to see the solution of the problem which their tumult heralds.

Still, there the problem is; and we must take a final glance at it before we quit the subject. It is an old problem in a new form: a fresh presentation of the problem propounded by that Resettlement of Europe in 1815, which served as our historical starting-point—the problem arising out of the claims of ignored but inextinguishable nationalities. The shifting of the orientation of the Austrian outlook from the Italian to the Balkan peninsula, so often acclaimed as an act of wise statesmanship, has only restated that problem in a fresh shape. For the Italia Irredenta which was a thorn in the side of Austria in the past, it has substituted a Servia Irredenta which will prove a thorn in the side of Austria in the future.

In the days when the change was effected, the Servians were a despised people; and the Austrians and Hungarians believed the Turks, who declared that, in their many battles with the Servians, they had only seen their backs. They took that view alike of the Servians within the Empire—the Servians of Illyria, Dalmatia, Croatia, and other regions—and of the Servians of the independent kingdom of Servia. The former, it seemed to them, were naturally their slaves; the latter were a feeble folk, incapable, and never likely to be capable, of delivering those slaves from servitude. But now they are not so sure. Their Bosnian war established the unexpected truth that men of Servian race not only hated Austrian domination, but could make a good fight for their independence. The recent Balkan war has renewed the warning; and it remains to be seen what will happen now that there is a strong Servia—at least as strong as the old kingdom of Sardinia—to which the unredeemed Servians can look for their redemption. The situation, in short, reproduces in almost every particular the conditions which led to the formation of the kingdom of United Italy.

It is a situation in which there is one incalculable factor: the internal dissensions of the Balkan peoples. Those enmities are undeniably acute; and Austria is clearly determined to foment them, in order to postpone, if not to frustrate, the welding together of a formidable Balkan Confederation. That is the obvious inwardness of her recent support of Bulgaria and Albania. The plan may answer for the moment; but it can hardly avail in the long run, for two reasons. Albania is too disorganised to count; Bulgaria is too weak to have any future except as a member of a Balkan

Confederation; and there is also Roumania to be reckoned with—Roumania, which may prove to be at once a consolidating influence in the Balkans, and an influence hostile to Austria.

The fact that there is a Roumania Irredenta as well as a Servia Irredenta may be expected to draw the Servians and the Roumanians together; and their ultimate purpose in drawing together would obviously be to raise the questions of the two unredeemed territories simultaneously. If that should happen, the history of United Italy can hardly fail to repeat itself in the Danubian States. That it would so repeat itself there was one of Mazzini's political predictions; and he exhorted his countrymen, when the day came, to go over to Macedonia and help the Slavs. If they should ever do so, they will certainly want to help themselves to the Trentino at the same time; and they might alternatively—Triple Alliance or no Triple Alliance—demand the Trentino as the price of their neutrality.

The danger is perceived, of course, in Vienna; and there are those in Vienna who have their plan for meeting it. The Archduke Francis Ferdinand himself is generally understood to have a plan: the transformation of the Dual Monarchy into a Triple Monarchy—the third of his Trinity of Kingdoms to be a Kingdom of Slavs. To some the idea seems a brilliant inspiration; to others a counsel of despair. It derives most of the value which it has from the fact that a majority of the Slavs within the Empire are Catholics, whereas a majority of the Slavs without the Empire belong to the Orthodox Church, and that the Catholics despise the Orthodox as their inferiors in piety and civilisation. The Archduke, as a very religious man—the sort of man whom people speak of as being "in the hands of the Jesuits"—relies, apparently, upon differences of creed to keep the Slavs divided and weak, in spite of the brotherhood of race.

He may be right; but there are not wanting indications that he is wrong. Even in the Balkans religious fanaticism is no longer the force that it used to be; and the Austrian police has recently had all its work cut out to prevent inopportune explosions of sympathy with Servian successes, in Croatia. There, and in Bosnia, and in Dalmatia, just as of old in

Lombardy and in Venetia, explosions have only been prevented—perhaps one should say have only been deferred—by the policy of sitting on the safety-valve; and when that policy has to be adopted, things never fail to happen which make the oppressed difficult to reconcile. Moreover, there is a further difficulty, already indicated on a previous page: the difficulty which has its double root in Slav numbers and Austro-Hungarian pride.

Of all the races which make up the composite Empire, the Slavs are the most numerous. Admitted to the Empire on equal terms, they will be in a position to control it—to control, that is to say, the Austrians and Hungarians who have hitherto controlled them. If that were allowed to happen, the condition of things created might be as intolerable to the Austrians and Hungarians as is the existing state of things to the Slavs. Foreseeing this, they will be reluctant to take the step which will compel them to bow their necks; and, if they do take it, yet another "unredeemed" question will be raised: the question whether the Teutonic portion of the Habsburg dominions should not be regarded as Germania Irredenta. The Pangermanists of Prussia already, as we know, take that view of it; and Slav predominance might easily create a Pangermanist party in Austria also. Indeed, the nucleus of a Pangermanist party already exists there.

One doubts, therefore, whether the plan of the Archduke Francis Ferdinand—bold though the conception is—will prove to be a panacea. It strikes one as an artifice—a piece of diplomatic jugglery; and the forces which really determine the course of history are forces which mere juggling is powerless to control. The real rivalry of the Europe of to-day and to-morrow is the rivalry between Teuton and Slav; and that is a rivalry which has its origin, not merely in conflicting material interests, but in fundamental antipathies of character. As long as Teutons are anywhere ruling over Slavs, no policy of "live and let live" is feasible; and as the Slavs increase in numbers and in racial self-consciousness, the clash is bound to come. When it does come—when the unredeemed Slavs, assisted by the unredeemed Roumanians, insist upon their redemption—Austria will have played her part on the stage of European history, and the curtain may be rung down.

That is one of the predictions with which we may leave our subject; but there is also another speculation which it would be difficult to avoid. What of that House of Habsburg which has so long been the personal incarnation of the Austrian Empire? Whither is it tending? On what will its ultimate destiny depend? Will the family problems prove to be more easily soluble than those of the Empire itself? Will it still be in the future, as it has been in the past, the unifying principle of a complex political system? One doubts it—one cannot help doubting it—for various reasons.

The question before us—before Austria, rather—is the question of the importance which the world of the immediate future will attach to family pride and the exclusiveness of an imperial caste; and that is a question about which the world of to-day does not quite seem to have made up its mind. It has gained a little knowledge without losing an equal proportion of prejudice, and has reached a point at which it finds it equally difficult to live either with its superstitions or without them. It is moved—it cannot help being moved—by the formidable array of facts by which the Eugenists demonstrate that the path to degeneracy is paved with consanguineous marriages; but, at the same time, it cannot easily shake off its instinctive reluctance to accord imperial dignity to the offspring of a healthy young woman of what it regards as the "lower orders." It is, the world feels, very embarrassing to have to choose between a degenerate and a person of inferior social status.

That, nevertheless, is the choice which lies before Austria in the immediate future. Francis Ferdinand, as we have seen, has married beneath him; his marriage is "morganatic." That is to say that, when he comes to the throne, the heir to the throne will not be his son, but his nephew. That nephew is a young man about whom comparatively little is known; but when Francis Ferdinand goes into the matter, he will do so with the following facts before him:—

1. The heir to the throne is the son of the family scapegrace, who used to dance in cafés *in puris naturalibus*.

2. This heir is married to a lady who comes of the decadent Bourbon Parma stock.

3. This young man, and his wife, and his family are taking precedence of his own wife, whom he loves, and the healthy[7] children whom she has borne him.

The superstition of caste would, indeed, be strong in Francis Ferdinand if he regarded that as a right and proper state of things; and the mere fact that he married as he did, in the face of the opposition which he encountered, shows clearly that, whatever superstitions may still retain a hold on him, that particular superstition has relaxed its grip. Is he likely—human nature being what we know it to be—to accept an affront inflicted in the name of a superstition which he has abandoned? Can we expect his wife and his children to press him to do so?

Obviously we cannot. The thing might have happened in bygone ages—or even in comparatively recent ages—when universal opinion drew a religious as well as a social distinction between hereditary sovereigns and their subjects, and the personal dignity of the individual counted for nothing in comparison with that great impersonal principle. It cannot happen now that all impersonal principles are in the melting-pot and so many postulates which men used to grant as they now grant the law of gravitation are being brought to the bar of opinion to be cross-examined. The postulate which bids the progeny of an Emperor who married for love take a lower seat than the son and grandsons of the family scapegrace will assuredly be questioned by the next Emperor of Austria; and it will be found that it has nothing to say for itself. It may die fighting; but it will die; and the whole of the Habsburg superstition will die with it. What will happen then lies in the lap of the Gods.

It is, however, precisely because of its gradual approach to such problems as these that one finds the reign of Francis Joseph such an intensely interesting period of history. It is interesting from the personal point of view as the story of Nemesis overtaking the oppressor; the story which we have

---

[7] Apparently healthy, though there is, unhappily, a strain of insanity in the Chotek family also. Nothing was known or suspected of it at the time of the marriage; but the Duchess of Hohenberg's father had to be placed under restraint before his death. One may hope that the weakness was developed too late in life to be transmitted.

presented symbolically as the story of the fulfilment of Countess Karolyi's curse. Philosophically it is interesting as the age of transition from mediæval to modern ideas: the age in which both nationalities and individuals have stormily asserted their right to live their own lives in their own way. In both these matters we see, in Austria more clearly than anywhere else, the hungry generations treading down the past.

It is seldom that so complete an evolution of outlook is co-extensive with the life of a single sovereign; perhaps, indeed, Francis Joseph's reign has been unique in that respect. In any case, he has witnessed all these changes, and lived through all these intellectual and emotional experiences. His *rôle*, while doing so, has been to keep up appearances; but, if we could penetrate to the realities behind the appearances, we should assuredly find that he had not himself been unaffected by the transformations going on around him. That is the true moral of the story of his affection for Frau Schratt, and of the rumour of his desire to give that lady his left hand in marriage. He felt what the other Habsburgs felt, though he controlled his feelings better. Seeing what the other Habsburgs were doing, he had the impulse to be "in the movement," though he resisted it. He, like the rest, has sometimes had the intuition that happiness lay in living one's own life rather than the corporate life of one's country; and there are moments when his biographer feels that, in spite of all the pomp and glory which have attended his public career, the day of days for him must have been the day on which he met Frau Schratt, who, after twenty-eight years of mutual devotion, now totters down the hill with him at the journey's end.

Daily, for a little while, when health permits, he sits with her and wonders.... We will leave him wondering.

FRAU SCHRATT.

www.ingramcontent.com/pod-product-compliance
Lightning Source LLC
Chambersburg PA
CBHW020320160726
47992CB00004B/1616